Printed by ADAMS BROTHERS & SHARDLOW, LTD., and Published by the Proprietors, THE WEST AFRICA PUBLISHING Co., LTD., at their Editorial, Advertisement and Publishing Offices, Temple Bar House, 28, Fleet Street, London, E.C. 4.

The
Development of Capitalism
in Northern Nigeria

The Development of Capitalism in Northern Nigeria

Robert W. Shenton

University of Toronto Press

TORONTO AND BUFFALO

Published in Canada and the United States 1986 by
University of Toronto Press
University of Toronto
Toronto M5S 1A6

Canadian Cataloguing in Publication Data

Shenton, Robert William
The development of capitalism in Northern
Nigeria

Based on the author's thesis (Ph.D.) – University
of Toronto (1982).
Bibliography: p.
Includes index.
ISBN 0-8020-5651-2 (bound) ISBN 0-8020-6573-2 (pbk.)

1. Nigeria, Northern – Economic conditions.
2. Nigeria, Northern – History. 3. Capitalism.
I. Title.

HC1055.Z7N67 1984 330.9669'5 C84-099108-8

Set in 10/11pt Baskerville
Set, printed and bound in Great Britain

This work is dedicated to my parents,
William H. Shenton and Ruth C. Shenton,
as well as to the other members of the working
classes whose surplus made it possible.

Contents

Acknowledgements

This work has taken me a very long time to complete and I have become indebted to many in the course of its production. First of all, I would like to thank my best friend, Linda Hudson, who also happens to be my sister. I would also like to thank Jim and Richard Shenton who provided encouragement to a young and curious mind. To T. M. Ali and Mike Watts it is impossible to express my gratitude. The same situation prevails with regard to John Olinger and Bill Freund, two steadfast and invaluable companions. Constant inspiration came from Dr Y. B. Usman and George Kwanashie. Heavy debts are owed to Louise Lennihan, Robert Johnston, Hans-Heino Kopietz, Jonathan Barker, Gavin and Gillian Williams and to my ever patient supervisor, Martin Klein. In addition, thanks are due to Professor A. P. Thornton, John and Baba Lavers, Marion Johnson, Sam Jackson, Jay Jackson, Richard Palmer-Jones, Mark Duffil, Mike and Mary Mason, Charles Stewart, Ian Linden, Lorne Larson, Brian and 'Nana Crow, Kate Davies, Jan van Apeldoorn, Richard Jeffries, Tony Humphries, Magda Szlenkier, Jack Wayne, Gavin Smith, and the support staffs of Ahmadu Bello University, of the Nigerian National Archives in Kaduna, and of the University of Toronto. In particular, I would like to express my gratitude to Maria Pinto Carland and Nancy Gottschalk who continually assisted me in circumventing the regulations. I would also like to express my gratitude to Frank Spitzer and the University of Toronto Computer Services. The average Ph.D thesis now costs approximately $1000 to have typed. Without their help in instructing me in the use of the Advanced Text Management Service word processing system through which I was able to produce this thesis, I would have been forced to spend approximately one-fifth of my annual income on typing alone.

Financial support for this work was limited to the following: University of Toronto, $3000; University of Toronto International Studies Programme, $1500; Ahmadu Bello University, $4500. I express my thanks to these donors and especially to Ahmadu Bello University for supporting a foreign scholar. This support was especially welcome at a time when support was not forthcoming from my home institution, and all the more remarkable because it came at a time when my own institution insisted on increasing foreign students' tuition.

Finally, I would like to express my thanks to my comrades in the Canadian Union of Educational Workers and in particular, Christine Brown, Gary Watson and Brian A. Robinson for permitting me to have the opportunity to unite theory with action.

Preface

Geoffrey Kay has observed that:

> the law of value poses the most immediate problem for radical development theory. What meaning can be given to its claim that exploitation is the cause of underdevelopment if the rate of exploitation is higher in the developed than in the underdeveloped countries? Or to put the same question in a different way: capitalism has undeniably brought about development in one part of the world, why did it not do the same in the other? . . . If we square up to it, we have to face the unpalatable fact that capitalism has created underdevelopment not simply because it has exploited the underdeveloped countries but because it has not exploited them enough.[1]

This enigmatic and, perhaps for some, overly economistic Marxian proposition is nevertheless both unsettling and challenging. It is so because it seems to attack our common sense. If exploitation is given as the explanation for underdevelopment, how can the relative absence of exploitation be accepted as an explanation for the same phenomenon? And yet the contradiction embodied in Kay's proposition is firmly embedded in a great deal of radical writing on Africa. Central to Walter Rodney's critique of colonialism, for example, was his comment that the peasants of Africa went into the colonial period with hoes in their hands and emerged from that period in the same technologically deficient position.[2] Colonizers are attacked not only for what they did but for what they failed to do – criticized not only for the railways built, but also because they did not build more of them; not only for the creation of a particular educational system, but also for the paucity of schools; not only for the factories erected, but also because they were not built in greater numbers. Nor do such views pertain only to the past.[3] One need only reflect on the comment of Amir Jamal, former Tanzanian Minister of Finance, that the only thing worse than being exploited by a multinational corporation was not being exploited by one.[4] Kay, then, is not alone in raising the issue of the contradictory nature of exploitation. He has, however, attempted to analyze this contradiction through an investigation of the reality which is hidden behind the appearances which have given rise to the views noted above.

Read at its broadest, the present work is an investigation of Nigeria as a case study of the contradictory nature of exploitation. Today Nigeria, like much of the rest of the African continent, faces a grave socio-economic crisis. Central to this crisis is the near-collapse of the agrarian sector in Nigeria and, indeed in Africa. Once major exporters of agricultural commodities to the world, Nigerians, like many other Africans, have now become unable to produce enough food to feed themselves adequately. Once heralded as the developmental 'engine of growth', the agrarian sector has now become the single most important fetter on the further progress of the Nigerian economy. What follows is an examination of the genesis of the agrarian crisis in Nigeria. Its geographic focus is the Nigerian north – a great centre of grain and oilseed production – clearly a crucial point of departure for any analysis of Nigeria's agricultural economy.

Of late, it has become fashionable in academic discourse to minimize the impact of the colonial period in analyses of poverty in contemporary Africa. This fashion will not be followed here. In 1900, that portion of the West African savannah which was to become Northern Nigeria was a pre-capitalist society which was, in turn, part of a distinct regional economy; by 1939, it was part of a colonial state which was itself fully integrated into a worldwide system of capitalist relations of production and exchange. It is a central argument of this work that the first four decades of the present century were a crucible in which Northern Nigerian society was transformed as a result of this process of integration and, further, that Nigeria's present agrarian crisis is inexplicable without a prior understanding of this process of integration and transformation. Hence, it is these four decades which are the temporal focus of this study.

In large measure, my investigation of the parallel processes of integration and transformation has been an attempt to understand and elucidate Kay's 'unpalatable fact' in a concrete and historical fashion. I have sought to do so through an examination of the manner in which a particular historical type of capitalist and form of capital acted respectively as the historical agent and agency of the integration and transformation of Northern Nigerian society. In so doing I have endeavoured to unlock the answer to the question posed by Kay of how a particular society could be integrated into the world capitalist system and yet could not only fail to develop the vastly augmented forces of production integral to the development of capitalism in the West, but also – even more strikingly – could undergo a process of social transformation which undermined the ability of that society to reproduce itself in a manner consistent with its own continued survival.

In answering this question I will argue that a particular form of capital

– merchant capital – was the crucial agency of the integration of Northern Nigeria into the world capitalist economy. I will argue further that the dominance of this particular form of capital had a profound impact on the transformation of Northern Nigerian society. More particularly, I will demonstrate that merchant capital in Northern Nigeria was essentially parasitical in nature, that it sought to batten on to pre-existing forms of surplus appropriation, and that it sought, in a profoundly conservative fashion, to preserve rather than to transform the pre-existing forces and social relations of production in Northern Nigeria.

However, I will argue that in contradiction to its own objectives, merchant capital in Northern Nigeria was a powerful catalyst of social transformation which, through its operation, worked to undermine the pre-existing social relations of production and in so doing to alter dramatically the manner in which that society was able to reproduce itself. It is my contention that far from creating the conditions in which this overwhelmingly agrarian society could reproduce itself in such a manner as to permit it to assume the role of a springboard of advanced capitalist development, the twin processes of integration and transformation set the stage for the current agrarian crisis in Northern Nigeria. In particular, I will argue that the outcome of these processes was such that the age-old vulnerability of Northern Nigerian society to the threats of famine and disease was not only preserved but intensified, while at the same time the working of these processes exposed Northern Nigerian society to the new threat of capitalist crises.

The work is structured chronologically. The reader will find, however, that the coverage of each period is also concerned with a specific theme. The choice of this overlapping chronological/thematic structure has meant that I have been forced to choose what I felt was the dominant theme for each successive period. Chapter 1 is an attempt to draw a baseline for the work as a whole by means of an examination of the pre-capitalist social formation of what was to become Northern Nigeria. Here I have focused on the peoples of the Sokoto Caliphate, which ruled a large portion of the region, at the expense of the other inhabitants of the area. I have done so primarily because it is the peoples of the Caliphate who play a central role in the remainder of the work. In attempting to analyze the social formation of the Sokoto Caliphate I have had to come to grips with the question of pre-capitalist social formations as a whole, including the large literature that makes up the debate over the nature of pre-capitalist modes of production. Unfortunately this debate, which began as an attempt to comprehend the nature of pre-capitalist societies in order to assess the manner in which they were transformed, has largely degenerated into scholasticism, with its participants often engaging in the strikingly un-Marxist enterprise of 'naming' or cataloguing pre-capitalist societies on the basis of some *a priori* schema or recipe. My own interests are more in keeping with the debate's origins. I am interested in understanding how once-living societies functioned, in order to understand better how they have been transformed. Hence, I have presented an analytical description of the Sokoto Caliphate as it was in the years immediately preceding its conquest by the British and have eschewed any attempt to categorize it as, for example, 'feudal' or 'Asiatic'.

In Chapter 2, I examine the origins of the colonial state. I find these to be located in the competition among different elements and forms of capital as well as between capital as a whole and the pre-capitalist forms of appropriation which characterized pre-colonial Nigeria. Central to this discussion is an examination of how and why merchant capital came to be the dominant form of capital in the creation of the colonial state.

Chapters 3 and 4 have as their central concern the nature and evolution of the colonial state. In this discussion I have relied heavily on the arguments advanced by Philip Corrigan, Harvie Ramsey and Derek Sayer (and more recently by Nicos Poulantzas) that the state in capitalist society is best understood as a relation of production indispensable for the production and reproduction of capital and capitalism.[5] Seen in this way, the state in capitalist society is neither simply an 'instrument' of ruling class interests nor is it a 'structure' dictated by some supposed 'logic of capital'. Rather, the state is here seen as an arena in which not only class conflicts but also intra-class conflicts are constantly being fought out. However, in opposition to 'pluralist' conceptions of the state, the analytical framework of the state as a relation of production retains the concept of class rule. Yet, in doing so it permits the explanation of actions on the part of the state which although in opposition to certain elements of the ruling class, or at times even in opposition to that class as a whole, are necessitated by the balance of class factions and/or forces at a particular historical moment.

In examining the creation, development and actions of the colonial state in Northern Nigeria the use of such an approach was warranted for several reasons. First, given its limited sovereignty, the colonial state was not simply a committee of those capitalists with interests in the region. Rather, it can be viewed as a sub-committee of the larger British imperial ruling class in which capitalists with local interests had to contend with the 'ex-officio' representatives of British capital proper and imperial interests at large. Moreover, it was a forum in which different forms of capital – finance, merchant, and industrial – contended as well. Further, it was not only capitalist interests which were represented in the colonial state but also the interests of Northern Nigeria's pre-colonial rulers, themselves rooted in pre-capitalist modes of surplus appropriation. The representation of this latter group was the price paid for its co-operation in maintaining a quiescent population.

The formation of state policy was rarely the result of the pursuit of the single-minded interests of any one of these groups. This is not to deny, however, that it was on behalf of these interests as a whole that the state ruled. It did not, however, rule with impunity, for the threat of revolt by the underclass of peasants and craftsmen continually bulked large in the minds of the colony's rulers. This threat was not only continuously taken into account in the formation of state policy but was also used at times by various elements of the colonial state as a lever with which to promote their own particular interests.

Given this plurality of ruling class forces, it was often possible for the state *apparatchiks* themselves to play a decisive role in the formation of policy. The opportunity for such action was often the outcome of a balance of contending ruling-class forces. In such a situation the 'man on the spot' could often function in a 'relatively autonomous' fashion. In addition to such opportunities for independent action, the state apparatus itself was a major appropriator of the social surplus of the workers and peasants of the region. The provision of the state's services to capital – most importantly the creation and preservation of colonial 'law and order' – was a *sine qua non* for the reproduction of capital. Yet, as capitalist expansion occurred, a commensurate expansion in the state's apparatus and thus in its surplus appropriation was also necessary. The representatives of the state apparatus in the colonial sub-committee of the bourgeoisie thus wore two hats. On the one hand they functioned as arbitrators among contending capitalist interests as well as between those interests as a whole and Northern Nigeria's subject population. On the other, they were themselves mindful of their own interests as appropriators. These two roles could and often did conflict. Once again, the outcome of such conflicts was the stuff of which state policy was wrought.

Chapter 5 and 6 although concerned with seemingly separate issues are intimately intertwined. Chapter 5 is a straightforward depiction of the process of the concentration and centralization of capital in Northern Nigeria. Chapter 6 is concerned with the fiscal crisis of the colonial state and the origins of the idea of state-promoted and -controlled 'development' during the capitalist crisis of the 1930s. In writing these two chapters it has been my intention to show the manner in which the concentration and centralization of capital in the context of the depression was a generative factor in the creation of both the fiscal and political crises of the colonial state in the 1930s and how these crises gave birth to the 'development' idea. I have done this because a mythology has grown up around the origins of state intervention. Central to this mythology is the idea that state intervention in the colonial economy began in the post-war period as an attempt by left-leaning Colonial Office mandarins to supplant private capital. In reality, this could hardly be further from the truth. First, state intervention in the colonial economy was present – indeed a necessary element – in the creation and development of colonial capitalism from the conquest of Northern Nigeria onwards. Secondly, increased state intervention began in the late 1930s as an attempt to save colonial capitalism, not to supplant it.

With Chapter 6 the historical narrative comes to an end. I have chosen to end this study at the outbreak of the Second World War rather than to follow the more traditional periodization of African history which sees the colonial period in its entirety as a coherent historical entity. This decision requires explanation. To put matters simply, the periodization adopted here is not one dictated by the superficial criterion of the complexion of Nigeria's rulers but one more in keeping with the development of capitalism. Before the Second World War, the primary form of capitalist accumulation in Northern Nigeria was characterized by the appropriation of the absolute surplus labour or product of the region's agricultural producers. This form of appropriation involved little or no technical change or conscious reorganization of the social relations of production. Under this regime, increases in the amount of surplus appropriated were largely the result of a greater commitment by individual producers to the production of commodities for the world market, an extension of the geographic area involved in such production, and/or a lengthening of the agricultural season through the device of labour migration. Such activities can be seen as loosely parallel to those depicted by Karl Marx in his discussion of increases in the appropriation of absolute surplus value through the lengthening of the working day in the early phase of the development of industrial capitalism.

The crisis of the 1930s laid bare the weaknesses of a situation in which commercial expansion was based on the extraction of an increasing surplus from an economy characterized by a stagnant level of physical output per unit of labour. The Second World War and its aftermath were to force the colonial state to address these weaknesses. Thus, from 1939 onwards the state itself was to embark on a conscious project to 'develop' Northern Nigerian agriculture. The hallmark of this project of development was to be an attempt – continued to the present day – to increase the level of appropriation from rural producers through an intensification of production. To put this in other terms, the development effort has been characterized from its inception by an attempt to shift the basis of appropriation from an absolute to a relative form in a manner roughly analogous to the shift in appropriation from absolute to relative surplus value which Marx depicted as the central element in the emergence of industrial capitalism. Virtually the entire development arsenal of irrigation, mechanization, settlement schemes and inputs provision has been geared toward this end – the intensification of agricultural labour. Crucial to this project would be the question of labour control. It is tempting to go on! This, however, is the story of 'development' and as such it constitutes a separate era with which I hope to concern myself in the near future.

Chapter 7 is offered both by way of a summation of the main arguments of the text and also as an attempt to evaluate the social transformation of Northern Nigerian society which was wrought during the period under discussion. In so doing I have endeavoured to give life to the dead record of history and to humanize the antiseptic dissection of analysis. I have tried to do so in order to do justice to the peoples of Northern Nigeria who lived through the period covered by this study. They deserved to live better lives, but how they did live should not be forgotten. Two final comments on the nature of the present work are in order. First, although I believe that the present work falls within the Marxist tradition, I have deliberately kept theoretical comments and discussion to a minimum. If I have been skilful enough in telling the story at hand, the theoretical implications to be drawn from it should be clear. Second, I have deliberately shunned overt engagement with the interpretations of other writers. This has been done largely because I am not a skilful enough craftsman to tell a story and carry on an argument at the same time. However, it should be clear to the well-versed reader when and how I differ from other writers in my interpretation of events. Finally, I would simply like to say that I hope I have been skilful enough to have made a contribution to my friends and colleagues in Nigeria and their struggle for justice.

NOTES

1 Geoffrey Kay, *Development and Underdevelopment: A Marxist Analysis* (London: Macmillan, 1975), pp. 54–5.
2 Walter Rodney, *How Europe Underdeveloped Africa* (London: Bogle L'Ouverture, 1972), p. 239.
3 For a recent analysis in this vein, see Bade Onimode, *Imperialism and Underdevelopment in Nigeria: Dialectics of Mass Poverty* (London: Zed Press, 1983).
4 Speech by Amir Jamal to the Conference on the Global Impact of the International Monetary Fund and the World Bank, Toronto, 7 September 1982.
5 Philip Corrigan, Harvie Ramsey and Derek Sayer, *Socialist Construction and Marxist Theory: Bolshevism and its Critique* (London: Macmillan, 1973) and Nicos Poulantzas, *State, Power, Socialism* (London: New Left Books, 1978).

Where speculation ends, where real life starts, there consequently begins real, positive, science, the expounding of practical activity, of the practical process of the development of men. Empty phrases about consciousness end, and real knowledge has to take their place. When the reality is described, a self-sufficient philosophy loses its medium of existence. At the best its place can only be taken by a summing up of the most general results, abstractions which are derived from the observation of the historical development of men. These abstractions in themselves, divorced from real history, have no value whatsoever. They can only serve to facilitate the arrangement of historical material, to indicate the sequence of its separate strata. But they by no means afford a recipe or schema, as does philosophy, for neatly trimming the epochs of history. On the contrary, the difficulties begin only when one sets about the examination and arrangement of the material – whether of a past epoch or the present – and its actual presentation. The removal of these difficulties is governed by premises which certainly cannot be stated here, but which only the life process of the individuals of each epoch will make evident . . .

Karl Marx, *The German Ideology* (1846)

1

Pre-Colonial State and Economy

Although the central concern of this work is the development of the forces and relations of production of Northern Nigerian society under colonial rule, it is impossible to commence our discussion with the colonial period itself. The conquest did not create the social formation of Northern Nigeria *ex nihilo*. Rather, under British rule that society continued to carry with it the marks of earlier material developments and class struggles. Therefore a brief outline of the historical legacy is in order.[1]

The task of reconstructing the central elements of Northern Nigerian society before the advent of colonial rule is complicated by the nature of the secondary sources available. The chief difficulty has been that nearly all of those writing on the pre-colonial period have been concerned to legitimize or, alternatively, to challenge the legitimacy of, the Sokoto Caliphate which emerged in the early years of the nineteenth century. Of the few major works which have managed to rise above this limited political exercise, that of Y. B. Usman is the most useful for the purposes of this chapter. Usman's work is specifically concerned with the political transformations which brought the Caliphate into being, and his work is that of a scholar rooted in historical materialism. Thus, Usman's is one of the few works which have sought to find the hidden material basis for social and political change in the region. Although its scope is limited to the Emirate of Katsina, one of a number of emirates which composed the Sokoto Caliphate, the developments he portrays broadly reflect developments in the region as a whole, thus making the work sufficiently representative for the purposes of this brief historical introduction.[2]

The pre-jihad period

The earliest agricultural communities which can be associated with a Hausa-speaking population were collections of patrilineal family groups (*gidaje*, sing. *gida*) in villages (*kauyuka*, sing. *kauye*) recognizing no higher authority than the individual household/lineage head (*mai gida*, pl. *masu gida*). These early settlements were characterized by a rudimentary division of labour and the existence of lineage totems (*kan gida*) as well as ancestor worship. The only positions of authority beyond the household/ lineage heads were those associated with particular occupations; thus the *sarkin noma* or head of the farmers, and the *uban farauta* or head of the hunters. These positions were primarily ritualistic and concerned with the success of the crops or the hunt and were in no sense governing offices.[3]

At some point well before the fifteenth century this characteristic form of rural life had given way in a number of areas to the development of towns (*garuruwa*, sing. *gari*) which were initially agglomerations of several lineage-based units. With the beginning of urban life and the emergence of a *mai gari* or town head who was usually the head of a senior lineage and who held authority over the other *masu gida*, Hausa society began to evolve a state structure. Although the *garuruwa* were able to attain a greater division of labour than the *kauyuka*, including the emergence of full-time craftsmen, they remained essentially agricultural communities heavily dependent on the lineage as the central form of social organization.[4]

By the fourteenth century the walled town (*birni*, pl. *birane*) had replaced the *gari* as the most significant form of urban settlement. The *birni*, a true city, contained a population which no longer consisted simply of a mere handful of lineage groups. Rather, it was populated by migrants attracted by the proximity of a scarce resource such as iron, or by good farming land, or drawn by the power of an especially potent spirit cult. The city would almost certainly be situated at the intersection of several important trading routes.[5]

Significantly, the title of the rulers of such cities was not *mai birni*, master of the city, but *sarkin kasa*, or ruler of the land, for they ruled not just the population of the *birni* itself but that of the surrounding *garuruwa* and *kauyuka* as well. Thus perhaps the most important development associated with the rise of the *birni* was the elaboration of the state apparatus and the investiture of senior lineages with hereditary state offices or, to put the matter more succinctly, the emergence of class society. This change necessitated a shift in the ideological structure of Hausa society. The old spirit cults, linked to the founding lineages of the old *garuruwa* and *kauyuka*, would have been inaccessible to the large migrant population of each *birni*; thus new forms of worship, which

2

transcended lineage divisions but which were still intimately linked to the ruling houses of each *birni*, emerged as the dominant force in Hausa society. Many of these new cults were directly concerned with the forces of nature and the agricultural cycle.[6]

Islamization

The Islamization of Hausa society seems to have run parallel with the rise of the *birni*. The fifteenth and sixteenth centuries witnessed the adoption of Islam by a significant section of the urban commoner class which was employed in commercial and other non-agricultural pursuits. Islam was especially attractive to this group because it provided a legal framework amenable to the increasing commoditization of everyday life in the city. As Usman cogently notes, the old religion was chiefly concerned with defining and controlling man's relationship with nature, while Islam was chiefly concerned with the regulation of man's relationship with man. The ideological position of the ruling lineages in the *birni* with respect to Islam was ambiguous. On the one hand, their legitimacy was in large measure dependent upon their association through the lineage structure with the various cults. On the other, they were increasingly dependent upon the significant Muslim commoner community for support in war and in dynastic struggles. As the commoditization of Hausa society continued apace, the latter group became increasingly important. Attempts to resolve this problem on the part of the rulers led to syncretism in religion as the ruling class made appeals to both the Muslim and non-Muslim communities. This conflict and the various attempts to resolve it reflected the fundamental political split of the *birni*, between the *cikin gida* or palace clique on the one hand and the *cikin fada* or influential Muslim commoner class on the other.[7]

The inherent contradictions in this situation were compounded in the eighteenth century by a rising level of inter-*birni* conflict stimulated by the struggle of each *birni* to control its respective hinterland. This necessitated both increased taxation and the increased use of enslaved troops, and had as its consequence agricultural and commercial disruption. This crisis provided the immediate background to the jihad of Usman dan Fodio and the establishment of the Sokoto Caliphate.[8]

The establishment of the Sokoto Caliphate

It was the literate, scholarly stratum of the Muslim commoners which generated, in the person of Usman dan Fodio, a revolutionary challenge to the ruling lineages of the Hausa *birane*. Dan Fodio, preaching and writing in all the important languages of the region, called upon the ruling lineages to adhere to Islamic norms in law and taxation while chastising them for their religious syncretism. Over a remarkably brief period at the beginning of the nineteenth century he was able to recruit a substantial following not only from Muslim commoners but from many other groups who were alienated by the severity of *birni* government. The establishment of dan Fodio's community, or *umma*, posed a direct challenge to the legitimacy of the old ruling houses, and they made several attempts to liquidate it. These attacks forced the community from its early defensive position and provoked the proclamation of an offensive war, or jihad, on the part of the *umma*.[9]

The jihad, which was ultimately to sweep aside all but a few of the ruling lineages of the Hausa *birane*, has most often been described in tribal terms as a Fulani revolt against a Hausa ruling class. While this description may have been functional for the ideologues of the colonial state, it bears little relation to historical reality. As Usman argues, this dichotomy conceals the complexity of the social and political relations embodied in the jihad and the resistance to it. Fulani and Hausa were to be found on both sides of the revolution as, for that matter, were professed Muslims themselves. Although the revolution was justified in religious language, the jihad was primarily concerned with the relation of ruler to ruled, and royalty to commoner. The term 'Fulani' came to be associated with the jihad's adherents by those who opposed the movement; it was a political label rather than an ethnic or tribal category.[10]

The objective of the jihad was the establishment of a state whose legal and ideological norms would be those of the Muslim commoner class of the *birane* and whose leaders would be clearly charged with the upholding of those norms in matters of war, taxation and government. Perhaps more important, the jihad was concerned with opening the doors of high state office to the literate scholars (*malamai*, sing. *malami*), who were the ideologists of the revolution and who had previously been barred from high state office by reason of their common birth.[11]

Although we are not directly concerned here with the military aspects of the revolution, it is important to note that the jihad armies were initially composed of a lightly armed and highly mobile force fighting an essentially guerrilla war against a heavily armed slave cavalry and a conscripted commoner infantry. The jihad forces lived off the countryside amongst the rural population and were able to rally the commoner class against the taxation and conscription policies of the rulers of the *birane*. Ultimately the old ruling classes of most of the *birane* were isolated and overthrown.[12]

The success of the jihad was followed by a politically fluid period in which the jihad leaders ruled the various *birane* in a loose confederation. Those who were closest to leaders of the jihad or who had earned a position of high esteem through piety or by virtue of military prowess, were given the title *amir* ('emir') and ruled the major *birane* of Hausaland and beyond under the nominal authority of dan Fodio, the *amir al-muminin*, or commander of the faithful, who made the *birni* of Sokoto the capital of this new theocratic state, the Sokoto Caliphate.

The existing political climate augured ill, however, for this fluid form of political organization. The gains of the jihad forces were continually under attack from the remnants of the conquered dynasties. The defence of the conquered *birane* necessitated a far more regularized military force than the guerrilla forces of the jihad. Moreover, the jihad forces had inherited a centralized state apparatus of tax and tribute collection, which although reformed still necessitated a significant bureaucratic structure. More ominously, rivalries between elements of the jihad forces soon surfaced, the struggle for control of the new state commencing even before the initial phase of the jihad was brought to a close.

The series of revolts that broke out against the new emirates in the period immediately following the death of dan Fodio in 1817 forced the crystallization of the state apparatus. Although focused around the remnants of the pre-jihad aristocracy, these revolts gained the support of dissident jihadists and rural elements who were opposed to any form of centralized state control.

In order to deal effectively with these challenges and to continue to extend the area under jihad control, it became increasingly necessary to regularize and centralize the emirate state apparatuses. Thus, the appointment of kin members and close associates to political office became the norm and an increasingly large number of offices became the preserve of particular lineages. Significantly, the nomenclature for these offices was borrowed wholesale from the pre-jihad state structure.

By 1870, Hausa society was once more divided between ruling lineages and commoners, with the ruling class divided into three distinct elements. The composition of the three elements of the ruling class provides us with an essential key to the structure of each emirate. The immediate palace coterie which supervised the emir's household, the control of craft and merchant organizations and the collection of taxes at the emirate level was termed the *bayin sarki* (literally 'slaves of the emir'). A portion of this group had a juridically servile origin, but the name more closely connoted the immediate relationship of loyalty and dependence of this group rather than its legal position. This group had no independent base, thus it formed a cadre of politically loyal functionaries upon whom the Emir could rely without fear of creating rivals. The *sarakunan sarki*, or 'king's kings', formed a kind of *noblesse d'épée*. These were the descendants of prominent jihad figures and formed a group which exercised an important influence on royal succession. Some controlled second-level *birane*, and most held some territorial jurisdiction.

They were, as a group, especially important in the realm of military affairs and often could not be deposed without Caliphal approval. The last group, the *'yayan sarki* formed the administrative apex of each emirate's state apparatus beyond the capital. They often resided for most of the year in the capital itself and administered the countryside through *jakadu* (sing. *jakada*) or slave messengers. Together, these groups made up a class of office-holders, the *hakimai* (sing. *hakimi*).[13]

Below the ruling class of the emirate capital, the local government of the *garuruwa* and the *kauyuka* was the preserve of a lower class of officaldom consisting of town heads (*masu gari* sing. *mai gari*). In the larger *garuruwa* and second-level *birane* much of the capital apparatus was reproduced on a more modest scale. These lesser officials constituted the interface between the emirate and the local government. The lowest level of the state apparatus consisted of the rural village heads (*dagatai*, sing. *dagaci*) and urban ward heads (*masu unguwa*, sing. *mai unguwa*) who were of little importance but who were responsible to the *masu gari* and *hakimai* for the maintenance of law and order.[14]

Social relations of production in the Sokoto Caliphate

The fundamental unit of production in the Sokoto Caliphate in the late nineteenth century was the household farm, or *gandu* (pl. *gandaye*), which was the productive expression of the *gida*, or household. The *gandu*, which embraced not simply the nuclear family but extended kin as well, was a joint production/consumption unit which seems to have survived the decrease in importance of the lineage as a political unit. Non-kin members could be, and often were, integrated into the *gandu* unit as slaves or clients, eventually becoming, over several generations, full-fledged family members. The *mai gida* took charge of the organization of the production and distribution of *gandu* produce and was responsible for the fulfilment of the unit's social obligations including taxation. Secondary agricultural and craft production by *gida* members could take place outside the *gandu* framework, in which case the proceeds accrued to the individual members involved.[15]

The village formed a second level of productive organization. Aside from the integrative aspects of village food and craft markets, a system of communal workgroups, or *gayya*, was common. Land and labour exchanges were also of importance and a rudimentary craft organization was to be found. In urban areas craft organization was more sophisticated, resembling the guild system and corresponding to a higher division of labour and a more highly differentiated market. Yet it was the household which remained the fundamental unit of social production. Significantly, it was the household which was the unit of tax assessment as well.[16]

As has already been suggested, a considerable portion of the socially defined surplus of craft and agricultural production was appropriated by the office-holding class, through the state. Although the taxation system was complex and varied both among and within emirates, it is possible to outline its basic aspects for the Caliphate as a whole. The most important tax was that on land, the *kudin kasa*. The assessment of this tax was intimately linked, as was that of nearly all taxes, with the ideological framework of the state itself. Under the Caliphate, all land was theoretically vested in the *amir al-muminin*, who with the various emirs held it in trust for the *umma*. Thus, while ideologically all land was communally owned, it was at any given moment in the gift of the ruling class. Juridically private property in land could not exist; however, in reality, land, where scarce, was jealously guarded by the household and the village and was often bought and sold. The ideological fiction of communal land tenure administered by the state did, however, provide the legal basis for the taxation of land by the office-holding class. In addition to the land tax the state collected religious tithes (*zakka*), taxes on crafts and taxes on special crops such as sugar, indigo and cotton. The exact nature of these other taxes differed greatly from place to place within the Caliphate. The collection of these taxes was made through what can best be described as a tax-farming system composed of the levels of officialdom which have been outlined above, all of which appropriated a share of the proceeds which passed through their hands.[17]

In addition to the taxation system proper, the office-holding class held private estates through which a further portion of the social surplus could be appropriated. These estates, the *gandayen sarauta*, were worked by various combinations of slave, corvée and wage labour and provided both items of consumption for the office-holding class as well as commodities to be sold in the market. Recent work has attempted to describe this aspect of the Caliphate economy as a 'plantation sector' which is seen as the basis of the Caliphate's economy as a whole. The evidence for this view remains unconvincing. On the contrary, there is more evidence to suggest that here too production was organized on the basis of the household, whether slave or free, and that the *gandayen sarauta* were of secondary importance in the social relations of production as a whole. To say this is not to minimize the overall importance of slavery. Slaves, whether as trusted political agents, members of the military, or as agricultural or craft labourers, provided their owners in the office-holding class with a direct and independent source of surplus appropriation. Yet to admit this is not to say that the institution provided the basis of the economy. The latter was clearly the household, bound to the office-holding class through both ideological and material ties and subjected to surplus appropriation. Slavery remained a clearly subordinate, if important, relation of production.[18]

By the end of the nineteenth century it is clear that the production of

7

craftsmen and agriculturalists went far beyond the needs of local subsistence. Moreover, a substantial stratum of the commoner class was engaged in wage labour. Most important, the existence of a sizeable number of urban craftsmen, divorced from agriculture and producing almost exclusively for the market, enables us to note the extent of commoditization in Caliphate society. This process of commoditization was greatly facilitated by a common currency zone throughout much of the central Sudanic belt and Guinea coast in which the cowrie shell was the primary medium of exchange.[19]

Perhaps the major ramification of the commoditization of production within the Caliphate was the emergence of a distinctive division of labour between town and country, with certain cities, notably the great *birni* of Kano, dependent on regular importation of foodstuffs. As a result of this division of labour a significant category of the social surplus was appropriated by a merchant capitalist class trading in basic foodstuffs, craft products, and luxury goods. Because a significant portion of the Caliphate's trade was carried on over long distances and between different social formations, this class was able to reap the benefits of unequal exchange. It is important to note that while some merchants did invest in slaves and other productive resources and in some cases came to dominate the production of specific commodities, their ability to penetrate either urban craft guilds or the rural household appears to have been miminal. Sumptuary laws, Maliki inheritance laws, and the land tenure system all mitigated against long-term accumulation of private property by merchants as a class. Thus, the development of merchant capitalism in the Caliphate was clearly subordinated to the continued predominance of a mode of production which was based on the control of agrarian producers by an aristocratic, office-holding class which monopolized the means of violence and controlled ideology. The basic lines of class cleavage remained those of royalty and commoner, office-holder and labourer.[20]

Class consciousness was not, however, merely a reflection of this material reality. Although the basic issues around which class conflict centred were those of land tenure and taxation, the ideological framework of the Caliphate mediated class conflict. From the jihad on, grievances were expressed through support or opposition to the structure of the Caliphate itself through the choice of sides in a dynastic quarrel, through a personal commitment to a particular Muslim brotherhood, or through belief in the coming of a redeemer or *Mahdi*. Tyranny was primarily understood as a deviation from or violation of Islamic norms, and rebellion was usually aimed at a particular ruler rather than at the ruling class as a whole, and thus did not pose a direct threat to the hegemony of the state system of the Caliphate.[21]

This then, in brief outline, was the nature of the social formation of the

Sokoto Caliphate in its last years of independence. Neither stagnant nor traditional, the possibilities presented by its social relations of production were continuing to unfold on all levels. Urbanization and commoditization continued apace and the class relations of both urban and rural society continued to be elaborated.[22]

NOTES

1 This interpretation of the social structure of pre-colonial Northern Nigeria has received much stimulus from the work of Y. B. Usman, Bill Freund and John Lavers as well as from the graduate students who organized, participated in, and welcomed me to the Seminar on the Political Economy of Northern Nigeria at Ahmadu Bello University, 1976–8. In writing this chapter I have relied heavily on the work of Y. B. Usman. I have been unable to utilize the more recent work of Murray Last and M. G. Smith which may radically alter our view of early state structure and development in the central Sudan.

2 In addition to Y. B. Usman, 'The transformation of Katsina, *c.*1796–1903: the overthrow of the sarauta system and the establishment and evolution of the emirate' (PhD thesis, Ahmadu Bello University, Zaria, 1974), this chapter is also informed by A. Smith, 'Some considerations relating to the formation of states in Hausaland', *Journal of the Historical Society of Nigeria*, vol. 5, no. 3, (1970), pp. 329–46. Another interesting treatment of state formation in the central Sudan is Nicole Echard, *L'expérience du passé, histoire de la société paysanne hausa de l'Ader* (Niamey: Institut de Recherche en Sciences Humaines, Etudes nigériennes no. 36, 1975).

3 For the political role of lineages, see M. B. Alkali, 'A Hausa community in crisis. Kebbi in the nineteenth century' (MA thesis, Ahmadu Bello University, Zaria, 1969).

4 Usman, 'Transformation of Katsina', pp. 44–5; Smith, 'Some considerations'.

5 See Usman, 'Transformation of Katsina', p. 47; also A. Smith, 'The early states of the Central Sudan', in J. F. A. Ajayi and M. Crowder (eds), *History of West Africa*, Vol. 1 (London: Longman, 1971), pp. 158–201.

6 The term 'feudalism' has been uncritically applied to the states of the central Sudan by M. G. Smith in his *Government in Zazzau* (London: Oxford University Press, 1960). Its application to Africa has been uncritically attacked by J. Goody in his *Technology, Tradition and the State in Africa* (London Oxford University Press, 1971) and given a measured and well-argued defence by L. E. Koubebel, *The Songhay Empire: Essay in the Analysis of its Socio-Political Structure* (Moscow, n.d.). Marx himself felt the term 'feudal' was Eurocentric, and was, in his last years reworking the idea of an 'Asiatic mode of production'. A number of writers have attempted to apply this idea to African societies. Ultimately I have found this idea and that of a distinct 'African mode of production' unworkable. For a very useful discussion of

Marx's writings on the Asiatic mode of production, see L. Krader, *The Asiatic Mode of Production: Sources, Development and Critique in the Writings of Karl Marx* (Assen: Van Gorcum, 1975). For a critique see P. Anderson, *Lineages of the Absolutist State* (London: New Left Books, 1974). See also D. Crummey 'Abyssinian feudalism', *Past & Present*, no. 89 (November 1980), pp. 115–38

7   See Usman, 'Transformation of Katsina', pp. 66–9, 115–16, 148, 181–2.

8   ibid., pp. 192–204.

9   See M. Last, *The Sokoto Caliphate* (London: Longmans, 1967).

10 See Usman, 'Transformation of Katsina', pp. 183–93.

11 See Last, *Sokoto Caliphate*, for a comprehensive discussion of the *malamai* and the revolution they made.

12 See J. Smaldone, *Warfare in the Sokoto Caliphate: Historical and Sociological Perspectives* (Cambridge: Cambridge University Press, 1977).

13 Usman, 'Transformation of Katsina', pp. 229–32.

14 ibid, p. 413; see also Y. B. Usman, 'Some notes on three basic weaknesses in the study of African cultural history', paper presented to the Seminar on the History of Culture in West Africa in the Second Millenium AD, Zaria, Nigeria, 1977.

15 For an interesting discussion of *gandu* see Christine C. Wallace, 'The concept of gandu: how useful is it in understanding labour relations in rural Hausa society?', *Savanna*, vol. 7, no. 2 (December 1978), pp. 137–50. See also R. W Shenton and L. Lennihan, 'Capital and class: peasant differentiation in Northern Nigeria', *Journal of Peasant Studies*, vol. 9, no. 1 (1981), pp. 47–70 and Chapter 7 of the present work.

16 This is my own interpretation based on the sources examined in Chapter 3 of the present work.

17 ibid.

18 See Paul Lovejoy, 'Plantation economy of the Sokoto Caliphate', paper presented to the American Historical Association, 1976. Lovejoy's view of the economy of the nineteenth-century Sokoto Caliphate is poorly documented and, in my own view, perhaps apocryphal. See also Echard *L'expérience du passé*.

19 See P. Shea, 'The development of an export oriented dyed cloth industry in Kano Emirate in the nineteenth century' (PhD thesis, University of Wisconsin, 1975). On commoditization in Zaria, see Nigerian Archive Kaduna, Secretariat Northern Provinces (hereafter NAK SNP), 7, 4252/09 'Notes on Taxation and Industrial Organization in Hausa Towns of Zaria Emirate'. Fuller details of the contents of these files appear in the Bibliography.

20 See Shea, 'Cloth industry'. See also Garba Na Dama, 'Rise and collapse of a Hausa state: social and political history of Zamfara' (PhD thesis, Ahmadu Bello University, 1976); and Usman, 'Transformation of Katsina', pp. 103, 124–5.

21 Usman, 'Transformation of Katsina', p. 481. The Ningi rebellion and the Kano civil war are examples of such conflicts.

22 On late nineteenth century developments see M. Mason, 'Trade and state in nineteenth century Nupe', paper presented to the Seminar on the Economic History of the Central Savanna of West Africa, Zaria, Nigeria, 1977.

2

Capital and the Origins of the Colonial State in Northern Nigeria

The colonial state in Northern Nigeria did not simply come into being with the hoisting of the Union Jack over Lokoja on the river Niger on 1 January 1900. Rather, it was created by the competition among various forms and fragments of capital.[1]

Until the end of the nineteenth century the Sokoto Caliphate had largely escaped direct incorporation into the expanding capitalist system of production and exchange. It had done so primarily because of its relative inaccessibility to the probings of capital. Situated in the heart of the West African land mass, its contact with the capitalist world had been mediated by the great commercial cities of the Maghreb to the north and by the coastal states of the Bight of Benin to the south. Thus, our story must begin well outside the Caliphate itself.[2]

The region which in the nineteenth century comprised the Sokoto Caliphate was, for most of its earlier history, the southern limit of the ancient commercial world of the Mediterranean Ocean. This world was a crucial one for the development of capital in its first historic form, merchant capital, and thus for the history of capital itself. The links between the trading cities of the Maghreb and their counterparts in the central Sudan are ancient and, upon examination, they reveal much about the nature of merchant capital as a form. The Sahara constituted a major obstacle to the exchange of commodities. Transport was difficult and slow. Yet, if trading conditions were difficult in a physical sense, they were ideal for the development of merchant capital.[3]

In trading between the Maghreb and the central Sudan the merchant capitalist was exchanging commodities between two social formations and in doing so was able to appropriate the difference in the value of commodities between them. In other words, he was able to realize profit from unequal exchange. Moreover, he was able, by virtue of his position as the middleman merchant between Europe and the central Sudan, to exploit the difference in the value of commodities between three or more social formations. It was these conditions which made the trade a profitable one, and it was its profitability which led to the circumnavigation of the Maghrebian traders by their European counterparts.

Much of the impetus for the European voyages of exploration and trade which, from the late fifteenth century onward, slipped cautiously down the West African coast, came from the desire to bypass the Islamic middlemen of the Maghreb. Yet this desire was only realized as a result of a crucial change in the nature of the social formations of Western Europe. In feudal Europe the development of merchant capital, much as that of merchant capital the world over, had been checked by the prevalence of pre-capitalist relations of production. By the end of the fifteenth century, however, the transformation from feudalism to the absolutist state was well under way and with it merchant capital was increasingly liberated from its feudal bonds. The absolute monarch had need of merchant capital in the form of loans which would release him from his dependence on the feudal nobility. More precisely, he needed such loans to raise armies which would be loyal to his person. In return, merchant capital received royal approval and patronage in its expansion into Africa, Asia and the New World.[4]

The period from 1500 to 1800 was the classical period of merchant capital. It was also the period of the primary accumulation of capital which was to launch Western Europe on its industrial future. Moreover, it was the initial period of contact between European merchants and their counterparts on the West African coast. At first, European merchants skirted the coast, trading in the products of European, Asian and African craftsmen and agriculturalists, making their profits in the same manner as their Maghrebian counterparts. The development of plantation slavery in the New World and the consequent expansion of the trade in slaves, however, altered these conditions of trade to a considerable extent. The trade in slaves enabled European merchants to trade in the one commodity, labour power, which has the capacity to create value. In doing so, they were able to exploit the difference in the price of labour power between the social formations of West Africa and the New World.

Why should this difference in the price of labour power between the two regions have existed? The answer to this question is to be found in the conditions of the production of labour power itself. The destruction of the indigenous populations of the West Indies and much of Latin America through conquest, disease and the general disruption of society had created a massive need for labour to mine precious metals and to cultivate high-value commodities such as sugar. An attempt was made to fill this need through the use of free and indentured labour of European origin but this was only marginally successful. The social cost of reproduction of European labour power, the minimum it would require in recompense, was too high. It was left to West Africa to provide the solution. It could do so for one reason only. West African labour could be purchased at below its cost. The costs of social reproduction did not have to be borne by the slave raiders and traders, nor by the plantation owners in the New World. The development of the slave trade and the plantation economies of the New World which relied upon it had a differential effect on the social formations of Europe and West Africa. In Europe the development of the slave trade, the plantation economies and other related activities such as the plunder of India and the civilizations of Latin America catapulted merchant capital into the dominant position in the social formations of Western Europe.[5]

Important areas of merchant capitalist endeavour became sacred and protected preserves, often through the device of the granting of royal charters to companies such as the Hudson's Bay Company and the East India Company. Moreover, this state of affairs was generalized to colonial relationships as a whole. Mercantilism and monopoly were the order of the day. The effect of this development, the creation of protected spheres of trade, was a stimulus to the expansion of commodity production in Western Europe itself. In West Africa, the effects of the growth of merchant capital were different. To a certain extent, the growth of European merchant capital stimulated the development of its African counterpart, which soon came to play an imposing role in many of the coastal states. Yet the expansion of this indigenous merchant capital could only continue as a result of a further expansion of the plunder of human labour, slaving, a practice which by its very nature ultimately had detrimental effects on other forms of commodity production.[6]

From 1776 on, however, the dominance of merchant capital and its monopoly form in particular came under severe attack. The publication of Adam Smith's *Wealth of Nations* and the declaration of their independence by thirteen of Britain's North American colonies were the twin harbingers of this assault. Free trade was the standard rallied to in the fight against mercantilism and monopoly and thus against the dominance of merchant capital itself. In Britain this battle would not cease until the repeal of the Corn Laws in 1846, until merchant capital had been subsumed by its own creation – industrial capital. It is in the context of this attack that the abolition of the trade in slaves is to be understood.[7]

The abolition of the trade in slaves altered the commodities traded, and the position of merchant capital on the West African coast. To a certain extent the trade in slaves itself had prepared the way for a commerce in agricultural produce. Slaves had never been the sole commodity of the trade. The provisioning of slave ships was one factor which gave rise to alterations in the relations of production and exchange in a number of slave-exporting areas. In addition, many of the slave entrepôts themselves were situated in infertile areas and had to import food, which in turn stimulated the production of agricultural commodities. Yet the transition from the trade in slaves to the trade in agricultural produce would not have been possible without the rise of industrial capitalism in Western Europe and, in particular, in Britain.

The development of industrial capitalism marked a clear break with the mercantilist past. Merchant capital could only appropriate value through unequal exchange. Merchant capital was in other words, limited to the sphere of the circulation of commodities. This remained true even in the trade in slaves. Industrial capital, by contrast, directly intervened in the production process. The divorce of labour from its direct means of production resulting from and combined with the primary accumulation of capital gave rise to the generalization of the wage labour form. Capital in its industrial form was thus able not only to appropriate the surplus product of labour but also the surplus value produced by labour. In short, while merchant capital could only appropriate value, industrial capital could produce it and produce it on an ever-expanding scale. The triumph of industrial capitalism was the triumph of capitalism as a system, a system characterized by the self-expanding production of commodities and value. Under such a system merchant capital was continually thrust further and further afield in search of the ever-larger amounts of raw materials necessary for the continued expanded production of industrial capital and in search of new markets to realize the ever-larger amounts of value and surplus value embodied in the commodities which industrial capital produced.

The period from 1848 to 1873 was one of previously unparalleled expansion of capitalism as a whole and of the West African trade in particular. British imports of palm oil alone doubled between 1842 and 1855. In large measure this rapid expansion of West African commerce was directly due to the application of steam-power technology to ocean transport. Originally, the European merchant firm on the West African coast had been merchant and shipper combined; the sailing ships were owned by the merchants themselves and functioned as trading depots when moored. The application of steam to the West African trade created a division of labour between shipper and merchant and thus introduced yet another form of capital, transport capital, into the competition over the appropriation of surplus value and profit.

Although the potential of steam transport in the West African trade had been recognized since the MacGregor Laird expedition first utilized steamships in its journey to and travels on the Niger river in 1832, it was not until the spring tide of capitalist expansion that a regular steamship service between Britain and the West African coast was begun. In 1852, the African Steam Ship Company, owned by Laird, began service between Liverpool and the heart of the palm oil trade, the Oil Rivers, or eastern portion of the Niger Delta. It is important to note that it was not a merchant but a shipbuilder who inaugurated this service. The reason for this is clear. No merchant operating in the Oil Rivers was large enough to amass the initial capital outlay necessary for the acquisition of the new technology, nor did any single merchant have a sufficient volume of trade to keep a steamship fleet in constant motion, a necessity if the initial outlay was to be recouped before the ship went out of service. One steamship company could, however, serve a large number of merchants. Moreover, it could place itself in a monopoly position vis-à-vis those whom it served.[9]

In addition to bringing a new form of capital into existence in the West African trade, the period of capitalist expansion, through the introduction of steam transport, brought with it the expansion of the number of merchant capitalists, both European and African. It did so largely because the introduction of steam technology, while increasing the initial outlay for shippers, greatly reduced that necessary for the individual merchant capitalist. This greatly increased the level of competition and set the stage for a dramatic transformation of the trade. The trade in palm-oil in the Oil Rivers of the Niger Delta may be characterized as a system in which African merchants served as middlemen between palm-oil producers farther inland and the European, predominantly British, merchants on the fringe of the Delta itself. These African merchants performed a useful service to capital but they also appropriated a share of surplus value and profit. During the period of capitalist expansion their activities were seen as necessary; during the period of capitalist contraction, commencing in the 1870s, their usefulness was called severely into question.

The period between 1874 and 1893 was, for capital, one of a general and gradual deceleration in the rate of profit and resulted in a marked fall in the rate of growth of industrial output of the Western European nations, particularly Britain. This crisis of industrial development in turn lowered the prices of agricultural commodities such as palm oil exported from the West African coast. The result of this fall in prices was a drastic decrease in the mass of merchants' profits. In the Niger Delta the specific result was the introduction of a period of Hobbesian economic warfare pitting transport capital against industrial capital and British against African merchant capital, as well as British and other European merchant capitalists against each other.

In the face of the general fall in the rate of profit and the consequent reduction in the mass of profit in the Niger Delta trade, the initial reaction of British merchant capitalists was an attempt to maintain their own profit margins by passing on the fall in prices to their African counterparts. African middlemen resisted this attempt with some success and thus forced British merchant capitalists to seek their circumvention or elimination as independent entities.[10]

It was recognized that the elimination or circumvention of the Delta middlemen would be an expensive process well beyond the means of the small-scale British merchant capital of the region. The answer was to be found in the centralization and concentration of capital. Such a process required its human agent, and found it in the person of George Taubman Goldie, an adventurer and hitherto ne'er-do-well who would ultimately be responsible for the conquest of the Sokoto Caliphate. As Goldie's biographer John E. Flint has concisely noted, 'Goldie was to bring trade and politics together as a unity . . . [his] desire for political power in the Niger arose directly from his analysis of the difficulties of the Niger trade; without political power there could be no stable commerce with Europe, and no secure profit.' Commercial supremacy, the monopoly of trade: this was Goldie's route to political power.[11]

To this end Goldie, whose family had entered the Delta trade in 1876 through their participation in the Central African Trading Company, placed himself at the head of an amalgamation of British merchant firms trading in the Delta region and subsequently, in 1879, formed the United African Company, the express purposes of which was to circumvent the Delta middlemen and to trade directly with palm-oil producers on the Niger River proper. In response to this initiative there rapidly followed a second amalgamation of merchant capital creating the African Association, which sought to check the activities of the United African Company by bringing the Delta middlemen to terms.[12]

Goldie had only just completed his amalgamation of the firms trading on the river proper when a challenge to his firm's commercial supremacy presented itself in the form of an intrusion on the river by French merchant capital. His response was further to increase the size of his firm through a financial reorganization which resulted in the creation of the National African Company in 1882. He then used this improved commercial instrument to engage the French in a brief but sharp price war which eventually resulted in the capitulation and absorption of the remaining French firm – the Compagnie Française de l'Afrique equatoriale – in 1884. The concentration and centralization of capital on the River Niger was no isolated event. Similar processes were underway elsewhere. These concentrations of capital were to bring into play the various merchants' respective nation-states through the intervention of consuls, gunboats and military expeditions. Such actions on the part of Britain, France and Germany throughout Asia and Africa were inevitably bound up with the political and economic struggles in Europe itself which were ultimately to bring the European powers into armed conflict. In the short run, however, diplomacy was substituted for arms, and thus at Germany's behest a conference of the powers was called together at Berlin to consider the question of the division of Africa.[13]

One of the results of this conference was the Niger Navigation Act, which declared the River Niger open, without hindrance, to traders of all nationalities. The act was to be administered by the British state, largely as a result of the National African Company's *de facto* control of the river. Thus, as a result of the concentration of merchant capital, the British state was now poised to assume directly formal control of the Niger, the highway to the heart of the Sokoto Caliphate. However, it refused to do so.

The reasons why it refused to do so are complex and in many ways beyond the scope of this work. It suffices to say that the British state, like any other, was neither the direct instrument of the social classes and class fragments of British society nor an impartial arbitrator between them. Not all of the capitalist class fragments contained within it were favourable to the extension of formal control in West Africa and not all supported the interests of the particular fragment of British merchant capital operating on the River Niger. Colonies involved expense, a reallocation of surplus value and profit, with immediate benefits only to those in the area concerned. Moreover, even those directly concerned with trade on the river drew back from formal colonial rule, which would have imposed financial obligations and commercial restrictions for what were seen as somewhat dubious benefits. Goldie's firm was among this latter group for whom formal colonial rule would spell the end of a carefully constructed commercial monopoly.

Goldie responded to this situation by pressing for the revival of an archaic, early form of colonial control, a throwback to the age of mercantilism, the company armed with a royal charter. A chartered company would have the authority of the British government behind it but would be autonomous and wholly self-supporting. More to the point, it would place state power in Goldie's hands, allowing him to dispense at will with both European and African competition. In 1886 such a charter was granted and the National African Company was transformed into the Royal Niger Company, Chartered and Limited.[14]

The granting of the charter was immediately followed by a complex series of hostilities and negotiations between the Royal Niger Company and the British merchants of the Delta. The Delta traders, whose firms were organized as the African Association, attacked the charter on the grounds that it constituted a commercial monopoly which would drive them into ruin. They followed this attack with an aggressive push on to the river. Goldie countered with the offer of a grand amalgamation of the firms and of a campaign to have the charter extended to the Delta itself.

An agreement was within sight in 1888 when it was blocked by the steamship lines under Alfred Jones.[15]

Jones had begun his career as a clerk in the offices of Laird's African Steam Ship Company and had later moved to Elder Dempster, which became the principal agent for Laird's company and for a second firm which entered the West African trade, the British and African Steam Navigation Company. Jones was able to gain control of Elder Dempster and to utilize its position as a principal agent to gain control over both steamship lines in 1891. Jones understood clearly the threat posed to the shippers by Goldie's plans. Isolated, the merchant firms could not profitably finance their own shipping line. United, they would force the shippers to the wall. Thus in 1888 Jones fostered opposition to the extension of the charter and to the amalgamation of the merchant firms. He was successful largely because he was able to being to bear the full weight of the shippers, including those not directly concerned with the West African trade. The charter was not extended and the further concentration of merchant capital was temporarily blocked.[16]

The choice of the archaic instrument of a royal charter to invest Goldie's company with state power has often been commented upon but its deeper significance has not been well understood. It has generally been explained that such a device met the desire of the British Treasury for economy while extending colonial control. It has been seen as 'empire on the cheap', and so, to a certain extent, it was. Yet there is a deeper logic to this form of rule which was to become a crucial heritage for the formal colonial successor state of Northern Nigeria, a logic which would ultimately lead to the Royal Niger Company's demise.

The chartered company was, in the mercantilist period, the instrument of merchant capital *par excellence*. It was the direct political expression of colonization through and for this form of capital. The conditions which gave rise to it, in its original form, were those of the period of the primary accumulation of capital, the destruction of commercial competition to insure monopoly profit. Such conditions were resurrected by the capitalist crisis of the late nineteenth century which brought the Royal Niger Company into existence. Yet, if there appeared to be a new mercantilist era in the offing, the reality which lay behind this appearance was radically different. For this was the era of industrial capitalism, which fostered free trade in order to obtain continually expanding sources of raw materials at ever lower prices. From the very moment of the institution of its charter, the Royal Niger Company was to come under attack.[17]

Article 14 of the charter itself prohibited a monopoly of trade: 'Nothing in this Our Charter shall be deemed to authorise the Company to set up or grant any monopoly of trade . . . trade with the Company's territories shall be free.' Why then did Goldie accept the terms if his object was state power? The answer is to be found in the same article. Trade was to be free but it was also to be subject to customs duties and charges 'authorised . . . for the purpose of defraying the necessary expenses of government'. Taxation was to be the weapon Goldie would wield to carry to fruition his plans for the construction of a commercial monopoly.

Upon receiving the charter, Goldie reorganized the company, transforming its board of directors into a governing council, its manager into a senior executive officer, and its trading agents into the district agents of the company's rule. A senior judicial officer (Samuel Moore, first translator of the first volume of Marx's *Capital*) was appointed as well as a commandant of the constabulary, the latter being the company's army. Thus, in large measure the instruments of commerce and state power became one.

This situation, and Goldie's deliberate attempts at obfuscation, made it extremely difficult for the British government to distinguish between the administrative and commercial aspects of the Royal Niger Company and thus to judge whether the taxes levied by it were to cover administrative expenses or to control commercial opposition. With more than a little justification, the company's rivals believed the latter to be the case.

The British rivals of the Royal Niger Company were not the only group to protest against its monopolistic policies. French and German merchants hoping to take advantage of freedom of navigation on the Niger were vocal in their opposition. Moreover, the rulers of the various African states which had fallen within the company's territories were not pleased with the curtailment of commercial competition. The protests of these groups resulted in the MacDonald Commission of 1889, the outcome of which was inconclusive.[18] The immediate threat from French and German interests was diplomatically resolved by the Anglo-French Agreement of 1890 and the Anglo-German Agreement of 1893. The threat from British merchant capital was handled by other means, with the transport capital of Jones playing a crucial role.

While Goldie and the Royal Niger Company pursued the goal of monopoly on the river, Jones pursued it on the high seas. By 1892 he directly controlled some 92 per cent of West African shipping. This situation proved intolerable to the African Association which in 1891 decided to go into shipping itself. In addition, the African Association was attempting to obtain a royal charter similar to that of the Royal Niger Company. Jones realized that the success of the African Association on these two fronts would pose grave threats to his own position and hurriedly made an alliance with the Royal Niger Company. Goldie needed this alliance badly because of the gains which the African Association had made in its attempts to invade the river trade. He offered

Jones the lure of higher freight rates and the promise that the Royal Niger Company would not go into shipping. In return, he received Jones's promise that Elder Dempster would stay out of the river. The results of this alliance were threefold. It brought to an end the possibility of the African Association being granted a charter, forced it out of shipping and ultimately forced the sale of the Association's river interests to the Royal Niger Company.

The centre of the storm, however, had not yet passed. The temporary frustration of the French initiative had been blocked by fragile means. The Anglo-French Agreement of 1890 had been negotiated on the French side largely out of ignorance of the bogus character of the treaties between the Royal Niger Company and various African rulers. Awakened to these facts, French interests began, in 1892, a renewed attempt to gain access to the River Niger.[19]

A second source of conflict was to be found in the rebellion of the African middlemen whose positions had been undercut by the Royal Niger Company's advances on the Niger. Until 1893 their protests had found a voice in the propaganda of the African Association. However, the Association's capitulation to Jones and the Royal Niger Company now left them isolated. Deprived of their political allies, the most important of these middlemen, the Nembe, prepared for war.[20]

Yet a third source of trouble for the Royal Niger Company was posed by the difficult relations between the Colony of Lagos, established in 1861, and the Emirate of Ilorin, which lay within the Royal Niger Company's supposed sphere of influence. Lagosian merchants sought to expand their commercial sphere through the state of Ibadan into the Ilorin area. The almost permanent state of hostilities between Ilorin and Ibadan, however, checked such efforts. Ilorin's rulers were supposedly under the Royal Niger Company's control although they had in fact never ceded their sovereignty, and thus the Lagos government held the company responsible for Ilorin's actions. In doing so it demanded that the company bring the Emir of Ilorin to heel, threatening to launch an expedition of its own if the company failed to act.[21]

In the event, this triple attack on the Royal Niger Company proved too great for it. Formal British intervention was needed to maintain control over the company's sphere of influence. Such intervention foretold the company's demise. Yet the Royal Niger Company's territory was not to be transformed into a formal colonial state until it had subjugated the Kabba and the emirates of Bida and Ilorin and had so begun the conquest of the Sokoto Caliphate.[22]

Throughout its existence this colonial state was to bear the marks of its birth, the marks of merchant capital. Moreover, the competition among the forms of capital and capitalists had created, in what is today Nigeria, three separate states: Lagos in the west, the Oil Rivers Protectorate in the east and the Protectorate of Northern Nigeria. In doing so it presented the Nigerian people with an inheritance which some sixty-odd years later was to lead to civil war.

NOTES

1 This chapter draws heavily on the empirical material presented in J. E. Flint, *Sir George Goldie and the Making of Nigeria* (London: Oxford University Press, 1960). It is theoretically informed by G. Kay, *Development and Underdevelopment: A Marxist Analysis*, (London: Macmillan, 1975). For an alternative interpretation of these events, see A. G. Hopkins, *An Economic History of West Africa* (London: Longman, 1973).

2 See F. Braudel, *The Mediterranean and the Mediterranean World in the Age of Philip II*, 2 vols (London: Collins, 1972–3).

3 For a discussion of the trans-Saharan trade, see Hopkins, *Economic History*, especially Chapter 3.

4 See C. R. Boxer, *Four Centuries of Portuguese Expansion 1415–1825: A Succinct Survey* (Johannesburg: Witwatersrand University Press, 1961); also K. M. Panikkar, *Asia and Western Dominance. A Survey of the Vasco da Gama Era of Asian History, 1498–1945* (London: Allen & Unwin, rev. edn, 1959).

5 See W. Rodney, *How Europe Underdeveloped Africa* (London: Bogle L'Ouverture, 1972) and a review of this work by R. Shenton in the *Canadian Journal of African Studies*, vol. 9, no. 1 (1975), pp. 146–50.

6 See Rodney, *How Europe Underdeveloped Africa*, especially Chapters 3 and 4.

7 Eric Williams, *Capitalism and Slavery* (London: André Deutsch, 1964).

8 David Northrup, 'The compatibility of the slave and palm-oil trades in the Bight of Biafra', *Journal of African History*, vol. 18, no. 3 (1976), pp. 353–64.

9 P. N. Davies, *The Trade Makers. Elder Dempster in West Africa, 1862–1972* (London: Allen & Unwin, 1973).

10 See Hopkins, *Economic History*, Chapter 4. Hopkins, however, does not understand the relationship between competition, technology, monopoly and imperialism. His analysis is, therefore, of limited value.

11 Flint, *Goldie*, p. 9; see also D. J. M. Muffett, *Empire Builder Extraordinary: Sir George Goldie* (Ramsey, IOM: Shearwater Press, 1978).

12 Flint, *Goldie*, Chapter 2.

13 ibid., Chapters 3 and 4.

14 ibid., Chapter 5.

15 ibid., Chapter 6.

16 P. N. Davies, *Sir Alfred Jones: Shipping Entrepreneur par excellence* (London: Europa, 1978); see also Davies, *Trade Makers*.

17 Flint's failure to analyze this point is an important flaw in what is, otherwise, one of the most impressive studies of imperialism in West Africa.

18 Flint, *Goldie*, Chapters 5, 6, and 7.

19 ibid., Chapter 10.

20 ibid., Chapter 9.

21 ibid., Chapter 11.

22 ibid., Chapters 12 and 13.

3

The Foundation of Colonial Capitalism in Northern Nigeria

The first objective of the government of Northern Nigeria, which supplanted the Royal Niger Company, was the completion of the military conquest of the Sokoto Caliphate and the surrounding region. This enterprise, led by the first High Commissioner, Sir Frederic Lugard, took a mere three years and it took that long only because of difficulties of supply and the parsimony of the British Treasury. From 1901, when the armies of the emirates of Kontagora and Adamawa were crushed, to 1903, when the conquest of Kano and Sokoto ended all serious resistance to the British, the imperial armies were never seriously threatened. Throughout the Caliphate the issue was decided in a series of pitched battles in which the superior firepower and military organization of the British-officered troops were the deciding factors.[1]

The tale of the conquest itself has been told often enough to need no further reiteration here. Yet it is worth noting that in the aftermath of the conquest there were only two important instances of large-scale resistance within the Caliphate itself. Prolonged resistance was carried on almost exclusively by peoples who had never been fully incorporated into the political structure of the Caliphate. It was the hill peoples of the Jos Plateau, the peoples of southern Zaria, those of Bussa and those of Fika who militarily troubled the new rulers, not the organized armies of the Caliphate. It is no accident that resistance was fiercest and most prolonged among those peoples who comprised smaller-scale and less highly stratified societies than that of the Caliphate itself. In general, the greater the degree of social equality, the fiercer and more prolonged resistance seems to have been. The massed armies of an emirate could be destroyed in an afternoon; the armed people of the Jos Plateau, fighting to preserve not an emirate but their land, could resist for years. Yet, once the Caliphate itself was conquered the resistance of the surrounding societies was of no real lasting political importance. After 1903 the new rulers had arrived for good.[2]

In order to understand the policies of these new rulers – how they were to rule – we must understand how they comprehended their new domain. What did they know of Caliphal society? How did they see it? We must also determine what they sought from it, and how they believed what they wanted could be secured. Finally, we must understand the strategic limitations of their own position, their assessment of the resources at their disposal and the possibilities of augmenting these through local means.

The British view of the Sokoto Caliphate had been largely shaped by the imperial experience, on the one hand, and the overlapping belief in imperial political propaganda on the other. The Protectorate of Northern Nigeria was created at the end of the long period of British imperialist expansion and thus the conquerors carried with them the heritage of the subjugation and government of the peoples of Ireland, India, the Caribbean, Egypt, and elsewhere. The more thoughtful among these new rulers also carried with them the intellectual heritage of empire and administration as expressed in the works of Sir John Budd Phear, Henry Maine, James Mill and Sir William Jones, scholars who had written the major interpretations of the law and society of the peoples under imperial rule. A more immediate if less rigorous heritage was that of the political propaganda which had formed the public justification for British conquest and rule in Africa. It is with this latter element that we will be immediately concerned.[3]

From the early nineteenth century on, there is one theme which remains constant in the British view of the African continent; the evils of slavery and the raiding for and trading in slaves. From the campaign to abolish the trans-Atlantic slave trade to the conquest of Northern Nigeria nearly a century later, the view of Africa as a single mass peopled by enslaved unfortunates on the one hand, and rapacious slave raiders and traders on the other, prevailed.[4] Attitudes toward the Sokoto Caliphate were no exception to this general view. It is a great irony that this, in many cases genuine, concern with human freedom was to provide the moral justification for the conquest of the African continent.[5] In the case of the Sokoto Caliphate this view was compounded by late nineteenth-century attitudes toward race. In the eyes of the new rulers, there was only one possible explanation for the existence of a highly stratified society such as the Caliphate which was in keeping with their racism. This was that the Caliphate had originally been founded by a supposedly light-skinned and hence more intelligent racial group. Seizing upon the political nomenclature of the Caliphate, the British then identified this light-skinned group as 'Fulani'. There was a major problem with this analysis. Ruler and ruled were virtually indistinguishable on the basis of colour. Faced with this reality, the British then concocted an imagined history for the area in which the light-skinned rulers had been racially debased through interbreeding with their darker subjects. Thus, the political situation that existed was comprehended only through the most circuitous and tortuous logic. This logic, once constituted, was also brought to bear in comprehending the nature of the Caliphate itself. The conquerors presumed that the Caliphate had fallen from a golden age to become corrupt and degenerate. This corruption and degeneration was thought to be the result of the darkening of the ruling class. It is a view which tells us less about the conquered than the conquerors themselves.[6]

The broad British view of the people of the Sokoto Caliphate was thus one of a once-great light-skinned ruling class which had conquered a backward black people and enslaved them only to be corrupted themselves through the mixing of races. According to this interpretation the century of rule by the Sokoto Caliphate could be reduced to a century of warfare and slave raiding. It was a view that had much in common with those held towards other parts of the empire in which the British had found stratified societies and centralized states.[7]

The views of the rulers would have been of little import had it not been for the fact that they shaped the manner in which the aims and goals of British rule were to be realized. What were these aims and goals? They can be summed up in a phrase – the continued expansion of British capitalism or, in the parlance of the day, 'trade'. Everything else was rhetorical decoration. With the arrival of Joseph Chamberlain as the Secretary of State for the Colonies at the end of the century this aim was laid bare. The Birmingham screwmaker saw the issue clearly. The colonies were imperial estates, and estates were held in order to be developed. They were to provide the raw materials and the markets which would support and renew British industrial capitalism in an inceasingly competitive world. Chamberlain held shares in the Royal Niger Company and was prepared to see the work it had initiated brought to fruition. Moreover, Chamberlain recognized the importance of state intervention in achieving the goal he had set out. Like many others in the British government, he realized that colonialism meant expense, but as a capitalist himself he also understood what many of his colleagues did not – if money is to be made, money must be spent. He was not alone in this view. Alfred Jones, the great shipping magnate, shared it. So did Winston Churchill, Mary Kingsley, and Edmund Morel, all influential writers who predicted a great future for the new colony as well as sharing Chamberlain's aims for its development. For a brief period at the dawn of the present century, Northern Nigeria loomed in the public's imagination as a kind of miniature China, a limitless market of unbounded productive potential. The land was such, it was said, that its bare scratching brought forth the harvest in abundance.[8]

Yet if these were the views of the most progressive element of British capitalism, they were decidedly not those of the imperial book-keepers, the British Treasury. For the Treasury, whence the funds for the conquest and administration of the colonies were forthcoming, colonies were a dubious venture which could be reluctantly accepted only if they were made to pay for themselves. Northern Nigeria, in the short run, could not do this. There was no loot, no booty to be shipped home. The Treasury therefore had to bear the burden of the expense of conquest. This was the logical outcome of the splitting of commerce from state power which resulted from the Royal Niger Company's demise. Moreover, the demise of the Royal Niger Company itself constituted an added burden, for its holdings had not simply been seized by the state but rather purchased. The compensation paid to its successor, the Niger Company, and the debts assumed from it, totalled some £865 000 sterling and an attachment on the mineral production of the colony for ninety-nine years.[9] In the Treasury's eyes this was no mean sum. Thus, the Treasury view was one that called for parsimony and self-support at the earliest possible date. It set the limits on the manner in which the development of the Northern Nigerian estate was to be undertaken. There would be few administrators and no large standing army. Development was to be undertaken by private initiative or through the utilization of local resources. Above all, the post-conquest peace was to be maintained. Of all the forces impinging on the new colonial state it was this last which was the most real and most important. It presents us with the twin demands of colonial political economy, the maintenance of political order and the satisfaction of the fiscal demands of the state. It was the satisfaction of these demands which was to make possible the development of capitalism in Northern Nigeria.

The problem of the maintenance of political order presented itself with the greatest immediacy. The Caliphate had been conquered but how, in the absence of a massive army of occupation, was it to be held? The early writings of the first generation of British administrators are filled – with good reason – with the fear of incipient and widespread revolt. The memory of the Indian Mutiny of 1857 was not dead, and if it needed refreshing the experience of the Mahdist movement in the Anglo-Egyptian Sudan, the Bai Bureh rising in Sierra Leone, the conquest of Asante and the South African War provided contemporary examples of the possibility of prolonged, bloody, and expensive imperial warfare.[10]

In part these fears tempered the nature of the conquest itself. Where deemed feasible, as in the emirates of Zaria and Hadejia, the emir in office was left in place. Where resistance made this path of action impossible, great care was taken to find a co-operative member of the ruling house on whom to bestow authority. Guarantees were given as to the sanctity of Islam and it was given to be understood that Christian missionaries would be frowned upon. These policies were not the invention of the colonial state and its operatives. Rather, they had been the guiding light of Goldie and his merchant state, the Royal Niger Company.[11]

Given its position as an agent of merchant capital, the Royal Niger Company had had little interest in transforming either the relations of production or the nature of state power in Northern Nigeria, save for those actions which would expand the size of its own trading sphere, guarantee its monopoly position, and increase its profits. Neither did its colonial successor, which operated in the interests of British merchant capital as a whole. Nowhere can this attitude be more plainly seen at work than in the evolution of the theory and practice of colonial rule regarding slavery.

As early as 1886 the official British position towards slavery had been made clear in the Royal Niger Company's charter. Slavery was to be abolished within the Company's territories. Article 6 of the charter stated:

> The Company shall, to the best of its power, discourage and, as far as may be practicable, abolish by degrees any system of domestic servitude existing among the native inhabitants.[12]

Given this policy and given that the supposed ubiquity of slavery had been one of the major ideological justifications of the conquest itself, it might be reasonably supposed that the abolition of slavery would have been high on the agenda of the colonial state. The truth was quite the reverse. While decrees were made abolishing the trade in slaves and slave raiding, setting up procedures for manumission and proclaiming that any individual born after the inception of British rule was legally free, the institution of slavery itself was systematically maintained in the early years of colonial rule. Lugard's own position regarding fugitive slaves was made clear in his 1906 *Political Memoranda:*

> If, after inquiry the Resident comes to the conclusion that the slave has no good case, that there has been no cruelty and that the person is simply a bad character or loafer desirous of escaping from work, however light, he would discourage the assertion of freedom. More especially in the case of farm slaves if desertion has become prevalent in the district, and in the case of household slaves if the case occurred near a large native centre containing a considerable slave population.[13]

Moreover, while the hunting down of runaway slaves by their owners was distinctly frowned upon by the colonial authorities and while cases to reclaim runaways could not be heard in a Protectorate court of law,

Lugard instructed his Residents to:

> inform each other either of fugitive slaves from their own, or arriving from neighbouring provinces and if, after investigation it transpires that there was no sufficient cause for running away, and that they have not redeemed themselves, the Resident in the province in which they desire to take up land may decline to grant permission.[14]

This attitude was a far cry from that of the British anti-slavery blockade of the early nineteeth century and the establishment of the freed slave colony at Freetown in Sierra Leone. Why had this rapid and dramatic *volte-face* occurred? The answer is clear. The colonial government could not transform the social relations of production of the Sokoto Caliphate at a stroke, nor would such action have been in the interests of the forces which the state represented – merchant capital, the Treasury, and the state bureaucracy. Slavery represented an important prop of the indigenous ruling class, one of the forms through which the surplus labour of the mass of agricultural producers was appropriated. Any attack on slavery as an institution would also have been an attack on the indigenous ruling class which was now aligned with the colonial state.

The danger in such an attack was underlined by the single major instance of post-conquest rebellion within the Caliphate. In February 1906 a Mahdist-inspired revolt took place in the village of Satiru, located immediately north of the *birni* of Sokoto. The British attempted to contain the situation by sending a small armed party to disperse the rebels. In the ensuing encounter the Resident, two white officers and twenty-five African troops were killed. British supply lines were incapable of meeting this challenge and the task of crushing the rebellion fell to the army of the emirate of Sokoto under the advice, if not the direct command, of a British officer. The rebellion was crushed with great ferocity, and over 2000 of the rebels were killed.[15] The following year, Lugard's brother Edward, communicating the details of the massacre, noted that 'they killed every living thing before them'. He also described how, in atrocities committed after the battle, the Sultan's troops had cut off women's breasts and had spitted the leader of the rebellion on a stake.[16] Walter Miller, one of the few missionaries in the north and a sometime confidant of Lugard, wrote that it 'would be worth Leopold of Belgium's while to pay ten thousand pounds to get hold of what we know of this'.[17]

The British-appointed Sultan had saved the British from what they feared most, a religiously inspired rebellion which might have set the entire Protectorate aflame. He had done so because the Satiru rising was as much an assault on his own position as spiritual and temporal head of the Muslim community as it was an assault on the colonial state. The logic of the British position was clear. Nothing must be done to undercut the position of the indigenous ruling class. Rather, if British rule was to survive, the positions of Sultan, emirs, and *hakimai* must be maintained. The implications for the institution of slavery were clear as well. As one Resident put it:

> I am very much afraid that if slavery disappears and with it the wealthy class we will find in some ten to twenty years time that the Fulani administrative machinery has disappeared and that we have nothing to replace it with. The only solution I can think of . . . is that domestic slavery in some modified form be legalised, it would be a temporary measure and help to bridge the next twenty years at the end of which one hopes that the revenue of the country will have increased so much that it will be possible to provide adequate remuneration for native administrators.[18]

In the climate of the day, however, the open legalization of slavery even as a temporary measure would have been incompatible with public and parliamentary opinion. Other options were available, and these flowed from the pen of that much renowned Imperial mercenary-turned-political-philosopher, Frederick Lugard, who was now High Comissioner for the Protectorate. Lugard's later writings enshrined respect for local society, slow change and continuity of policy as the basic tenets of the theology of British colonial administration but in 1906 he proposed what amounted to a mammoth transformation of the social system of the Caliphate. Starting from the premise that the vast bulk of the population was enslaved, he wrote:

> Government, by the very act of introducing security for life and property, and by throwing open fertile land to cultivation, adds to the difficulty of the problem it has to solve, namely, the creation of a labouring class to till the lands of the ruling classes.[19]

Lugard believed that the ruling class could be transformed into a class of landlords employing wage labour to maintain its position – perhaps along the lines of mid-Victorian England. A firm but steady hand could show the indigenous ruling class the error of its slave-holding ways and point it down the road to progress:

> The practical advantage to him [the former slave owner] lies in the fact that whereas the British courts lend him no assistance in compelling his slave to do a proper day's work or in punishing him if he runs away – while the assistance of the native court is but a very precarious one – he can, if he employs free labour, obtain the full assistance of the Administration in enforcing the contract and punishing its breach, and it should be explained to him how he should enter a contract enforcable in law.[20]

Lugard sought then, almost as an act of sheer will, to carry through a social transformation in Northern Nigeria which had taken the better part of half a millennium in England. His facile view of historical change was compounded by his contempt for those who labour for wages. 'Nor,' he wrote:

> is the difference great between the free labour and the slave labour contract in the case of farm slaves, since sale, already greatly restricted by the Koran, is now illegal under Protectorate law. It amounts to hardly more than a difference in method, rather than in principle.[21]

Thus, in Lugard's eyes the Sokoto Caliphate and the rest of Northern Nigeria was to be transformed into a version of post-manumission British West Indies, in which slaves, while freed, were compelled to remain on the plantations. Slaves were not to be permitted to 'desert', and the Caliphate aristocracy was to become a wage-paying landlord class. The linchpin of the system was to be the recognition of the right of private property in land:

> The majority of the cases of the assertion of freedom take place among the agricultural population, and the most effective way of preventing too sudden and premature tendency to desertion, is, as I have said . . . by enforcing proprietary rights in land. In other words, by not permitting fugitive farm slaves to occupy land to which they have no title, nor to build new villages at will, and by upholding the landlord's right to charge rent to his tenants . . .[22]

Lugard may have seen this, his vision, as the future. Many of his colleagues, however, had decidedly different ideas, ideas which if somewhat more in keeping with the early years of the present century were equally bizarre in their intent. These were the theories of the American utopian socialist Henry George, as adopted by one of the Senior Residents of Northern Nigeria, Charles Temple, and as taught by him to the High Commissioner who took over from Lugard in 1907, Percy Girouard.

George, whose ideas had a far greater impact in Britain than in his native United States, believed that the real social cleavage in capitalist society was not between capitalist and worker but rather between both of these on the one hand and landlords, as a class, on the other. In his book *Progress and Poverty*, first published in 1879, George argued that:

> The increase of rent which goes on in progressive countries is at once seen to be the key which explains why wages and interest fail to increase with increase of productive power. For the wealth produced in every community is divided into two parts by what may be called the rent line, which is fixed by the margin of cultivation, or the return

which labour and capital could obtain from such natural opportunities as are free to them without the payment of rent. From the part of the produce below this line wages and interest must be paid. All that is above goes to the owners of the land. Thus, where the value of the land is low, there may be a small production of wealth, and yet a high rate of wages and interest as we see in the new countries. And where the value of land is high, there may be a very large production of wealth, and yet a low rate of wages and interest, as we see in old countries.[23]

George further argued that the landowner reaped the benefit of the exertions of others who built the cities, railways and factories which enhanced the value of his land. His solution to the problem was that the state should hold all land and, while guaranteeing the right of the user, tax away all rent which would have accrued to the private landowner. This tax would become a 'single tax' approximately equal to the 'economic rent' on land, and its introduction, so George believed, would free that portion of society's wealth which normally accrued as unearned income to the landowners.

Such a theory appealed greatly to that strange British blend of aristocrat and 'rather speculative and individual kind of socialist' of which Charles Temple, son of Sir Richard Temple of the Indian Civil Service, was a representative.[24] Moreover, Temple had the sort of connections which allowed him to have his views not only heard but acted upon. He was a close personal friend of the Colonial Office civil servant, Charles Strachey, who Margery Perham refers to as one of 'the three officials most concerned with [Lugard's] administration at this time.'[25] Even Lugard, who was Temple's official superior was forced to realize that:

> my opinions count for nothing at the Colonial Office. It is astonishing how difficult it is to efface oneself to the proper degree . . . I rarely dare speak of anything in regard to Native Administration in the North unless I can base myself on Temple.[26]

The departure of Lugard in 1906 and the appointment of Girouard in 1907 as High Commissioner presented Temple and his principal ally in the Colonial Office, Strachey, with the opportunity to develop a theory of social organization diametrically opposed to that of Lugard. Once implemented this would nationalize all land in Northern Nigeria, eliminate any prospect of the development of a landlord class, and have as its corollary the transformation of the indigenous ruling class into a mock-feudal, salaried bureaucracy. The mechanism through which this theory was to be enshrined in Protectorate law was that of the convening of a Colonial Office Committee on the subject of Land Tenure in Northern Nigeria while Lugard was conveniently half a world away governing Hong Kong. Preparation for this committee was Girouard's first priority on taking up office. To this end, his first act was to circulate to the Residents in charge of the emirates and Provinces a copy of B. H. Baden-Powell's work on Indian land tenure and a memorandum of his own composition on the evolution of land tenure and land revenue in Northern Nigeria. Attached was a letter soliciting their responses.[27]

The memorandum commenced with the argument that the eventual completion of a railway to the north from the coast 'will very probably result in a large access to the white population and a probable demand for land for agricultural purposes'. Such a large influx of whites demanding land, Girouard feared, might, 'if it occurred before the determination of Native Tenure', result in 'injustice to the present holders of the land . . . tending to unsettle the country and shake the faith in our rule now becoming firmly established'. After a brief historical discussion, in which he outlined the differences he believed to prevail concerning land tenure between the emirates and those areas of the Protectorate which had not been a part of the Sokoto Caliphate, Girouard commented on the prior practice of the colonial adminstration:[28]

> Since the British occupation the principle of the right of the Natives to their landholdings has never been questioned, Residents of Provinces invariably maintaining even individual right of possession, providing cesses of taxes on it were forthcoming . . . thus securing to the landholder of cultivated ground continuous occupation of the land.[29]

Concerning unoccupied land, Girouard noted that 'Village claim is laid to far greater areas than the actually cultivated or fallow land . . . In all the Provinces there would appear to be no land which was not subject to such a claim'[30] and that 'no serious investigation has been made as to the claims or rights in this unoccupied land.'[31]

Having thus justified the exercise on the grounds of prevailing ignorance and immediate political importance, Girouard proceeded to an examination of the thoughts and writings of Lugard. Lugard, in No. 16 of his *Political Memoranda* 'Title to Land', written in 1906, had been primarily interested in justifying the control of the colonial administration over all the land within the Protectorate without directly raising the question of its ownership. The first class of land Lugard had concerned himself with was the territory which the British government had acquired from the Royal Niger Company upon the revocation of the latter's charter. These lands included a one-mile-wide strip on either side of the River Niger from the frontier of Southern Nigeria, as the remainder of the country was now called, to Lokoja within the Protectorate, as well as other extensive holdings. Lugard maintained that these lands were 'by presumption, the absolute property of the Government', or Crown Lands.[32] He added, though, in a moment of candour, that the inhabitants of these areas:

> so far as I am aware have no knowledge that their rights in the land they occupy have ever been alienated. Since, moreover, the greater parts are situated in Pagan districts, where rights in land are communal, it was doubtful whether it was in point of fact alienable by any Chief under treaty.[33]

Having thus undercut his former employers' claims to these lands and thus those of his present employers, Lugard papered over the contradiction:

> It must, however, in fairness to the Company, be borne in mind that the treaties under which they had claimed to acquire these lands, and also the mineral rights, were often (probably almost always) the same by which they had acquired such political control as formed the basis of our own claim to what is now Northern Nigeria, as opposed to the claims of Foreign Powers.[34]

In addition to those lands purchased from the Royal Niger Company, Crown Lands also included the sites of various administrative offices and cantonments.

Aside from Crown Lands, which Lugard described as the 'private property of the Government', he identified a second class of land which he called 'Public Lands'. These Public Lands were those in which 'ultimate title . . . is vested in the Government by right of conquest, a right to which legal sanction was given by Proclamation 13 of 1902'. They became government property 'owing to the fact that the Fulani, when they conquered the country, assumed the ultimate title to all land, and when a Fulani chief was conquered or deposed by the Government, the title vested in him lapsed to the Government'.[35] On the basis of this claim Lugard maintained that the government had:

> the right of disposal of all such land as is included in a district declared to be Public Lands, provided that it is not in actual occupation, and cannot be proved to be the private property of an individual. In this latter case Government could not alienate it, for conquest by a civilized government does not confer the right to confiscate private property.[36]

This statement, in Lugard's opinion, justified the appropriation of 'practically all the territory under Fulani rule'. Yet the Protectorate of Northern Nigeria included vast areas which had never been a part of the

Caliphate, 'the enormous area which is occupied by Pagans', as Lugard put it. Here, he confessed, 'I have no legal instrument by which to legitimate to the hyper-critical legal mind the *de facto* consequences of conquest in this case.'[37] In those cases where such peoples had been conquered, the same argument of the 'rights of conquest' as in the Caliphate were applied. Yet it was not to be announced to them as such. 'I have,' Lugard noted, 'a strong dislike to going through formulae – be they treaties or public proclamations – which are not understood by the parties concerned.'[38] Given the tenous nature of the British claim to land in these areas it is questionable whether it was either the need to satisfy the 'hyper-critical legal mind' or the ignorance of the peoples involved which really brought Lugard to his new-found dislike of announcing treaties and proclamations.

Finally, according to Lugard, there were the lands in those emirates and 'Pagan' areas whose leaders and peoples had peacefully submitted to British rule. These were to be declared Public Lands as well:

> In these cases the submission may be due to the fact that the Chief or tribe did not consider themselves strong enough to oppose the advent of British rule and yielded to circumstances they could not control, or it may be that they welcomed the British friendship against aggressive neighbours. It seems clear that in such cases, the Government would be justified in assuming the same rights as in the Districts already discussed, since they are only such as may be rightly exercised by a Suzerain, and do not involve the confiscation of private property; but some difference in procedure would be necessary, and the wishes of the Chiefs and people would have to be consulted before any waste lands were sold or leased to non-Natives or aliens.[39]

Taken together, these writings had justified, if only to Lugard himself, British control of virtually the entire Protectorate. Yet Lugard realized that he would have to make provision for private property in land if his scheme for the social transformation of Northern Nigerian society was to come to fruition. Thus, he ended his treatise on the Protectorate's land law with the following plea:

> In my opinion the ownership of land by the upper classes is a most useful principle to inculcate, so that Native Rulers and Alkalis who devote their time to executive and administrative work, may be provided with a private income to supplement their official salaries, and replace the wealth which formerly consisted of slaves. But while encouraging the principle of private ownership in estates, Residents should be careful to make the peasantry (and indeed all classes) clearly understand the distinction between rent paid to a landlord and taxes paid to the state.[40]

Girouard, if his and Temple's theories were to be implemented, could not let such views on land ownership stand unchallenged. In his comments on Lugard's memorandum, Girouard maintained that 'both in definition as to class and in definition as to right the foregoing appear to me to be, from a legal point of view cumbersome and, in practice indefinite. They, moreover, have no standing in the laws of the Protectorate.'[41] In addition he argued that 'no account is taken as to village claims as to boundaries', on the basis of which Girouard maintained that there 'was practically no land which was not subject to such a claim'.[42] Most of this was window-dressing. The real problem with Lugard's view was given only a passing mention by Girouard, when he noted that 'the right to private freehold ownership is apparently contemplated . . .' If this latter policy was not contested, the Girouard/Temple scheme would be lost.[43] Pressing the point home, Girouard argued:

> My predecessor denies the right to Government of seizing cultivated lands or house property, or of interfering with private titles, transfers or sales between individuals.
>
> In another Memorandum, in referring to the difficulty of the free labour problem, mention is made of the necessity of 'the creation of a labouring class to till the lands of the ruling classes' and 'the enforcement of proprietory rights in land'. I can only presume that this means the creation of a landlord class. Though I am altogether in favour of the definition and recognition of the native rights in land, I am not at all certain that it would be in their best interest to create a landlord class where apparently they have been non-existent.[44]

Having clarified the points on which he and Lugard differed with regard to land tenure, Girouard next tackled the necessary accompaniment to any settlement of the land tenure question – land revenue. He did so, once again, through a review of Lugard's previous policy statements and an examination of the prevailing reality.

Here the issues, if as complex as those regarding land tenure, were at least more concrete. The colonial government needed a source of revenue. As Lugard noted, the Protectorate was landlocked and hence could not raise sufficient funds through indirect taxes such as customs levies without adding to the duties paid by European merchants at the coast. Increased impositions, it was feared, might stifle commerce in the Protectorate completely. The implication of this view was clear. The bulk of state revenue would have to be raised through some form of direct taxation.

Although Girouard makes little mention of it, during the immediate post-conquest period Lugard and the Residents under him had simply approached the emirs and demanded a large share of the taxes and tribute which the latter had collected. This system of plunder had problematic results. In the emirate of Katsina, for example, the emir increased taxes dramatically so as not to eliminate a large proportion of his own income. As a result, tax gathering parties required an armed guard of several hundred men to proceed through the countryside and resembled raiding parties far more than an arm of 'civilized government'. In areas outside the Caliphate the situation was worse. Here, many peoples had never paid a levy to an outside authority and resisted its introduction. An example of the result of attempts to enforce taxation in such areas was noted in a letter from a Niger Company agent to Lord Scarbrough, the Company's Chairman:

> We have had another disaster . . . and lost 8 men and 11 wounded and their guns and 3000 rounds and all through this beer tax which is really the people's food. I should not write this but can't help it for you know and understand.[45]

As the writer's comments imply, reports of such events were not for public consumption. Yet the situation was so problematic that Lugard was forced to issue instructions stating precisely under what circumstances villages were to be burned and their food supplies destroyed. 'A Resident,' wrote Lugard, 'is not justified in deporting a Chief or burning his village, because he refuses to pay tribute'. A village might only be put to the torch after its inhabitants had committed some 'outrage', or had had a fine levied against them which they refused to pay and insufficient livestock could be found to liquidate the fine. In such cases only the huts themselves were to be burnt. Only in extreme cases of repeated offences were grain supplies to be destroyed. Moreover, looting on the part of the government's troops was not to be permitted but they might 'if the work has been very arduous, be awarded with the sanction of the High Commissioner, a certain portion of the captured livestock as a reward.'[46]

It is difficult to believe that the problem with such instructions was not apparent even at the time they were issued. Refusal to pay taxes might very possibly take the form of armed resistance to what would, in the presence of several dozen armed troops approaching a village, look very much like a raiding party. Resistance might involve the loss of life on the government side and thus constitute an 'outrage', and as such, be dealt with, barring the payment of a fine, by the burning of the villagers' huts. Continued resistance or 'repeated outrages' would mean the destruction of grain stores. A series of events very much along these lines happened repeatedly to the peoples of southern Zaria and the Jos Plateau.

Needless to say, Lugard, in his Memorandum on the subject of taxation, did not dwell on the difficulties described above. Rather, he first set out to justify the principle of direct taxation. He did so on various grounds. First, he maintained that direct taxation was well understood by the peoples of the Caliphate because such a system was 'an accomplished fact . . . being based chiefly on the Koranic model'. Second, he argued that although the system of taxation had fallen into:

> gross abuse in the greater part of the country . . . the administration could not tolerate the extortion and corruption which had become so prevalent and had driven the people to repudiate their taxes, nor could it, on the other hand, allow the absolute impoverishment of the ruling classes, who were now without arms and without power to enforce their dues. The abolition of the slave trade had also decreased the wealth of all Emirs and also altered the whole basis of taxation.[47]

Once again, Lugard's desire to maintain the position of the indigenous ruling class was carefully spelled out:

> The disarmament of the armies of the great chiefs, which has been necessary to stop slave raiding and internecine war and to enable us to hold the country with a small force, has, at the same time imposed upon the Government the obligation of enforcing taxes by which alone the native rulers are able to maintain their position.[48]

Lugard justified the Administration's policy of sharing in these taxes with the 'native rulers' by arguing that 'by this means the British rule becomes more closely associated with the Native Administration, which will now form an integral part of it. The interests of the native rulers thus become identified with those of the Government.'[49]

Lugard proposed to 'retain as far as possible the ancient forms of taxation known to the people and sanctioned by tradition; to utilise the existing machinery, while simplifying the modes of collection.'[50] However, the existing taxes themselves, he found, were characterized by such a 'bewildering' number of regional differences 'as to make it an almost impossible task' to summarize them.[51] For the areas which had been beyond the taxation of the Caliphate, he believed that relief from slave raiding, which he repeatedly argued had been endemic, was of sufficient benefit to compensate the inhabitants for the direct taxes now levied on them.[52]

Lugard next proceeded to discuss the main forms of taxation in force in the Caliphate before the British conquest, a summary of which has already been presented. His crucial point here concerned the *kudin kasa* and the *zakka*. These were, Lugard stated (as if in anticipation of the onslaught by Temple and Girouard) taxes and not rents 'since the farms were acquired by purchase, and, in default of male heir, lapsed to the

Chief.'[53] Lugard next addressed himself to the simplification of the mode of collection. The *jakadu* of the emirs and *hakimai* who had served as tax collectors and who had received a percentage of the receipts were, as a class, to be eliminated. The *hakimai* would now be forced to live in the districts which they ruled rather than the emirate capitals and were to be transformed into district heads. Initially, the district heads, the village heads below them and the emirs above them were to be given a percentage of the tax collected. Later – when 'on the other hand, the system has become fully established and effective, and, on the other hand, it has become clear what incomes are to be required by the various grades and individuals in order to maintain their position'[54] – they were to be put on a salary. The intended result of such a policy was that 'the Native Administration . . . as in India, become incorporated with the British'.[55] In addition, the practice of assigning 'official estates' to office-holders where these did not already exist, and the maintenance of such a practice where it did, was to be adhered to. Income with which to maintain these estates and to hire free labour to replace 'serfs or slaves' now employed was to come from the realization of rent on a portion of these estates.[56]

The actual amount of taxes which was to be collected was to approach a uniform limit based on the taxes which had previously generally been in force, and was to be assessed by the political officer (Resident, district officer, etc) himself. The sums to be demanded were to be fixed. They were also to be 'amended and brought up to date from time to time (but not too frequently) . . . this fact should be explained to the peasantry, who otherwise might fear that increased industry and production would involve them in higher taxation'. The taxes were to be 'fixed rather too low than too high at first'. It was to be explained to all from emir to peasant that the proceeds were to pay for administration and levied 'in return for security to life and property, and the consequent increase in trade and wealth' and were not 'a personal perquisite of the High Commissioner or Resident (as they are likely to imagine)'.[57]

In the case of peoples beyond the boundaries of the Caliphate, taxation was to be levied on the community and not the individual and was to be assessed by the political officer but collected by the 'Village Chiefs and Elders'. Lugard's view of these peoples and their future was summed up in his comments on the usefulness of taxation as a civilizing influence. 'Obviously,' he noted, 'there will exist many grades varying between the wholly uncivilised savage and those . . . with a recognised chief and some form of law.'[58] Taxation, therefore, was seen as one of the ways in which the Government was to fulfil its responsibility to 'push each community a stage further up the ladder of progress and of individual and communal responsibility'.[59] Finally, the assessment of taxation was to 'bring the Political Officer in touch with his people'. All of this was to be done with a gentle hand. 'The primary test of a Resident's value and fitness for promotion' was 'the content and satisfaction prevailing in his Province'.[60] Once again, however, reality was at some variance with theory. As the Niger Company's representative in the north wrote to Lord Scarbrough in 1904:

> Taxation is really getting too funny. One Resident writes, 'I have taken so much Plantation Tax'. Sir F. [Lugard]: 'Plantation Tax! What is this! However don't stop until I can go into the matter.' Another – 'I have instituted something like a poll tax'. Sir F: 'Oh you have have you, you know that that is directly against my ideas! How dare you! However, leave matters until I can get around to see for myself.'[61]

The same source also provides us with a clue to a less obvious reason for the opposition of Girouard and Temple to the Lugardian system; its deleterious impact on trade. 'What a clean sweep the next man will make of this humbugging of trade,' a Niger Company agent wrote hopefully in 1904, 'we could not do a worse job for the country.'[62] A second Niger Company agent wrote along similar lines in 1905:

> I find that taxation in Northern Nigeria is still as vigorous as ever and I wonder that it does not crush trade altogether, anything and everything appears to be mulcted if taken from one place to another – even food is not exempt . . . under the present regime the case is hopeless. The incidence of taxation continues to change in the most capricious manner, and it is the industrious traders who suffer and are discouraged.[63]

In general, taxation was seen by the merchant community as an unavoidable evil. Every shilling which went to the government in taxes was a shilling which could not be used to purchase imported wares. As such a drain on commerce, taxation was to be kept as low as possible. The irony here is clear. While Henry George's Utopian socialism, as preached by Temple and Girouard sought to benefit capital through the elimination of landlords, capital knew better. It was government and taxation which were the evils. Neither Temple nor Girouard recognized this point. Others, however, did. In 1909, Resident Arnett noted to himself the problems which the application of George's theories raised:

> It is asserted that if the state appropriates the full economic rent of the land the private landowner is kept out of existence or driven out if he already exists . . . As a theory and an ideal it seems perfect but in practice does it not require a minutely inquisitorial machinery for the assessment of the economic rent of the land and a supernatural omniscience on the part of the administration? Does it not necessitate

that the state should incline to over-taxation with all its fruitful sources of disaster for a subject country like this . . . ? For the moment an occupier is called upon to pay less rent for his land than his neighbours are willing to pay for it he will inevitably tend to become a private landlord instead of a state tenant . . . If we are to preserve the principle of state ownership of land we will have to start as soon as possible an uphill fight against the inroads of the private landlord, we must proclaim the receipt of sale or rent money illegal and forthwith increase taxation in every district where it occurs.[64]

In his review of Lugard's writings on taxation Girouard sidestepped such issues, preferring to outline the mechanism through which taxes could be made to constitute an economic rent. Having implicitly criticized Lugard's writings and past practice, he now set about erecting, in time-honoured bureaucratic tradition, a precedent on which to base his call for a change. This he found in the Indian empire and, specifically, in Burma. Why was this example used? It is my opinion – an opinion based on an examination of Baden-Powell's *The Land Systems of British India*, the source which Girouard utilized, excerpted and distributed to his Residents – that an example from the Indian empire was chosen because any citation of imperial precedent from the Indian case explicitly carried a good deal of authority. However the specific example of Burma was probably chosen because it was the only tenure system in British India which does not *explicitly* recognize private property in land. As Baden-Powell notes, and as Girouard noticeably omits from his review of the work, Burma finds 'no direct parallel to the case of land tenures in India'.[65] However, in utilizing Burma, and, specifically, Lower Burma, as his case for the establishment of a legal basis for the construction of George's utopia in Northern Nigeria, Girouard was on extremely shaky ground. For while Baden-Powell had maintained that private property in land did not exist in Lower Burma, he had also been at great pains to point out that private property in land hardly existed anywhere – even in Britain. What did exist, he had argued, were forms of tenure which approached private property in land, or 'proprietary rights'. Thus he wrote concerning the Burmese example, 'It can hardly be doubted that the idea of proprietary right in land has long existed in Burma'.[66]

In order to justify the validity of the example of Lower Burma, Girouard was forced to lean heavily on the provisions of the 1876 Land Act of Burma, The Land Act was divided into two parts. Part I of the Act recognized, according to Baden-Powell, the right to permanently occupied land. In addition, the first part of the Act places all other land at the 'unfettered disposal of the state, *unless* some private person has acquired a specific right to it, i.e. some kind of right recognized and defined by the Act'.[67] In other words, all lands were vested in the state *unless* they were permanently occupied lands.

By sleight of hand, Girouard erased this distinction. He did so by citing a passage from Baden-Powell referring to Part II of the Act and omitting to mention that it referred to Part II, to wit:

GIROUARD: To sum up shortly as regards private rights, the land is *prima facie*, subject to no rights of private persons . . .[68]

BADEN-POWELL: To sum up shortly, it means that, generally speaking, as regards private lands, the land to which Part II applies is *prima facie* subject to no rights of private persons . . .[69]

Needless to say, Part II of the Land Act was not referring to the 'permanently occupied lands' of Part I of the Act. In short, in his utilization of the Lower Burma example as a precedent for Northern Nigeria, Girouard had nary a leg to stand on, except that of his own dubious construction.

Girouard also sought to utilize the Lower Burma taxation system as a guide post for Northern Nigeria's future. Here he was on somewhat safer ground, but only because the highly developed taxation system in Lower Burma established a precedent for the finely tuned assessment system which would be needed in Northern Nigeria if an economic rent was to be established and maintained. Such a system necessitated:

1 the complete survey of all lands.
2 registration of all cultivators . . .
3 the equitable assessment of land revenue.
4 punctual registration of all transfers and all changes in the occupation and use of the land.[70]

In other words it necessitated the creation of a Northern Nigerian Domesday Book. Collection was to be made by the presentation of a ticket stating the demand, and payment would be acknowledged by a receipt.

Girouard completed his analogy between Burma and Northern Nigeria by drawing the parallel between Upper Burma and the regions of Northern Nigeria which had been beyond the control of the Sokoto Caliphate. In both, what would initially appear to be a poll- or hut-tax would gradually be transformed into the more elaborate system of assessment described above.

In conclusion, Girouard launched a scarcely veiled attack on the policy of tax assessment in practice under Lugard in the Caliphate. Drawing on Assessment Reports, he demonstrated that far from a continuation of the Caliphate taxation system, assessment had degenerated into a poll tax. Coming only ten years after the Sierra Leone Hut Tax

War which was caused in large measure by the imposition of just such a tax, this was a damning indictment.[71]

Girouard's memorandum was now circulated to the Residents for comment in preparation for sittings of the Colonial Office Northern Nigerian Lands Committee. Only a complete incompetent would have failed to understand that a new broom was about to sweep the Lugardian system away. Writing to Lugard in Hong Kong, Girouard attempted to sweeten the pill:

> I am entirely with you on the Land Revenue policy though not entirely on Land Tenure . . . I can only say briefly that I favour the complete nationalization of land as a landholder's, not a landlord's system and full protection of the natives against the land grabber and usurer which such a system will permit.[72]

Temple expressed the same view to Lugard, only more bluntly:

> The fact that the land belongs to the community and not to the individual . . . is amply recognized throughout the report. Revenue is an 'economic rent' for the Government and guards against speculation, [and the report] defines taxation as 'payment for the use of land'.[73]

Temple also wrote to Lord Scarbrough in words designed to warm the heart of a merchant capitalist:

> The reason why I am so anxious that the prior claims of the natives should be acknowledged by the Government are two, 1) to justify the apparently arbitrary act on the part of the Government in assuming dominion over all land occupied and unoccupied 2) to provide for the unlikely, but possible, contingency of the exclusion of a section of natives from the land causing the primary interest of the Europeans, which are trade, to be subservient to the secondary interests i.e. planting and production.[74]

When the Northern Nigerian Lands Committee convened in London in 1908, its membership reflected the conclusions which the evidence already presented inescapably led to, with a proper leavening of expertise and authority designed to make these conclusions unassailable. It consisted of Strachey, Temple, Charles Orr, the Resident of Zaria who was clearly in Temple's camp, Sir James Diggs La Touche, former Lieutenant Governor of the United Provinces in India, T. Morison, a former member of the India Council, H. B. Cox of the Colonial Office, Sir Kenelm Digby, a former judge and Home Office official and J. C. Wedgwood, a Member of Parliament and a 'somewhat fanatical upholder of the single tax' theories.[75] The evidence laid before the committee consisted principally of the Residents' replies to Girouard's memorandum, the testimony of the Chief Justice of Southern Nigeria (who had no experience in the north), of Temple, Orr, and of Richmond Palmer, the Resident of Katsina and another Temple supporter.

Palmer's views on the land tenure question provide an interesting glimpse of how the committee's conclusions had been pre-ordained. Writing in 1907, in reply to Girouard's memorandum, Palmer stated that:

> the theory of Land Tenure at present *in being* . . . as an intelligent native would expound it, 1) The Governor owns all the land (or in other words the Crown). 2) He gives it to the Seriken Kano on payment of a certain amount of tribute. 3) The Seriken Kano gives the 'villages' or unit to a Sereki on payment of tribute.[76]

Palmer wrote further that he wished to maintain a peasant title in land and believed that 'it would be a pity to abolish the purchase system as in the mind of the native it gives him a title.'[77] Nonetheless, he also wished to restrict the sale of land to a system in which a farmer would legally be able to sell land only to the government, which would then sell it to other farmers. Yet, being a lawyer, he had very real doubts about such a procedure. While he staunchly maintained that the rural population did not hold a title of 'fee simple' to the land they occupied, the status generally recognized as ownership in England, he correctly pointed out that a 'fee simple' was, in strict legal terms, not ownership *per se* but merely a form of tenure granted by the Crown. However, he shied away from the logical conclusion of his own line of reasoning, which was that in strict legal definition there was little to distinguish the holder of a 'fee simple' tenure in England from the legal condition of the rural proprietor in Northern Nigeria.[78]

Palmer's evidence before the committee was contradictory. Compare his replies to two questions put to him by the committee's chairman on the same day:

Question 181
Q: Supposing that in a large town like Kano a person wants to transfer his land, does he have to go to a chief and if so what chief?
PALMER: In Kano itself?
Q: In Kano itself.
PALMER: To the Emir of Kano, I should say.[79]

Question 188
Q: Are houses bought and sold within Kano?
PALMER: Yes.
Q: Without reference to the Emir?
PALMER: Yes.[80]

The discrepancy in Palmer's answers was not even commented upon by the committee, for to have done so would have opened the whole question of the real status of landed property to an investigation, severely damaging the case put forward by Temple and Girouard. Why did Palmer hold so tenaciously to the view that private property in land had not existed within the Sokoto Caliphate? The answer is to be found in his reply to Girouard's memorandum on the land tenure question. It refers specifically to the consequences which Palmer thought would ensue if private property in land was recognized in the Protectorate. These would be, according to Palmer that 'they would all have their farms mortgaged in a year.'[81]

Palmer's evidence was reinforced by that of Temple and Orr, the testimony of the former comprising over a quarter of all evidence heard. Temple was clearly seen by the committee as the expert. Presented with such a unified front, the committee came to the obvious conclusion:

> The whole of the land whether occupied or unoccupied, is subject to the control of the Government.
>
> He [the occupier] has no legal right to security of possession: he cannot sell or mortgage the land so as to make secure title to the purchaser or mortgagee. Nor does he transmit indefeasible title to his heirs.[82]

On the basis of these conclusions it was decided by the committee that 'Government is entitled for any good cause to revoke the title of any occupier . . . ' and 'good cause' was defined as:

a) non-payment of taxes or dues
b) voluntary alienation by sale or mortgage or transfer of possession without the consent of the Government
c) requirement of the land by the Government for public purposes[83]

Clearly, from this point on, the ownership of private property in land ceased to exist in the Protectorate of Northern Nigeria. Had it ever existed? Given the nature of the evidence placed before the committee and the purpose for which it was collected, it is difficult to say. There were, however, those who clearly doubted the validity of the findings of the committee. The first of these was Lugard himself, who, safely in Hong Kong, had no voice in the committee's proceedings. There were others – like Watts, the Niger Company agent who wrote to his employer, Lord Scarbrough:

> Two facts strike me very forcibly in connection with the evidence taken before the committee, firstly the evidence of the parties principally interested i.e. the natives of Northern Nigeria was not

sought, and secondly benefit was not taken of Sir William Wallace . . .
in the country prior to British occupation . . . the socialistic principles
of the Land Committee will prove to be utopian and unworkable in
practice . . . I cannot agree with Mr Temple's conclusion that under
no possible conditions could a private estate exist in Northern
Nigeria . . . I am well aware that in the Emirate of Bida under emir
Maliki, circa 1885–1895 private individuals were fully allowed to
dispose of their interests in such property and this is confirmed by Dr
Cargill's assertion that in Kano the right of the user of a plot of land
could be purchased and such right was inheritable. This official had
experience in the country prior to British occupation and to my mind
his conception of land ownership under Fulani rule is [a] much more
accurate one than Mr Temple's . . .[84]

Such criticism of the committee's findings receives support from evidence
which appears in a 1914 tax assessment report for Raba District in Sokoto
Province. This states that 'in former times it was customary to sell farms
ranging from £1 to £5 to strangers, but since the Land Proclamation of
1910, (which put into effect the recommendations of the Lands
Committee) this has ceased.'[85] What was the situation regarding land
tenure in the Caliphate before British rule? Perhaps the best analysis of
the situation made at the time was that given by former Resident Arnett,
who had not been asked to present his views to the committee.
Commenting on the committee's deliberations, he wrote:

> State ownership of land is the customary tenure of the country and one
> which it is desired to maintain. It exists naturally where a people living
> in a patriarchal state of society settle in a country which offers them
> more fertile land than they require. So long as there is good land to
> spare it can acquire no private sale or rent value. But in the Hausa
> states and in this Emirate [Kano] especially land is so fully occupied
> that it has for years past acquired such a value and private ownership
> of land is therefore coming into being and must if the present course of
> events continues be eventually recognized as part of the customary law
> of the land . . .[86]

If Arnett's analysis of the situation was correct, and it is the view of this
author that it is, if anything, an understatement of the situation at that
time, then the findings of the Lands Committee had the effect of halting
the development of the ownership of private property in land in Northern
Nigeria and as such could only have enormous consequences for the
economic and social development of the Protectorate. What were these?
    First, in the absence of private property in land, Lugard's vision of the
creation of a landlord class was doomed. In its place the implementation
of the Girouard/Temple/Palmer policy set the stage for the transformation of the old ruling class into a mock-feudal bureaucracy. A major step

in this direction was accomplished by the introduction throughout the north of the *beit-el-mal*, or Native Treasury, which was first established in Katsina Emirate by Palmer in 1910–11. The Emir of Katsina, a British appointee with no legitimate claim to power, was heavily dependent on British goodwill. Thus, he submitted to the practice of depositing a share of the tax proceeds in a local government account or Native Treasury. In time these Native Treasuries became the material basis for the founding of the Native Administration bureaucracies. Gradually weaned away from their direct appropriation of a share of the agricultural surplus through the introduction of salaries, the emirs, district and village heads and Islamic judges formed the human material of the colonial state. Through them, the demands of the state for order, funds and the increased production of commodities were met. Physical control by the Native Administration rested ultimately on the colonial state, while ideological control was continued and enhanced by the maintenance of pre-colonial Islamic hegemony.

Law and order was maintained by a native police force, the *dogari*. Judges were trained by Islamic jurists from other colonies, notably the Sudan. Taxes were assessed by native surveyors and collected by native authorities. Taken as a whole, the creation and gradually increasing sophistication of the Native Administration was a rationalization of the colonial state. This was to operate harmoniously with the increased commoditization of the social formation of Northern Nigeria. Taxes were collected, order was maintained and the shell of ideological authority left little room for anything to emerge comparable to the quarrelsome voice of the southern Nigerian bourgeoisie. The Native Administration also operated as the instrument for the implementation of such development policy as existed. Initially, this was confined to road building and other construction, but later included greater attention to agricultural issues.

Secondly, and as a consequence of the fate of the ruling class, the rural producers of the region were to be transformed into a peasantry rather than the wage earning, agricultural proletariat which Lugard had envisaged.

Thirdly, the creation of a form of plantation agriculture originating from external capital was also blocked and the predominance of merchant capital within the Northern Nigerian social formation was guaranteed.

Fourthly, state control of landed property (and thus control of a major portion of the surplus appropriated from that source) blocked the indigenous accumulation of capital via the control of the principal means of production, land, a crucial feature of all societies which have made a full transition to capitalism as a system of production and exchange.

In addition, three important theoretical conclusions can be drawn from the resolution of the land tenure question. These concern the nature of the colonial state in Northern Nigeria. First, although state power had initially derived from the use of force, its later development was firmly rooted in the ability to appropriate the surplus product of rural producers through the mechanism of taxation, by virtue of its ownership of the means of production – land. Secondly, the manner in which the land question was resolved was itself a reflection of the power of the various forms of accumulation present in Northern Nigerian society. Initially, the power of the indigenous ruling class was recognized and an attempt was made to maintain the loyalty of this class to the colonial state via the attempt to create a landed aristocracy. When this attempt was blocked, the state fell back to the position of maintaining the old ruling class as state functionaries. In doing so, the ideological relation between the old ruling class and the rural producers was maintained and in large measure passed on to the colonial state while its economic base was undercut. The position of merchant capital as a whole, which was the most important bloc of capital within the state, was guaranteed. No attempt to undercut the power of this bloc through the establishment of capitalist relations of production whether generated internally or externally was to be permitted.

Thirdly, the abolition of the legal right to own property in land, although couched in humanitarian terminology and implemented under the pretext of saving Northern Nigeria's agricultural producers from the fate of expropriation and landlessness was in fact an action in the interests of capital as a whole. In his views concerning the iniquity of landlordism, Henry George was a lineal, if somewhat eccentric descendant of Ricardo whose thinly veiled attack on the parasitical nature of landlordism gained increasing ground during the course of the nineteenth century. By abolishing the ownership of private property in land, precluding the emergence of a landlord class and eliminating the possibility of local accumulation through the mechanism of ground rent, the colonial state ensured that no capitalist would face the possibility of having to pay tribute to landed property. This was, as Lenin said of other land nationalization schemes under capitalism, a bourgeois reform.

Capital would however be forced to pay a price for this intervention on its behalf. That price was to be the emergence of the state itself as a major accumulator. The colonial state would henceforth maintain two, often conflicting positions – as arbitrator among the various capitalist interests and as a major accumulator in its own right. The result was that from its origin, capitalism in Northern Nigeria was to be characterized by the distorted and truncated nature of its birth.

Moreover, the impact of the abolition of private property in land was not limited to Northern Nigeria. In the aftermath of the Lands Committee's report a similar committee – the West African Lands Committee – including three of the members of the Northern Nigerian committee was formed to consider the land tenure system in British West Africa as a whole. Although the findings of this committee – which collected evidence between 1912 and 1914 and reported in 1916 – were not published, its proceedings had a profound impact on the formation of land law in the Protectorate of Sierra Leone, the Northern Territories of the Gold Coast, Tanganyika and elsewhere. In each case the Northern Nigerian model was implemented in so far as previously held practice permitted. The impact of such legislation on the evolution of the societies concerned clearly deserves further study.[87]

NOTES

1   See J. Smaldone, *Warfare in the Sokoto Caliphate: Historical and Sociological Perspectives* (Cambridge: Cambridge University Press, 1977).

2   ibid.

3   Ironically Marx drew on the writings of many of the same authors in the formation of his ideas on the Asiastic Mode of Production. See L. Krader, *The Asiatic Mode of Production: Sources, Development and Critique in the Writings of Karl Marx* (Assen: Van Gorcum, 1975).

4   See P. Curtin, *The Image of Africa; British Ideas and Action, 1780-1850* (Madison: University of Wisconsin Press: 1964).

5   On the uses and abuses of humanitarianism, see Eric Williams, *Capitalism and Slavery* (London: André Deutsch, 1964).

6   F. Lugard, *Political Memoranda*, 1906. A copy of this work may be found in the Northern History Research Scheme at Ahmadu Bello University. It should not be confused with the similarly titled volume published in 1919 by Lugard. This latter work, *Political Memoranda. Revision of Instructions to Political Officers on Subjects Chiefly Political and Administrative, 1913-1918* is readily available as a reprint published in 1970 by Frank Cass, London with an introduction by A. H. M. Kirk-Greene. The two works are entirely distinct. It was on the basis of the 1906 volume that Northern Nigeria was governed. Ironically, it was on the basis of the 1919 volume that Lugard's reputation as a political theorist of colonialism was built. Lugard systematically attempted to destroy all copies of the 1906 volume.

7   ibid.

8   On Jones, Kingsley, and Morel see S. J. S. Cookey, *Britain and the Congo Question, 1885-1913* (London: Longmans, 1968).

9   On the Niger Company's mineral rights see J. E. Flint, *Sir George Goldie and the Making of Nigeria* (London: Oxford University Press, 1960), p. 307.

10 See La Ray Denzer, 'Sierra Leone-Bai Bureh', in M. Crowder (ed.), *West African Resistance* (London: Hutchinson, 1971), pp. 233-67

11 See D. J. M. Muffett, *Empire Builder Extraordinary: Sir George Goldie* (Ramsey, IOM: Shearwater Press, 1978).

12 Flint, *Goldie*, p. 333.

13 Lugard, *Political Memoranda* (1906), 'Slavery Questions,' para. 13.

14   ibid., para. 14.
15   See M. Perham, *Lugard, The Years of Authority 1898–1945* (London: Collins, 1960), pp. 252–65.
16   Rhodes House Manuscripts, British Empire (hereafter RH, Mss Brit. Emp.) s. 62, Lugard Papers, E. J. Lugard to F. D. Lugard, October 1907.
17   ibid., W. Miller to F. Lugard, 24 December 1907.
18   RH Mss, Brit. Emp. s. 63, Lugard Papers, Howard to Lugard, 21 May 1908.
19   Lugard, *Political Memoranda* (1906), 'Slavery Questions', para. 8.
20   ibid., para. 10.
21   ibid., para. 11.
22   ibid., para. 14.
23   Henry George, *Progress and Poverty* (London, Routledge & Kegan Paul, 1981), p. 154.
24   Perham, *Lugard*, p. 474.
25   ibid., p. 187.
26   ibid., p. 485.
27   NAK SNP 6 c162/1907, 'Memorandum on Land Tenure in Northern Nigeria'. Note that both the file cited here and NAK SNP 16 c4002 contain much of the same information. They appear to be two drafts of the same document. However, each contains a portion of the material to be found in the draft which appears as an appendix to Lugard's *Political Memoranda* (1906) which the other does not. See B. H. Baden-Powell, *The Land Systems of British India* (Oxford, OUP, 1892; reprinted 1972 New York, Johnson Reprint Corp.).
28   NAK SNP 6 c162/1907, p. 2.
29   ibid., p. 2.
30   ibid.
31   ibid.
32   Lugard, *Political Memoranda*, (1906), no. 16, para. 1.
33   ibid.
34   ibid.
35   ibid., para. 2.
36   ibid.
37   ibid., para. 4.
38   ibid., para. 5.
39   ibid., para. 6.
40   Lugard, *Political Memoranda* (1906), no. 5, para. 4.
41   NAK SNP 6 c162/1907, para. 4.
41   ibid., para. 4.
42   ibid., para. 2.
43   ibid., para. 4.
44   ibid.
45   RH Mss, Afr. s. 96, Royal Niger Company Papers (henceforth, RNC), vol. 12, Lenthall to Scarbrough, 1 October 1904.
46   Lugard, *Political Memoranda* (1906), no. 7, paras 6,7,8.
47   ibid., no. 5, para. 3.
48   ibid., para. 4.
49   ibid.

50 ibid.
51 ibid., para. 5.
52 ibid., para. 3.
53 ibid., para. 7.
54 ibid., para. 38.
55 ibid.
56 ibid., para. 41.
57 ibid., para. 26.
58 ibid., para. 65.
59 ibid.
60 ibid., para. 78.
61 RH Mss, Afr. s. 96, RNC, vol. 12, Lenthall to Scarbrough, 1 October 1904.
62 ibid.
63 ibid., Watts to Scarbrough, 8 June 1905. See also Watts to Scarbrough, 24 June 1905.
64 RH Mss, Afr. s. 952, Arnett Papers, box 6, 18 August 1909.
65 Baden-Powell, *Land Systems*, p. 489.
66 ibid., p. 490.
67 ibid., p. 495.
68 NAK SNP 16 c4002, p. 7.
69 Baden-Powell, *Land Systems*, p. 496.
70 United Kingdom, 1910 Cmd 5101, *Northern Nigerian Lands Committee*, 'Minutes of Evidence', p. 46.
71 Denzer, 'Bai Bureh'.
72 RH Mss, Brit. Emp. s. 63, Lugard Papers, Girouard to Lugard, 16 August 1908.
73 RH Mss, Afr. s. 87, RNC, vol. 3, Temple to Lugard, 16 August 1908.
74 ibid., vol. 12, Temple to Scarbrough, 27 July 1908.
75 RH Mss, Brit. Emp. s. 63, Lugard Papers, Girouard to Lugard, 28 April 1909.
76 NAK SNP 6 c162/1907, Submission by H. R. Palmer.
77 ibid.
78 ibid.
79 United Kingdom, 1910 Cmd 5103, *Northern Nigerian Lands Committee*, 'Proceedings', Question 181.
80 ibid., Question 188.
81 NAK SNP 6 c162/1907, Submission by Palmer.
82 United Kingdom, 1910 Cmd 5102, *Northern Nigerian Lands Committee* 'Summary of Conclusions and Recommendations'.
83 ibid., para. 72.
84 RH Mss, Afr. s. 99, RNC, vol 15, Watts to Scarbrough, 25 June 1910.
85 NAK SNP 10 609p/1914.
86 RH Mss, Afr. s. 952, Arnett Papers, box 6, 18 August 1909.
87 Copies of the draft report, minutes of evidence and correspondence and papers of the West African Lands Committee, printed for internal use in the Colonial Office (Confidential Print Afr. nos 1046, 1047, 1048), are to be found in PRO CO 897/117 and CO 897/118. A copy of the report is also to be found in the Foreign and Commonwealth Office Library, London.

4

The Origins
of Colonial Capitalism
in Northern Nigeria

If the proceedings culminating in the Northern Nigerian Lands Committee resolved the theoretical and legal problem of the financial basis of the colonial state, they did little to alleviate the concrete and immediate problem of the state's fiscal insolvency. The seriousness of this problem can be gauged from the fact that the colonial state ran deficits of over £400 000 per annum on an expenditure of just over £500 000 between 1903 and 1906. Continued deficit financing on this scale was out of the question. Northern Nigeria had to be made to pay for its colonial government. The quantity of tax realized by the state had to be increased.[1]

How was this goal achieved? The records of the colonial state give us a clear answer – by an increase in the tax assessed on the rural agricultural producers. This increase in the taxation of the rural population was the result of an increasingly stringent assessment procedure. In the years immediately following the conquest, all districts in the Caliphate were classified as being 'native assessed', that is, the customary taxes which had been paid, continued to be paid. This system was gradually replaced by the system of 'Resident assessment'. The customary taxes continued to be paid but were supplemented by a tax on compounds. Finally, all farms were to be measured and an assessment was to be made on the basis of each farm's estimated productivity. Initially, this assessment was to be made by a 'native' and later by a Resident. A later stage in which soil quality was to be taken into account was proposed but appears to have only been implemented in a small area around the city of Kano.[2]

While the ideological justification for the ascent of this increasingly sophisticated ladder of tax assessment systems was the reduction in the *number* of taxes which the agricultural producer paid, in reality it had the effect of increasing the *amount* paid.[3] For example, the reassessment of Azare District in 1912 by the Resident resulted in an increase of 120 per cent over the previous assessment.[4] The general level of assessment per adult male in Sokoto Province increased by over one-third during the period 1911 to 1913.[5] In Fawa District an increase from 1s 4d to 3s 3d per adult male was made in 1907, and in the adjoining district of Kotorkoshi taxes were increased by nearly 200 per cent.[6] Not only were taxes on land dramatically increased but so were taxes on livestock. The average annual increase of the cattle tax in three divisions of Kano Province was between 22 per cent and 39 per cent during the period 1908 to 1913, while the total increase was between 88 per cent and 136 per cent.[7]

Nor does the stated increase in taxation, as assessed, fully reveal the extent of the increased burden on the rural producer. As village and district heads struggled to maintain their own income in the face of the colonial state which had transformed them from tax farmers into mere tax collectors, customary taxes were imposed over and above the colonial state's demands. One Resident writing privately about Zaria Province estimated in 1910 that 'roughly 100% more taxes are being paid than are returned to us'.[8] The assessor of Gonyoro District in Sokoto Province stated that while local collectors 'were almost word perfect in their theory of the methods of assessment', they 'were undeniably collecting very largely in excess'.[9]

The burden of the state's demands was compounded for the poor by the assessors making their calculations of tax due on the basis of the market price of produce at the time of assessment; the producer was forced to sell his grain at harvest when the market was glutted. Thus in Dan Makoyo District in Kano Province, taxation was assessed on the value of guinea corn (sorghum) at 1s 6d per 60 lb bundle, yet the assessor commented that 'the value of a bundle of guinea corn of say 60 lbs. weight, at the time of year when the farmer must dispose of it to pay his taxes . . . is not more than -/6'. He concluded that 'on the new basis of taki assessment . . . he has to pay 40% of the produce of his farm in taxes.'[10] It is useful to remember here that this 40 per cent figure did not include the demands of local petty officials, nor the cost of conversion of cowries into silver, both of which the Dan Makoyo farmer might well have had to pay.

Finally, the assessment of the colonial state was by and large inflexible, taking little account of the quality of the harvest in any particular area or year. This led to a vast increase in the rate of taxation. Commenting on one particularly bad year, 1908, a district officer in southern Kano Province was moved to write:

As you are aware the Talakawa [commoners] have suffered greatly this last year . . . owing to the bad harvest last year and unfortunately owing to our not having realized how great was their want, for the last few months the old people, the women and the children have been literally starving. It was stated that although the corn last year was not a third of the usual crop, Zakka in kind was levied as usual making the amount claimed (but not taken) not a tithe as we like to think, nor a sixth as we sometimes admit, but as much as one-half of what was grown.[11]

In the above case the amount assessed was 'not taken'. The records of the colonial state are, however, ominously silent as to what transpired in other districts and provinces. There is silence as well on the immediate response to such increased exactions. For one town in one district, Gonyoro, we do, however, have eloquent and simple testimony of their effects on the local collectors who 'found the strain of apportioning the taxes among their people too great' in 1911 'and have gone away'.[12]

The increase in tax revenue realized by the colonial state was, however, only part of the problem. The question of the form in which taxes were paid was of equal, if not greater, importance. Only ,one-quarter to one-half of the state's obligations were local and not even all of these could be met in cowrie shells and grain. Moreover, grain often cost more to dispose of than was realized from its sale, while the state's holdings in cowries depreciated as a result of the state's own demands for cash.[13] The colonial state increasingly demanded that taxes be paid in British currency as opposed to the pre-colonial payments in kind or in cowrie shells, these being the predominant local currency. This demand fostered a brisk seasonal business for the local money changers, as is made clear by the report of Birtwistle, the government commercial intelligence officer in 1907:

> when I was in Sokoto an attempt was being made by the brokers who had large stocks of cowries to force the exchange, which had been unduly inflated up to 600 cowries for 3d down to 300. This situation was caused by the scarcity of silver in the province at the time the annual collection of tribute was made, the Government ruling that this . . . should not be accepted in either cowries or kind but only cash. Holders of silver realizing this position, naturally took advantage to get possession of cowries at a very cheap rate with a view to putting them back on the market at a very dear one.[14]

The banning of the importation of cowrie shells cut off any new supply but did little to replace the existing money supply with British coin. What was needed was the wholesale introduction of British currency into the Northern Nigerian economy. This was clearly seen by Lugard as the role of British merchant capital. Only merchant capital could make British currency current by paying it out for local produce and demanding it back for the sale of imported goods. It was this concern over currency which conditioned the colonial state's attitude towards the different forms of trade. Lugard stated this position most cogently:

> The trader who buys with a mere token of currency and exports produce, therefore benefits the Government and the country most of all. He who imports goods, and exports their equivalent value is the next most valuable class of trader, while the man who imports goods and receives a mere token in exchange adds to the indebtedness of the country, because no valuable commodity leaves the country in return for the commodities received, and because in the circumstances of this country he makes it impossible for the Government to realize its revenue from taxes.[15]

Thus the attitude of the state was an almost purely mercantilist one. 'The general principle,' Lugard continued, 'is, in fact sufficiently obvious, viz., that a country can only pay its debts by the produce or manufactures that it exports overseas.'[16] Taxation could not be realized unless it was paid in British silver and British silver could only be brought into circulation through the growth of the sale of locally produced commodities to British merchant firms for cash. Yet, before 1912, British merchants purchased very little local produce nor did they usually trade in cash, preferring barter. In order to understand why this preference for barter existed it is necessary to examine the position of British merchant capital within the Northern Nigerian economy.

Before 1910, the presence of British merchant capital in Northern Nigeria was exceedingly modest. The Niger Company largely clung to its riverain trade, while the fledgling London and Kano Trading Company, which represented the attempts of two former colonial officers to break into the Kano market, teetered on the brink of bankruptcy. Beginning in 1902, Lugard addressed a series of pleas to the Niger Company to open up the north. These fell on deaf ears, and for good reason.[17]

In the same year, Watts, the Niger Company's commercial intelligence officer, reported gloomily to Lord Scarbrough on the prospects of the Company opening up shop in the commercial capital of the north. 'Kano,' he noted, 'is a great central market for the distribution of goods and products which have no possible chance of a market in Europe and therefore it would not pay the Company or indeed any other firm of European merchants to trade in them.'[18] Scarbrough seconded these comments and relayed them to Oliver Lyttleton, the Secretary of State for the Colonies, remarking that although 'for Imperial reasons it has been necessary to hastily occupy this huge territory, from a commercial point of view there is no justification whatsoever for the immense expenditure that has been incurred.'[19] No doubt Lyttleton appreciated the niceties of the distinction between 'Imperial' and 'commercial' reasons for the occupation in the light of the history of the Royal Niger Company's machinations to create the requisite imperial reasons for the hasty occupation of this huge territory.[20]

If British merchant capital held a minimal position in the Protectorate, the position of British manufactured goods was little better. The Resident of Katsina was moved to comment in 1907 that it was 'remarkable in going through the country how little English cloth is to be seen.'[21] Birtwistle, the government's commercial intelligence officer, concurred, commenting in the same year 'that not more than two per cent of the clothes worn by the natives of this district are of European manufacture'.[22]

What were the reasons for this paucity of British trade? Undoubtedly the most important explanation was the self-sufficiency of the regional economy. Northern Nigeria itself possessed an old and well-developed handloom textile industry which rather than being shattered by cheap British cloth showed every sign of continued growth.[23] The vibrancy of this local craft provoked the Resident of Katsina to comment irately that '. . . the most paying [trade] at present is to take Hausa cloth and sell them [sic] at Lokoja. Thus in a market we *made* the native cloth is preferred to that the English firms import.'[24] This self-sufficiency was closely connected to the economics of the import-export trade, the characteristics of which it is now necessary to elucidate. This may be done through an examination of the Niger Company's operating methods.

The chief business of the Niger Company's stores along the Niger River and its tributaries was to sell British manufactures and to purchase local produce. So far, so simple. Yet, the business was an extremely complex one, complicated not least of all by the structure of merchant capital itself. The Niger Company could have sold British goods for cash and remitted the cash to its head office in England. It did not, however, choose to do so because the cost of remitting specie (including freight and insurance charges) was quite high. Alternatively, it could have imported specie and purchased local produce for cash and sent the produce home for sale. It did not choose to do this either, for equally compelling reasons. First, the Company had to pay a 1 per cent premium on all specie procured locally to the Bank of British West Africa which was owned by the Company's arch-rival, the shipping magnate Sir Alfred Jones.[25] Secondly, the Company would have had to have borne the freight rates which Sir Alfred charged. These were, to say the least, extravagant both for imports and exports. How extravagant can be assessed from a comparison of the freight rates charged for salt imported into West Africa by Jones's Elder Dempster line with the rates of other lines for the same commodity. In 1907 the freight on a ton of salt shipped from Liverpool to Calcutta cost (including Suez Canal duties), 4s 6d; to Buenos Aires the cost was 11s 4d; even to Yokohama the cost was only 15s. Yet, the freight rate from Liverpool to Lagos or any other West African port over which Elder Dempster had a stranglehold was 20s–30s a ton![26]

Exports were equally affected by heavy sea-freight rates, as a letter from Trigge, one of the Niger Company's managers, to Lord Scarbrough in 1908 makes clear:

> It is well to remember that until quite recently the Niger company paid the ridiculous freight of 57/9 per ton of groundnuts from Burutu to Liverpool which has subsequently been reduced to 40/- per ton . . . The Niger Company were urged by Government to push the groundnut industry for which at an early date there is a great future in northern Nigeria, but how can they compete when groundnuts are shipped from Bathurst to the continent direct 12/6 to 15/- per ton.[27]

Yet another strategy might have been for the Niger Company to have imported British manufactured goods in order to have sold them for cash and then to have used the cash to purchase produce for sale in Britain or in Europe. Here again the Company was blocked, since southern Nigerians, who did not have to remit their profits to a home office in Britain, could nearly always have undersold the Company in the northern markets. The Resident of Muri Province remarked that although:

> the trade upriver consists almost entirely of European manufactures practically every item that the factories have in stock for the native trade can be bought outside in the market for 1/6 to -/3 less than in the canteen, though of course not in large quantities. For instance salt can always be bought for 30% to 35% less in the market than from the factories . . . Croydon priced at the factories at 3/6, can be bought outside at 2/9–3/-, baft at 9/-, in the market at 8/- to 8/6.[28]

Given these conditions it is difficult to understand how the Niger Company could have managed to sell anything at all. Yet it did. It was able to do so by insisting that all transactions be carried out in barter form. As early as 1900 Resident Hewby of Bornu Province complained that '. . . no black man buy salt except for produce . . .'[29] Similar complaints continue right up until 1915. The Niger Company insisted on barter because it was the only way in which it could make a profit. The local inhabitants needed British currency to pay their taxes and this commodity was in very short supply. What little British silver there was in circulation was largely the result of payments made to the colonial state's army and staff and the result of their local purchases. One of the few ways in which this scarce commodity could be obtained by rural taxpayers was through the sale of agricultural goods to British merchants, primarily the Niger Company, which jealously guarded its near-monopoly position in the north through the harassment of competitors, through commercial agreements, and through its control of river transport. The Niger Company charged competitors 40s–60s per ton for a 300-mile voyage which it privately calculated as costing only 28s per ton.[30]

The industrious local inhabitants who brought their produce for sale to the Niger Company, however, were not given silver for their produce, but merely scrip good for the purchase of cloth or salt at its stores. In order to acquire British silver, these goods then had to be taken to the local market where they were sold for silver at a much reduced price. Hence, much of the imported merchandise which was observed to be available in the local markets at below the Niger Company's prices was, in fact, the company's own merchandise![31]

The reason why the Niger Company insisted on barter now becomes clearer. A 1918 memo by T. F. Burrows, the Nigerian government war-time food controller elucidates this matter. 'Before the war,' he noted, '[produce] was practically a form of remittance. They [British firms] made a normal profit on the produce and saved the cost of a money remittance. The profits of the firms were made on imports.'[32] A 1901 report by Watts had made a similar point, stating that the merchant made his profits on cotton cloth imports which constituted the bulk of the Niger Company's trade. The produce trade, then, began as a by-product of the extension of British markets for manufactured goods.[33]

The 'sale' of imported goods, actually bartered at well over their market value, also covered the heavy freight expenses of the shipment of agricultural produce to the European market. In addition, over-invoicing to avoid the payment of taxes was a common practice. This method of doing business presented the amazing contradiction of the Niger Company making a paper loss and a money profit at one and the same time. Lugard figured it out and explained it to Lyttleton at the Colonial Office in the following manner:

> Cloth is invoiced out of England to the Benue station at 100% over cost price and salt at much more. If the expenses of the station are calculated at the locally invoiced price of the goods with which these expenses are met, and the cost of ivory is similarly shown, the paradox is capable of a solution, that the Company are selling at a large loss and yet making a profit.[34]

A barter trade, however, no matter how profitable for the Niger Company, was not exactly what Lugard wanted to encourage, for it did not improve the prospects of realizing taxation in silver. Nor was a barter trade thought by the Resident in charge of Muri Province in 1910 to be the best method of promoting local industry. He asked:

Is it human nature for a Provincial Officer in charge of a pagan district to use his utmost legitimate pressure in inducing his savages to collect shea nuts or to cultivate beniseed or cotton when he knows that all they will be able to get in return is some piece of cloth said to be of the value of 2/- and which the pagan can only sell in order to obtain the cash wherewith to pay his taxes for 1/9 in the open market? So long as the country people only consider currency as an article of barter needed once a year to satisfy the demands of the Government so long will the development of the trade of the country be hampered. If the question be asked, 'What do you consider the chief desiderata for the further development of trade?' I would answer . . . cash for produce.[35]

If the Niger Company's methods of trade begin to explain the insignificant British commercial presence in the north, they also provide a clue to the tenacious persistence of another group of foreign merchants, the trans-Saharan caravan traders.[36] From W. B. Baikie's visit to Kano in 1862 onwards, the diversion of the caravan trade from the trans-Saharan routes south to the Bight of Benin was a more or less constant aim of British merchants and officials. Yet, as recent research has shown, the trans-Saharan merchants continued to pursue a substantial trade up to the end of the first decade of colonial rule in Northern Nigeria. The existence of this trade was in fact utilized as a subsidiary argument in the propaganda campaign justifying the Sokoto Caliphate's conquest. Yet, it failed to fall into the hands of coastal-oriented British merchant capital until the beginning of the First World War. It also failed to contribute to Lugard's plans for making the Protectorate pay for its debts out of exported produce. In order to understand both why the trans-Saharan trade survived in the face of British competition from the coast and why it failed to make its proper contribution to imperial revenue it is now necessary to discuss the trans-Saharan traders and their trade.[37]

The trans-Saharan trade was an ancient one. That is not to say, however, that it was a changeless one. Alterations in the political economy of its termini on the Mediterranean shore and in the Sudanic belt of West Africa as well as changes in the political economy of the desert which it crossed, made and unmade the routes which it followed. Such changes were taking place from the middle of the nineteenth century onwards, but they were of a different order from those which had previously occurred, for these new mutations were the product of European capitalist expansion which altered the goods traded, the identity of the merchants themselves, and eventually set the stage for the trade's demise.[38]

From the middle of the nineteenth century on, the northern 'ports' of the trans-Saharan trade were increasingly coming under the influence of European imperialism. The advance guard of European commerce took up forward positions all along the North African coast much as its counterparts were doing on the Bight of Benin. European powers established formal political control in some areas, while being content in others to establish a commanding but informal political presence. It was, however, the ruinous financial policies of the Beys of Tunis which provided European merchant capital with the necessary gap through which to intrude into the trans-Saharan trade, and ultimately into the Sokoto Caliphate.[39]

We need here to consider only briefly the process of fiscal folly through which the Tunisian government was ensnared. By 1862 it had borrowed some 28 million francs from European sources to finance a programme of modernization. The funds were borrowed on such usurious terms that by the following year a further loan of 65 million francs was necesssary to consolidate the Tunisian national debt. In addition to these external debts the Bey had borrowed a further 50 million francs from local merchants, many of whom were members of the Maltese and Jewish communities, resident in Tunis and on the island of Djerba. Attempts to forestall the impending collapse of the Tunisian state took the form of concessions to these commercial communities while the consuls of those countries which controlled the external debt grew in political influence in the court of the Bey. Attempted increases in taxation to meet the repayment of the debt were met with rebellion, which had a disturbing effect on the desert trade, itself an important source of revenue for the Tunisian state. The Bey, powerless to halt this rapidly worsening state of affairs, was forced in 1868 to surrender the control of state finances to an international commission made up of the representatives of those who held the Tunisian external debt. With the creation of the financial commission, the independence of Tunisia practically came to an end.[40]

The loss of economic independence by the Bey carried with it legal concessions to the power of the European consuls. The claim to extra-territorial rights by all those who were recognized by the consuls as being the subjects or protected persons of the countries which these consuls represented was guaranteed. Thus all those members of the local trading communities who could place themselves under the protection of the British, French or Italian authorities were able to have commercial legal cases (most of which involved the recovery of debts) adjudicated under European rather than Islamic law. The claims of many of these 'protected persons' were dubious in the extreme, while the final decision as to their status was often in the hands of the consuls themselves. Since many of these had commercial interests, the decisions taken were sometimes based upon considerations which had little to do with the validity of the claims themselves.[41]

Under the umbrella of consular protection, the importance of Maltese and Jewish merchants in the commerce of North Africa grew in the third quarter of the nineteenth century. Using Tunis as a base they were able to become an important force in the trans-Saharan trade, rivalling and later often providing the trading capital for the older commercial communities like the Ghadamasi. Local opposition to the European protégés was intense, yet indigenous merchants were powerless to halt their inroads.[42]

The penetration of the trans-Saharan trade by these representatives of European commerce came during a crucial period. The second quarter of the nineteenth century had been a period of commercial stagnation, if not decline. This situation was undoubtedly linked to the ultimate success of the British attempts to halt the trans-Saharan trade in slaves in the 1840s and 1850s. Although slaves – destined for the markets of North Africa and Constantinople – had never been the sole commodity traded across the desert, they had been one of the most important.[43]

It is important to note that Northern Nigeria was not a raw materials exporter during this period but rather an exporter of manufactured goods such as woven and dyed cloth, tanned and dyed skins, leather bags, shoes and such like. With the advent of the new trading networks, ushered in by the intervention of the European protégés, the destination of the goods produced in the Sokoto Caliphate and elsewhere in the central Sudan underwent a marked change.[44] The campaign to abolish the desert slave trade, much like its predecessor on the West African coast, was linked to a successful attempt to create a 'legitimate commerce' with a European bias. The relative success of abolition dovetailed nicely with the growing ascendancy of the European protégés in Tunis and in the last quarter of the nineteenth century the desert trade was subjected to the whims of the European market. First ivory, then ostrich feathers and, finally, tanned skins provided the inspiration for the peaks and slumps of Saharan exports, while cheap cotton cloth made up a larger and larger share of imports from the late 1860s on.[45]

Very little is known about the role of the European protégés in the trans-Saharan trade, yet for one family there is enough material to illustrate what is perhaps a representative origin and development. The Arbib family, Jews resident in Tunis under British protection, became principal financial backers of the trans-Saharan caravans in the last quarter of the nineteenth century. This family seems to have made its entry into the upper echelon of Tunisian merchants via participation in the esparto grass boom of the 1860s. Esparto grass was a raw material used in the manufacture of paper and for a brief period large amounts of money were to be made in the trade. By the end of the nineteenth century the Arbibs had members of the family in Manchester, Tunis, and Tripoli as well as a network of agents and sub-agents in the Sokoto Caliphate. By this time the chief articles of the trans-Saharan trade were tanned skins, destined for New York, and cotton cloth imported from Britain, which was perhaps in part the origin of the small amount of British cloth worn in

Northern Nigeria during the first decade of this century.[46]

That the trans-Saharan trade to and from Kano across the vast Sahara desert could be profitable while the Niger Company felt 'it would not pay' to open up shop in that city presents us with a problem. It is the problem of the survival of the trans-Saharan trade in the face of competition from the West African coast. The solution to this problem lies primarily in the qualitative difference between the exports of the trans-Saharan traders, primarily luxury goods and manufactured goods, and the exports of the coastal-based merchants which were mainly high-bulk, low-value raw materials. It was the comparatively high bulk-to-value ratio of the commodities exported to North Africa that made the trans-Saharan trade viable despite the high cost of transport across the desert. Moreover, the trans-Saharan traders had worked out a system by which they could convert the cowrie shells of the Northern Nigerian consumer into European currency through the use of intermediary currencies such as the Maria Theresa dollar.[47]

As should now be clear, those who funded and operated the trans-Saharan trade were neither ignorant desert nomads nor provincial traders. Rather, they were cosmopolitan merchants who had established themselves from Northern Nigeria to Manchester, and as such they were ready to respond to the possibilities which the British conquest of the Sokoto Caliphate offered. Thus it comes as no surprise that it was they who approached the colonial state in an attempt to investigate the possibilities of the new coastal route.

The Arbibs themselves were to make one of the first forays along the new route. In 1903, one of their agents, Haj Khalifa Zennad, described as the 'chief Sudanese agent' of the firm, had H. P. Hewby, the Resident of Bornu, then travelling in North Africa, write to Lugard requesting the assistance of the colonial state in travelling the route north from Lagos to Kano. Zennad proposed to carry several thousand pounds-worth of imports. Several other firms also contacted Hewby while he was in Tripoli requesting similar information. In the event, Zennad was provided with free ocean transport by Alfred Jones, who sought to promote competition with the Niger Company, and free river transport by the government itself. The immediate result of this trip is unclear, although Zennad was quite impressed by the safety of the roads and said that he would be only the first of many to use them.[48] The long-term result is more certain. This was the diversion of the trans-Saharan trade to the West African coast. By 1909 it was estimated that the value of the export trade across the desert had fallen to one-tenth its annual average value between 1890 and 1900.[49]

The trans-Saharan trade survived as long as it did because of the inefficiencies of British merchant capital, which were largely generated by the near-monopoly positions of the Niger Company and the Elder

Dempster shipping line. The end of the trade was the result of a conscious decision on the part of the merchants involved to take advantage of the new opportunities presented by British colonialism. Similarly, the first important attempts to establish a European commercial presence in Northern Nigeria did not stem from the inroads of coastal capital but were rather a continuation of the trans-Saharan trading networks in a modified form.

One of the earliest of these attempts was that of a firm which later became known as Ambrosini and Company. The founder of Ambrosini was Max Klein, the son of a German manufacturer who had been sent to New York to learn the hides and skins trade at the end of the nineteenth century. The techniques involved in the tanning of skins had changed little in several hundred years. The tanning technique used in the mid-nineteenth century involved long periods of soaking and waiting. This time-consuming process limited the mechanization of the shoe and glove industries, kept costs high and made the ownership of a pair of gloves or more than one pair of shoes or boots a luxury to the working classes of Europe and the United States. This in turn had limited the demand for hides and skins.[50]

The 1880s, however, saw a technical revolution in the tanning industry which enabled costs to be cut and a wider market created. Characteristically, these new techniques found their widest application in the United States, to the detriment of British industry. The immediate outcome of this change in technique was a dramatic increase in the demand for untanned skins, the raw material of the industry, of which goatskins were especially prized. Older areas of supply such as China and India were more intensely exploited, while new sources such as East and North Africa were cultivated. Tanners themselves began to circumvent middlemen as the competition for raw material increased while middlemen went farther afield to seek their profits.[51] In such an expanding market the high quality, tanned 'Sudan skins' being exported from Tunis and Tripoli attracted attention. Moreover, these had already found a ready market in New York with one American merchant resident in Tripoli exporting over a million skins a year to New York. What was wanted, however, was untanned skins. It was the search for such skins which brought Kano to the attention of Klein.[52]

After his apprenticeship in New York, Klein was sent on a tour of the Arabian Peninsula and East Africa where he began to set up buying stations at Aden, Mogadishu, Mombasa and Dar es Salaam. In order to keep buying prices low, he made it a practice to employ local personnel. More important, the use of local agents allowed Klein to attach himself to a ready-made network of local sub-agents and small traders in a highly efficient manner. By simply offering a marginally higher price than that of the indigenous tanners he could easily divert supplies of raw skins from the local industry to the New York market.[53]

After establishing himself on the East African coast, Klein began to investigate North Africa as a possible source of supply. Upon discovering that the majority of the high-quality skins exported from North Africa originated in the recently conquered region of Northern Nigeria, he made several attempts to establish a trading station there. In 1905 he was finally successful, and, utilizing one of his European managers, Luigi Ambrosini, began what was to become a profitable concern. As in East Africa, Klein attempted to make use of the pre-existing trade networks. He seems, however, to have met with some resistance from the trans-Saharan traders and was forced to import Yemeni skin selectors from Aden. His use of Yemenis was very successful, perhaps because they were Muslims and could more effectively deal with their coreligionists, perhaps because they were able to live at the level of their local counterparts. Whatever the explanation, they provided Klein with a skilled staff at low cost which, combined with an assured market, made the venture a success despite the costs of transport. Yet this success was on a small scale and not of the order which could transform the economy of the Protectorate.

If the outcome of the venture of Ambrosini and Company was positive, that of the contemporary venture of the London and Kano Company was less so. This firm was exceedingly small, its total assets being listed at £5842 10s 5d as late as 1910.[55] Originally, it was the venture of two former colonial officers, Donnisthorpe and Esmonde-White, who believed that they could succeed where the Niger Company had feared to tread. In its first year, 1904, the company foundered but was rescued by the London merchant, Lewis Way. Way had shown an interest in the Kano trade as early as 1902 and appears to have bought into the company in 1905, at which time he began to agitate for a special relationship with the colonial government in return for offering competition to the Niger Company in opening up the north.[56] Way wanted the exemption of the London and Kano Trading Company from import and export duties and trading licences, as well as access to some form of government-subsidized transport. Lugard looked favourably on these requests for reasons he expressed to the Colonial Office with great clarity:

> I may add that in my own private view, it is also a benefit to West Africa to enlist in a participation of its trade a firm unconnected with the Liverpool shipping monopoly and so to throw open the development of Nigeria to a larger circle than that which has (with the exception of the Niger Company) hitherto engrossed it.
>
> I have recently learned that Mr Way has joined the Directorate of the 'Kano Trading Company'; and I believe that it is his intention if the concern promises well, to amalgamate his business with it. This appears to me to afford the opportunity I have long sought to

introduce a valuable competitor to the Niger Company in N. Nigeria, and opening [sic] the interior to development – a policy to which the Niger Company, though they have advocated it in theory, have I think been lamentably slow in giving effect.[57]

Lugard was extremely sympathetic to Way's venture, providing government ox-carts to the company for the purpose of shipping its goods south and eventually securing the abolition of certain import duties. He had to be, if his own currency and taxation problems were to be resolved. Yet, even with this assistance the London and Kano Company grew only very slowly. Lacking the family connections, guaranteed markets, specialized trade, and low-paid skilled employees of Ambrosini it had to compete on unfavourable terms against the trans-Saharan traders.[58] Each in its own way, the endeavours of the Arbibs, Max Klein, and the London and Kano Trading Company demonstrate why the Niger Company stayed on the rivers and declined to enter the Kano market.

Our discussion of the difficulties of European commercial capital had taken us very far from the question with which this chapter commenced – the fiscal difficulties of the colonial state. The problem of the realization of the colonial state's revenue still remains, as it still remained for Lugard. Neither the efforts of Ambrosini and Company nor those of the floundering London and Kano Company could do much to provide its solution. It was to be resolved only through state intervention, in the shape of a railway.

The first impetus to the construction of a railway into the heart of the Sokoto Caliphate came even before its conquest and was the result of a dual thrust by both the Governor of Lagos and the imperial policy of Joseph Chamberlain at the Colonial Office. As early as 1895 the first halting steps were made with a railway being built from Iddo Island at Lagos to Abeokuta in Southern Nigeria. By 1901 the line was open to Ibadan. Once there, however, it stalled as a result of tight-fisted Treasury policy, with no date set for a recommencement of construction.[59]

The cessation of construction of the Lagos line to the north forced Lugard to begin to develop his own railway policy. His goal was modest, a railway from Kano to Baro on the River Niger. The completion of such a line would necessitate either the creation of a greatly expanded government steamer service on the river or more probably greater reliance on the Niger Company. The latter was a prospect that Lugard did not relish. It was, however, the only alternative to awaiting the arrival of a railway line from Lagos which might never reach the north. The question was where could Lugard and the Northern Nigerian government look for support for such a scheme? If money could not be found to complete the railway project of the relatively affluent south, how much more difficult would it be for the deeply indebted northern government to find such funds?[60]

Certainly, Lugard could not rely on the Niger Company for support, for its control of river transport was its guarantee of the maintenance of its monopoly position. In 1906, Miller, one of the Company's directors, made this clear when he wrote that the 'transport problem is our protection, and the more serious our opponents find it, the better for ourselves.'[61] What the Niger Company had, it meant to keep. Yet, if it opposed the construction of a railway, there were others who would welcome it. The most important of these was Sir Alfred Jones. For Jones, a railway would offer two advantages. It would seriously damage the position of the Niger Company and it would ultimately, if successful in opening up the north, provide an increase in the shipping tonnage that his Elder Dempster line would carry. In fact, it was Jones's ships which were to carry the railway material itself. Moreover, Jones's support for the railway would cost him little or nothing and he therefore became Lugard's ally in advocating it.

A second potential source of support for Lugard's plans was the textile industry of Lancashire which sought, as it had done throughout the nineteenth century, an expanding market. The intensification of competition from other newly industrialized powers, however, gave this search a new intensity. More important, the continued expansion of the British textile industry necessitated new sources of raw cotton. This latter need was given a great sense of urgency by the shortfalls in American cotton production and the ensuing price speculation which occurred at the turn of the twentieth century with disturbing frequency.[62] The cotton magnates, a powerful voice in British politics, had the potential to provide Lugard with a second crucial source of support if they felt it was in their interests to do so. In order to realize the support of the cotton barons Lugard orchestrated an extraordinary propaganda campaign describing the wondrous possibilities of cotton-growing in the north. Happily for Lugard he did not have to work on untilled ground.

As Michael Mason has documented, 'As early as 1839 Africa was seized upon as a new Alabama.' For a time attention was focused on South Africa, then Dahomey, then Southern Nigeria, then anywhere cotton was reported to be grown. With the exception of the states of the Nile basin, virtually all of these visions of Africa becoming a major cotton producer proved in reality to be mirages. Yet 'if Africa was not going to save Lancashire, Lancashire was not going to give up on Africa'. By the beginning of the present century Northern Nigeria had emerged as Lancashire's great white hope.[63] That it did so is due far more to official mendacity on the part of Lugard, his immediate subordinates and Jones than to any inherent virtues which either it or its inhabitants might have had.

Jones was at the centre of the web. Placing himself at the head of the cotton manufacturers, he became the first president of the British Cotton

Growing Association (BCGA) which was to spread the gospel of cotton production for export throughout West Africa and later the Empire as a whole. Inaugurated in 1902, the BCGA had by 1904 an authorized, but non-paid up capital of £500 000 and a Royal Charter.[64] Jones's manipulation of the cotton magnates was aided substantially by the publicity campaign carried on by Lugard's wife, Flora Shaw, colonial editor of *The Times*, and by Edmund Morel, a one-time employee of Jones who had broken with his employer over the latter's duplicity concerning the Congo reform movement. Morel, who published the influential *African Mail* and who also wrote for *The Times*, was the permanently misguided humanitarian. That he was drawn into this new venture by Jones is a tribute to his gullibility.[65] In 1907 he was warned by John Holt, a Liverpool merchant who had had his fingers burned by Jones in the Congo fiasco. In response to a plea by Morel for Holt's participation in the floating of the BCGA, Holt wrote:

> I do not object to it [the BCGA], but there is no reason why I should shout and tell people what I do not believe . . . I am not going to be dishonest to please anybody. I do not want anyone to put money in Africa and lose it on my advice . . . Would not Jones put £100 000 in it to give his steamers freight if he thought there was a margin in it to pay expenses, not to speak of profit? Don't be deluded.[66]

Nor was Holt alone in this view. Despite the propaganda barrage which drew in valuable allies such as Winston Churchill, chief parliamentary spokesman for the Lancashire interests, and Ralph Moor, the former High Commissioner for Southern Nigeria and now a director of Elder Dempster, many of those who knew Northern Nigeria remained sceptical.[67] In February 1904, Lord Scarbrough wrote to Lyttleton at the Colonial Office remarking that 'as regards cotton, about which so much has been said lately, we have the experience to know that as soon as an attempt is made on a commercial scale to grow cotton in Northern Nigeria the labour difficulty will instantly crop up.'[68] Alexander Miller, a merchant experienced in the West African trade, echoed this view. Writing to Scarbrough, he advised caution:

> I do not know whether your views are optimistic as to the possibilities of cotton growing or the Kano trade referred to, but my view is supported by all I have learned from our agent-general and is to the effect that there is not the requisite population in Northern Nigeria for cotton growing. Again what certainty is there that they will undertake it or that it will be attended with success if they do? Are there not many more indigenous products which can be cultivated with more profit and less labour than cotton?[69]

Miller's pessimism about the possibilities of cotton becoming a major export crop in Northern Nigeria was reinforced by his suspicion of the motives of Jones and Lugard in mounting the cotton campaign. Writing again to Scarbrough, he expressed these fears:

> cotton growing and buying – here again I told of my past experience that their predictions would be doomed to failure as on two previous occasions of scarcity and high prices. When prices of cotton come back to even a high normal, there will be nothing in it, at all events in Northern Nigeria. Of course, I understand your own view was to show some face on this subject – to meet the wild dreams of the Cotton Association and some government officials who have ulterior motives . . . whose names I need not mention.[70]

To be sceptical of Northern Nigeria's potential as a cotton producer was now to be unpatriotic. It stands as a glowing tribute to the Jones–Lugard campaign that as powerful a personage as Lord Scarbrough was forced to 'show some face' on the issue. But if Scarbrough equivocated he was constantly kept informed of the reality behind the 'wild dreams' of the Northern Nigerian Alabama and that reality was the commercial rivalry between his Niger Company and Jones. George Miller, Alexander's brother, put the matter succinctly:

> the greater enemy we have to fear is Sir Alfred Jones and his Cotton Growing Association which he may use as a tool for taking away from us the hinterland trade and I trust this matter may find us all united so as to enable us soon to occupy the ground which Sir Alfred and his friends will immediately occupy to our disadvantage.[71]

Nor were the merchants alone in their pessimistic view of the possibilities of cotton-growing for export in Northern Nigeria. Birtwistle, the government's commercial intelligence officer, thought a portion of the crop might be purchased but he warned in 1907 that:

> It must not be assumed that by running a railway to Kano and by establishing buying centres and ginneries, we shall secure the whole, or even the bulk of the present production of cotton for Lancashire. The spinning and weaving industries are so firmly established in every town and village – one might say in every compound – around Kano, that in my opinion a large share of the present crop will be kept for home use. It will be many years before the coarse but pure and strong Kano cloths are displaced by Manchester goods.[72]

The criticisms of merchant and government agent alike went unheard amid the din of the cotton euphoria. The result was that not only was Lugard's proposed railway from Kano to the Niger approved but the go-ahead was given to renew construction on the line from Lagos to the north. Yet, despite the free distribution of cotton seed, the erection of ginneries and all official government encouragement short of outright coercion, the populace of Northern Nigeria refused to transform their land into a West African Dixie.[73]

By 1910, it was beginning to dawn even on the lower levels of colonial officialdom that something was amiss. One District Officer wrote:

> It is becoming more and more evident that the estimates that have been made of the possibilities of an early production of cotton on a massive scale, in this Protectorate have been greatly exaggerated. The amount produced at present is not even enough for the requirements of the local weavers, and unless large areas of land are to be found where cotton can be grown year after year, without fertiliser, and at a reasonable cost, I doubt the possibility of developing a great industry in cotton.[74]

In the same year Watts, the Niger Company's agent in Northern Nigeria, concurred:

> I have a poor opinion of the prospects of this place as regards cotton for export, as the natives will doubtless turn their attention to the most profitable crop and groundnuts will surpass cotton in this respect. . . . quantities of cotton are raised annually . . . and form the basis of an important cloth weaving and dyeing industry. In Kano Province itself, due to the density of the population, the natives cannot survive on, or by, the land and not an inconsiderable proportion live by weaving and dyeing and making up the cloth . . . both for local use and for export. Before cotton can be profitably exported the demands of the local industries will have to be met.[75]

Even more bluntly the Kano Annual Report for 1910 stated that 'the Kano cloth industry is likely to become the mainstay of our revenue for years to come.'[76]

The 'wild dreams' of the cotton magnates had met with disaster. Why? The answer is clear. As Marion Johnson has convincingly demonstrated, local cloth could be more cheaply put on the local market; therefore local weavers could consistently outbid Lancashire for the Northern Nigerian cotton crop. The home of 'free trade' had met that beast in reality. Kano, the ancient and renowned 'Lancashire of Africa' had, for the moment, withstood the assault of the 'Kano of Britain'.[77] Had it really been expected that the result of the initial confrontation would be otherwise? The answer to this question is perhaps best found in a letter from William Wallace, the Lieutenant Governor of Northern Nigeria, to Lord Scarbrough in 1910. 'As you are aware,' he wrote, 'we raised the cotton cry to get the railway. Once that was assured and the money voted, the cry to a great extent ceased, as it had served its purpose.'[78] With the completion of the railway from Kano to the Niger in 1911 both Jones and Lugard had achieved their aims. The Niger Company's monopoly had been broken and the solution to the colonial government's financial problems was in sight. The BCGA continued its work, garnering meagre results. Northern Nigeria would eventually export some cotton, but the dreams of a new Alabama were not to be realized.[79] Faced with failure, the cotton barons began to look longingly at the recently conquered Anglo-Egyptian Sudan.

Perhaps the most important political consequence of the construction of the railway was the political unification or 'amalgamation' of Northern and Southern Nigeria in 1914, which was carried out by Lugard on his return from Hong Kong.[80] Although the union of the Nigerian colonies had been advanced as early as the Selbourne Report of 1898 and although it was clearly on Lugard's mind shortly thereafter, it was not until the construction of the rail links between north and south that these plans came to fruition.[81] Again, it was the need for financial solvency on the part of the colonial state in Northern Nigeria which necessitated amalgamation. In particular, it was the issue of which government would control the revenue from the rail lines and which would be responsible for the debts incurred in their construction which was the bone of contention.

The simple fact was that by authorizing the funds to build both the rail line from Lagos north and the line from Kano to the Niger the Colonial Office had committed a magnificent folly. From 1906 on the colonial states of Northern and Southern Nigeria had competed with each other for funds and imperial approval for their respective railway plans as fiercely as any two independent entrepreneurs. The prize in this contest was the economic control of the north–south trade and the potential revenue which would accrue therefrom. The madness of two competing rail links to the north was directly abetted by the Colonial Office, where Lord Elgin decided in 1907 that both rail lines should be completed and 'allowed to compete on equal terms, their construction being financed by public loans on the basis of Southern Nigeria's credit. The price of construction was approximately £5 millions.'[82] Clearly, competition between the two state owned lines was madness in the face of the enormity of such a debt, and so it was ended. Railways rates were rationalized and the system unified. It was this unification of the two systems which prompted the amalgamation of north and south.

The origins of this process of amalgamation were very much reflected in its results. These, for the north, were of an almost purely financial nature, leaving it, if not the south, to develop politically in an almost purely autonomous fashion. The legacy of this policy was to be instrumental in the pre- and post-independence crises of the Nigerian state. In order to understand more deeply why the amalgamation of the two Nigerias took the form it did and had such dire consequences it is necessary to examine the process of amalgamation itself.

In 1914 Northern and Southern Nigeria were not only separated by an arbitrary political boundary but by the historic gap imposed by the uneven development of capitalism. Many of the peoples and societies of the south had had long and direct contact with European capitalism stretching back to the sixteenth century, and the slave trade. As a result, colonization had taken place in a piecemeal fashion. Moreover, the gradually increasing fiscal needs of the colonial state in the south were met through import and export duties levied at the major seaports. Hence there was no need for the Southern Nigerian state to undertake the kind of social and political reorganization necessary to collect direct taxes as was the case in the north.[83]

These differing paths of capitalist development in the north and south were abundantly reflected in the economic policies of the two colonial states in the period before amalgamation. While Lugard and later Girouard and Temple struggled to finance the colonial state through direct taxation and faced the problems of commoditization of the agricultural surplus and the realization of taxes in silver, Sir William MacGregor, Governor of Lagos, spoke of Northern Nigeria to the incipient bourgeosie of Lagos in the language of a rampant sub-imperialist:

> You should look on it [the hinterland's trade] as your heritage. You should spare no efforts, shrink at no sacrifice, that would secure to you and your children's children such a splendid possession. If you can only have this railway carried on, as I hope you may, the increase in the value of property here will be enormous, the careers opened out to your sons would be numerous, you would then obtain a degree of comfort and prosperity that you never dreamed of.[84]

It was, however, Lugard and not MacGregor who was to be the architect of the amalgamation, and he had only one aim clearly in view. This was the appropriation of the vast bulk of the south's revenue to use as he saw fit. Thus in 1912 Lugard wrote to his wife:

> I think you would laugh if I explained the lines on which I have done this thing. I amalgamate the railways . . . The bulk of the public debt I transfer to the railways on which it has been incurred. I therefore take over the public debt into my combined estimates. This involves a net expenditure of about ½ a million. So I take over the customs duties also (of course in each case both revenue and expenditure) and as this has a rev. of about 1½ millions, I have a million to meet the deficits of both budgets. The S.N. revenue is reduced to £108 000 from £2,000 000 by this process . . . They will never arrive at the fact that in

reality they leave me with a large sum which I can devote to either N or S Nigeria as I like.[85]

It was in part this financial sleight of hand which necessitated the disastrous introduction of 'indirect rule' to the south. Stripping the south of its primary source of revenue, customs duties, necessitated the abortive introduction of direct taxation. Amalgamation, spurred on by the needs of state accumulation, thus gave rise to further opportunities for state appropriation.[86]

The construction of the railway to the north and the ensuing amalgamation of Northern and Southern Nigeria taken together with the Land Tenure Committee of 1910 and the establishment of the Native Administration system provided the conditions for the continued expansion of merchant capital in Northern Nigeria. It is to the story of the accumulation, centralization and concentration of that capital that we must now turn.

Notes

1   RH Mss, Brit. Emp. s. 62, Lugard Papers, vol. 33.
2   NAK SNP 10 134p/1913. See also NAK KatProf 1769.
3   Lugard, *Political Memoranda* (1906), 'Slavery Questions', para. 38.
4   NAK SNP 9 6249/1912.
5   NAK SNP 10 152p/1913.
6   NAK SNP 7 2390/1907. See also NAK SNP 7 2813/1907.
7   NAK KanoProf 98/1914.
8   RH Mss, Afr. s. 1379, Grier Papers, Grier to his mother, 15 February 1910
9   NAK SNP 7 2991/1911.
10 Dan Makoyo Assessment, extracted in NAK SNP 15 Acc 167.
11 NAK SNP 7 5490/1908.
12 NAK SNP 7 2991/1911.
13 See NAK SNP 1/1, vol. 1 no. 264 'Coinage in Northern Nigeria', 13 May 1902. See also NAK SNP 15 Acc 167.
14 NAK SNP 7 1765/1907.
15 Lugard, *Political Memoranda* (1906), 'Currency and Payments in Kind'.
16 ibid., para. 2.
17 NAK SNP 15 Acc 73, Lugard to Way, 14 January 1903.
18 RH Mss, Afr. s. 86, RNC, vol. 3, Watts to Scarbrough, 26 June 1902.
19 ibid., s. 96, vol. 12, Scarbrough to Lyttleton, 19 February 1904.
20 See J. E. Flint, *Sir George Goldie and the Making of Nigeria* (London: Oxford University Press, 1960.) See also NAK SNP 15 Acc 73, Lugard to Way, 14 January 1903.
21 Katsina Museum, KatProf 1263.
22 NAK SNP 7 1765/1907.
23 ibid. See also P. Shea, 'The Development of an export oriented dyed cloth industry in Kano Emirate in the nineteenth century' (PhD thesis, University

of Wisconsin, 1975).

24 Katsina Museum, KatProf 1263.

25 Public Record Office, Kew (hereafter PRO) CO446/30, Minute by F. G. A. Butler, 27 March 1903, on Lugard to Secretary of State for the Colonies, 27 January 1903.See also 'The silver monopoly', *West African Mail*, February–March 1907.

26 'Ocean Carriage and British Trade', *West African Mail*, February 1907.

27 RH Mss, Afr. s. 86, RNC, vol. 13, Trigge to Scarbrough, 23 October 1908

28 NAK MuriProf 6255/1910.

29 NAK SNP 7 918/1906.

30 T. Pflaummer, 'Railway policy in Nigeria: the first phase', paper presented to the Nigerian Historical Society Conference University of Benin, 1978.

31 NAK SNP 7 918/1906, NAK SNP 7521/1912, NAK SNP 10 332p/1913.

32 RH Mss, Brit. Emp. s. 64, Lugard Papers, vol. 35, 'Memo by T. F. Burrows'.

33 RH Mss, Afr. s. 97 RNC, vol. 13, Watts to Niger Company, 28 March 1908.

34 RH Mss, Afr. s. 86, vol. 12, Lugard to Lyttleton, 31 March 1904.

35 NAK MuriProf 6255/1910.

36 A. A. Boahen, *Britain, the Sahara, and the Western Sudan*, (Oxford: Clarendon Press, 1966). Also Marion Johnson, 'Calico caravans: the Tripoli–Kano trade after 1880', *Journal of African History*, vol. 17, no. 1, (1976), p. 110.

37 See R. W. Shenton, 'A note on the origins of European commerce in Northern Nigeria', *Kano Studies*, vol. 1, no. 2 (n.s.) (1974/77), pp. 63–7.

38 Johnson, 'Calico caravans'.

39 J. M. Abun-Nasr, *A History of the Maghrib* (Cambridge: Cambridge University Press, 2nd edn, 1975), pp. 268–9.

40 ibid.

41 A. Martel, *Les confins saharo-tripolitains de la Tunisie, 1881–1911* (Paris: Presse Universitaire de France, 1965)

42 ibid.

43 Boahen, *Britain, the Sahara*, p. 112.

44 See Shea, 'Cloth industry'.

45 See Johnson, 'Calico caravans'.

46 Martel, *Les confins*, pp. 152–63. See also PRO CO 446/84, Report by Resident, Kano Province (C. L. Temple), 2 October 1909, enclosure in Acting Governor Wallace to Secretary of State for the Colonies, 25 October 1909.

47 Johnson, 'Calico caravans'. See also NAK SNP 1/1, vol. 4, no. 265, 'Maria Theresa Dollars'. Also NAK SNP 136/1907 and NAK SNP 6 81/1907.

48 See NAK SNP 7 510/1904, Hewby to Lugard, 13 December 1903. Also NAK SNP 7 757/1905; NAK SNP 7 4000/1905. and PRO CO 446/51/00671 p. 104.

49 Johnson, 'Calico caravans'.

50 A. H. John, *A Liverpool Merchant House: Being the History of Albert Booth and Company, 1863–1958*. (London: Allen & Unwin, 1959) Chapters 3 and 4.

51 Shenton, 'Origins of European commerce'.

52 M. Mery, 'Renseignments commerciaux', *Bulletin du Comité de l'Afrique Française*, September 1893.

53 Personal communication from Max Klein Jr.

54   ibid.
55   PRO BT 31/17301/82061, Reports under the Company's Act for the London and Kano Company.
56   NAK SNP 7 1307/1905.
57   PRO CO 446/51, entry by Lugard dated 31 October 1905. See also NAK SNP 15 Acc 73, 14 January 1903.
58   NAK SNP 15 Acc. 73.
59   Pflaummer, 'Railway policy'.
60   ibid.
61   ibid.
62   See *Empire Cotton Growing Review*, vol. 1, no. 1 (1924).
63   M. Mason, 'Industry and empire: a note on the Manchester Cotton Supply Association and West Africa 1857-1872', unpublished mss. See also M Johnson, 'Cotton imperialism in West Africa', *African Affairs*, vol. 73, no 291, (1974), pp. 178-87.
64   RH Mss, Afr. s. 97, vol. 13, G. Miller to G. L. Gaiser. Jones was also chairman of the African Trade Section of the Liverpool Chamber of Commerce. See 'Minutes, African Trade Section of the Liverpool Chamber of Commerce', 26 January 1903, Liverpool Public Library.
65   S. J. S. Cookey, *Britain and the Congo Question 1885-1913*, (London Longmans, 1968)
66   Morel Papers, Holt to Morel, 5 November 1902, cited in K. D. Nworah 'The West African operations of the British Cotton Growing Association 1904-1914', *African Historical Studies*, vol. 4, no. 2 (1971), pp. 315-30.
67   *West African Mail*, 1 June 1906. See also, RH Mss, Afr. s. 86 RNC, vol. 12 Watts to Scarbrough, 18 October 1906. Also, NAK SNP 7 1552/1906.
68   RH Mss, Afr. s. 96, RNC, vol. 12, Scarbrough to Lyttleton, 19 Februar 1904.
69   RH Mss, Afr. s. 86, RNC, vol. 12, A. Miller to Scarbrough, 17 April 1905 See also Watts to Miller, 24 October 1904.
70   RH Mss, Afr. s. 96, RNC, vol. 12, A. Miller to Scarbrough, 27 March 1904
71   ibid., s. 97, vol. 13, G. Miller to G. L. Gaiser, n.d.
72   NAK SNP 7 1765/1907.
73   However, for the later history of the BCGA, see R. W. Shenton and L Lennihan 'Capital and class: peasant differentiation in Norther Nigeria' *Journal of Peasant Studies*, vol. 9, no. 1 (1981), pp. 47-70.
74   NAK SNP 7, 1515/1910.
75   RH Mss, Afr. s. 97, RNC, vol. 13, Watts to Niger Company, 28 March 1908
76   NAK SNP 15 Acc 167.
77   Johnson, 'Calico caravans.'
78   RH Mss, Afr. s. 96, RNC, vol. 12, Wallace to Scarbrough, 31 May 1910.
79   See Shenton and Lennihan, 'Capital and class'.
80   A. H. M. Kirk-Greene, *Lugard and the Amalgamation of Nigeria: a Documentary Record* (London: Frank Cass, 1968), Chapters 3 and 4.
81   RH Mss, Afr. s. 64 Lugard Papers, vol. 33, 'Confidential Memo on the State of Administration in Northern Nigeria', 11 July 1905.
82   Pflaummer, 'Railway policy'.

83   See M. Perham, *Lugard, The Years of Authority 1898–1945* (London: Collins, 1960), Chapters 22, 23.
84   Pflaummer, 'Railway policy'.
85   Perham, *Lugard*, p. 419.
86   ibid., Chapters 23, 24.

5

The Concentration and Centralization of Capital

The opening of the Kano rail line on 1 April 1912 cemented a link between the social formation of Northern Nigeria and the international system of capitalist relations of production and exchange which remains unbroken to the present day.[1] It was the last necessary link in the chain of conquest, occupation, and taxation which was to bind Northern Nigeria to the international economy. It was the final precondition of capitalist development, the course of which was to join the fortunes of millions of Northern Nigerian agricultural producers to the international market for one agricultural product – the groundnut – the price of which would be beyond their control. Hinged on the production of this one commodity would be wealth and poverty, well-being and misery, political order and chaos. Moreover, the production of this one commodity was to become an important part of the foundation of one of the largest multinational corporations in the world, the Unilever empire.[2] It is the corporate side of this phenomenon which is the subject of this chapter.

The groundnut is an oilseed which flourishes in warm climates. Whole it is a useful source of protein and like most oilseeds produces an oil which is liquid at room temperature. Groundnut oil can be used for cooking, as a condiment, and can be burned in a simple lamp to produce light. The residue, which remains when the oil had been expressed, can be eaten or be used to provide fodder for cattle, as can the remainder of the plant. Moreover, the plant itself fixes nitrogen from the atmosphere in the soil. All in all, the groundnut plant is a natural blessing to the tropical farmer which is no doubt the reason for its long-standing and wide cultivation in Northern Nigeria.[3] Yet none of these intrinsic qualities or uses of the groundnut plant can explain how or why it was to come to dominate the fortunes of the political economy of Northern Nigeria. To understand this we must journey to the historic heartland of capitalism – Western Europe.

The period from the formalization of British control over Northern Nigeria to the opening of the railroad to the north (1900–11) was one of low rates of growth for the capitalist powers of Western Europe and, in England in particular, a period of falling real wages.[4] In England both the poor economic growth rate and the fall in real wages were directly linked to the heavy British commitment to production of cotton textiles and coal, both of which were meeting increasingly stiff international competition, and to the failure of British capitalists to make use of the various new technological processes in industrial production. The latter was the case especially in iron and steel production.[5]

It was the English working class which bore the brunt of this period of stagnation. They did not, however, bear it quietly. Between 1900 and 1910 an average of 4.1 million working days were lost each year as a result of strikes, and in 1912 the figure climbed to the hitherto unheard of height of 40.9 million working days.[6] Yet if strikes were one of labour's answers to the failings of industrial capitalism, so also were the more prosaic changes in consumption brought about by the shrinking real wage. Among these changes was the increase in the consumption of the butter substitute, margarine.

At the instigation of Napoleon III, Hippolyte Mège-Mouriès, a French chemist, developed in the 1860s a chemical process through which animal fat could be transformed into a cheap butter substitute. The process continued to be developed and perfected until any edible animal or vegetable fat which was solid at room temperature could be used in the making of margarine. Margarine, over the period 1900 to 1910, was at least one-third cheaper than butter.[7] As a result the production of the two largest margarine makers alone grew from approximately 28 000 tons per annum in 1902 to 140 000 tons per annum in 1910. This rapid expansion placed a great strain on markets in the primary raw material for the margarine production process, animal fat.[8]

From 1906 on, however, strenuous efforts were made by the margarine producers to find the technological advances which would allow liquid vegetable oils to be substituted for animal fat. The central problem was that these oils, of which groundnut oil was one, were liquid at room temperature. By 1910 a series of processes for the hardening of fats, hydrogenation, was coming into use and a substantial portion of the world's vegetable-oil production, which made up two-thirds of the world's fat market, was now open to use in margarine production.[9] Thus, as with the case of hides and skins, the interaction of technological change and the needs of the European working class created the demand for the Northern Nigerian groundnut. Liverpool prices for groundnuts increased from below £10 per ton in 1905 to £13 per ton in 1911 and to over £16 per ton in 1913.[10] Exports from Northern Nigeria increased in turn from an average of 804 tons per annum during the period 1902–6, to an average of

1476 tons per annum from 1907–11, with 2518 tons being exported in 1912 and 19 228 tons in 1913, the first year in which the rail line to Kano was available to move the crop.[11]

The Niger Company was not taken unawares by this development. It and its rivals on the coast had a long experience in the buying and selling of palm produce, an important commodity in the world oilseeds market. Moreover, the Niger Company had shown particular interest in the fruit of the shea tree from which a 'butter', solid at room temperature, was extracted.[12] Groundnuts were highly considered as well, as we have seen from the comments of the Niger Company's agent Watts. However, until 1912 the export trade in groundnuts had been discouraged primarily because of the discriminatory high freight rate which Alfred Jones's Elder Dempster line had placed on groundnut shipments. According to the Niger Company, which protested against these high rates in 1906, the freight on groundnuts equalled 25 per cent of the value of the produce and made 'the development of the trade very difficult'.[13] However, no change in the freight rates for groundnuts was made. In 1908 the issue was raised once more, this time by Jones himself. In October of 1908 Jones circulated a letter to the principals of the Niger Company and those of its Liverpool rivals:

No doubt you are aware, and have been for many years, that there is a very large groundnut trade between Africa and France, Holland and Germany. England has not participated in this trade in any way much to her loss. She imports very largely the manufactured article. The position now is that these large steamers of ours pass the groundnut ports (Bathurst, Dakar) with empty space which could be utilized. The idea would be to get up a groundnut mill, and I propose to call a meeting at a convenient date to discuss this point. Capital will be required and the mill should commence on a very small scale to begin with: but it is not necessary for me to point out to you how greatly it would be in the interests of all concerned to centre this industry in Liverpool.[14]

Given the scepticism of the Niger Company and the major Liverpool merchants to Jones's cotton adventures, the reaction of the merchants to this new scheme was predictable. A Niger Company director wrote to Lord Scarbrough:

With reference to the groundnut mill in Liverpool . . . It is well to remember that until quite recently the Niger Company paid the quite ridiculous rate of 57/9d per ton of groundnuts from Burutu to Liverpool which has been subsequently reduced to 40s per ton with transit options . . . The Niger Company were urged by the government to push the groundnut industry for which at an early date there is a great future in Northern Nigeria, but how can they compete when groundnuts [are] shipped from Bathurst to continent at 12/6 to 15/- per ton . . . Is it not possible therefore that the right policy is firstly for Sir Alfred to agree to carry groundnuts to Liverpool at a bedrock rate?[15]

Even 40s a ton freight rate for groundnuts was, however, excessive when compared to the rates for other oilseeds from the same Nigerian port. Both shea nuts and palm kernels were at least 10s cheaper per ton to ship, while for a time even palm oil, which could only be shipped in casks, was cheaper to ship than groundnuts.[16] Why was this so?

There are a number of possible explanations for the maintenance of high freight rates for groundnuts. One is that so few groundnuts were shipped that a high freight rate was maintained to offset the lack of quantity. This argument, however, faces two serious objections. First, the shipping of groundnuts required little if any special handling. Secondly, it seems to have been the policy of the Elder Dempster line to provide low initial freight rates for new commodities in order to encourage their development. Elder Dempster was clearly interested in the development of groundnuts.[17] Why then were freight rates kept at prohibitive levels? There are two reasonable explanations. First, it is known that Jones had purchased an interest in an oilseed crushing plant in England in the 1890s – the African Oil Mills. Jones's Elder Dempster line had been severely criticized in the past for trading in its own right and thereby undercutting its merchant-customers. Certainly if it was Jones's intention to monopolize the trade in groundnuts to provide his own mills with raw materials, the maintenance of excessive freight rates would have given him a decisive edge.[18] Second, it was widely known that Jones often made rate concessions on certain articles to the German Woermann line, which had joined Elder Dempster as a junior partner in the West African shipping conference in 1894 after a costly and ineffective rate war. The prime conditions of the combination were that while Woermann might not enter British ports, Elder Dempster was free to ship to continental Europe. Between 1894 and 1914, however, the Woermann line continued to expand and, had the combination broken down, would have provided a formidable rival to Elder Dempster. Since Germany was one of the most important centres of oilseed milling, was it not possible that Elder Dempster, by maintaining prohibitive groundnut shipping rates to Liverpool, was deliberately steering the trade to Germany?[19]

Whatever the reason for the high freight rates which Jones maintained, they had a prohibitive effect on the development of the groundnut trade. They were, however, reduced to 32s 6d in 1912, the level to which the freight rates on palm kernels and shea nuts were increased in the same year.[20] Together, the fall in freight rates, the opening of the railway to the north and the abnormally high Liverpool price for groundnuts of over £16 per ton made Northern Nigerian groundnuts competitive on the world market.[21] Even these favourable conditions, however, probably would have been insufficient to transform Northern Nigeria into a major groundnut exporter if the Niger Company had continued to maintain its near monopoly position in the north. In this regard the completion of the railway played a decisive role, for it had broken the Niger Company's control of transport and in doing so opened the door to competition between the European firms. There were eight European firms present in Kano in 1912 and fifteen by the end of 1915.[22] In 1916 Trigge, a Niger Company agent, explained the results of this competition to the Edible Nuts and Seeds Commission:

> TRIGGE The ground nut trade was in its infancy just prior to the opening of Kano. The Niger Company, and other merchants and in fact the government sent up a large quantity of seed and distributed it among the natives and I think the crop was almost 5000 tons. In the second year we were all surprised to find the station literally buried in groundnuts.
> Q. Was that in 1913?
> TRIGGE Yes, the traders competed very strongly and paid £19 on the spot ton. Government Officials, the Agriculture Department and the merchants all agreed that the native could make a fair profit at £4.10s per ton in 1914 . . . The natives said they were not going to bring in groundnuts because they said they were going to hold them for a better price.[23]

This price agreement, however, did not hold, and by the end of 1913 the price had reached £10 per ton once again.[24]

As we have seen, the alternation of open competition with the concentration or combination of merchant capital had long been characteristic of the Southern Nigerian trade in palm kernels and oil. Price agreements, or 'pooling', on either an informal or formal basis, constituted an intermediate position between open competition and formal combination. As such, these arrangements were highly unstable and even when in force open to cheating by one or more of the firms involved. It was crucial for the development of the groundnut trade that the buying pool, which had been composed of the Niger Company and a number of its most important Liverpool rivals, including the African Association and Miller Brothers, had broken down in 1910.[25] This pool had been advantageous to the Niger Company in that it had maintained Northern Nigeria as the Company's preserve. Doubtless the construction of the railway to the north was one of the reasons for its collapse in 1910. The buying pool of 1901–10 was essentially a device for equalizing the returns to capital investment through the limitation of competition. The pool did not directly set buying prices, as the abortive groundnut buying agreement of 1913 had done, but rather ensured that at the end of a particular buying season tonnages of produce bought and sold and hence profits made were declared. Upon the basis of these declarations it could be seen whether firms had over-bought or under-bought in proportion to their declared capital. Transfers of profits were then effected in such a manner as to equalize returns to capital. Buying at high prices was thus penalized. On the other hand, the pool agreements were over a fixed period of time and their renewal was contingent on the settlement of the contentious issue of the validity of the declared capital of each firm over the life of the pool. If a firm consistently under-bought in relation to its declared capital, its share of the pool would shrink upon renewal. Thus under-buying or buying at low prices was discouraged as well. Since both over- and under-buying were directly related to the price offered, the pools had the effect of controlling prices and limiting competition.[26]

It is important to note the Niger Company's ideological justification for the limitation of competition, as it would continue to be the main argument for the concentration of capital throughout the colonial period:

If fair dealing, energy and enterprise be assured, an amalgamation of European interests may prevent the undue enhancement of prices and enable the amalgamated trading companies to set aside capital for extension and development which else would be absorbed in the struggle of competition. While the wants of the natives in a primitive state remain few, enhancement of prices, no doubt, decreases supply for the producers having acquired all they need will not exert themselves to tap the full resources of the land.[27]

In other words, the Niger Company postulated a backward sloping labour supply curve for export crops such as groundnuts. Behind this ideological position lay the threatening reality of open competition. Referring to the breakdown of the 1913 groundnut price agreement, a Niger Company report for 1914 stated:

A most determined attitude was adopted by the firms established at Kano, especially the French Company, to at once secure a strong and dominating position there. A common policy seems to have been adopted by each newcomer, namely to struggle for a position at any cost. This being the case it is probable that the Company's trading in Kano Division during 1913 was conducted without profit. The whole trade now realize that the policy pursued last year in connection with the groundnut industry can only prove detrimental to the best interests of the country and also render it impossible for the product to command a first rate position among the crushers of Europe.[28]

The hopes for a stronger price agreement among the European buyers in 1914 were also disappointed and once again prices reached 'absurd' heights.[29] Kano exports, however, fell to 4869 tons.[30] Drought and famine had intervened to limit groundnut production and sales. By 1915, the outbreak of the First World War had disrupted trade among the Niger Company, the Liverpool merchants and the continental oilseed crushers and created a great and general uncertainty in the world oilseed market. Correspondingly, Liverpool prices fell to £12 per ton, while prices in Kano fell below £5 per ton, half of what they had been in 1913.[31]

The adversity of the war and the fall in Liverpool prices strengthened the resolve of the European merchants in Kano. On 12 January 1915, the Niger Company reported that 'Natives have given in and prices in Kano and Zaria are £4.10s per ton.'[32] A new pool was soon in operation. On 18 January it was reported that an 'arrangement has been made by us today with the following firms, the French co., Holts, MacIvers, Tin Areas, L&K, Lagos Stores to pay 1/2d per lb. for groundnuts.'[33] The effects of this new agreement are made plain by a Niger Company memorandum on profits for 1915 which noted that the 'abnormal purchase of groundnuts at below £5 a ton' meant 'a possible profit of little short of £100 000.'[34] Despite the fall in prices, Kano exports increased to 12 579 tons.[35]

From 1916 to the end of the war shipping problems eased and European demand was renewed. Once again the pool broke down and in 1916 the local price for groundnuts soared to £9 10s per ton, nearly double that of the preceding year.[36] By February 1920 local prices for groundnuts had reached £47 per ton.[37] Even with the forced withdrawal of the German firms, open competition reigned. Liverpool prices were in excess of £52 per ton.[38] Northern Nigerian exports increased in turn, averaging 52 000 tons per annum between 1916 and 1921.[39] This extraordinary increase in prices created the condition for an important crisis and reconstruction of merchant capital. In order to understand the crisis of capitalism which immediately followed the First World War and its effects on European merchant capital in Nigeria, we must understand the nature of the crisis in world terms and the particular vulnerability to it of those firms which traded in primary produce, such as oilseeds.

The post-war capitalist boom, which lasted from about April of 1919 through the first months of 1920, was largely the result of 'a very sharp rise in prices as pent up demand for commodities was unleashed at a time when production was still recovering from the effects of war'.[40] Ports were congested and shipping was in short supply as the removal of wartime controls over the consumption of various commodities unleashed this demand. This, in turn, immediately led to speculation in stocks and commodities forcing both the price of commodities and company shares to absurd limits. Then, in 1920, when the surge of contained wartime demand had been met, the real and more lasting effects of the war began to be felt. The disruption of commerce and manufacturing and the impoverishment of war-torn Europe posed severe limits to markets, with continental countries importing only 52 per cent of the raw materials and semi-manufactures which they had in 1913.[41]

In the margarine industry the boom and bust of 1919-20 paralleled that of the economy as a whole. In Holland, home of the great margarine manufacturers, per-capita consumption had nearly doubled, while exports to England had increased from 47 000 tons in 1910 to 165 000 tons in 1916.[42] By 1920, the sales of the two largest Dutch manufacturers had increased from 81 000 tons to 139 000 tons.[43] The demand for raw materials increased correspondingly. At the end of 1920, however, the contraction became apparent. Total English consumption fell from over 350 000 tons in 1920 to 254 000 tons in 1921.[44] The main reason for this dramatic drop in consumption was a fall in the price of butter. Butter prices fell over one-third from 1919 to 1921, while butter sales in Britain increased from 146 000 tons to 239 000 tons over roughly the same period.[45] The relative changes in the prices of butter and margarine, occasioned by the unloading of stored supplies of butter from the British empire and the post-war recession in agriculture, combined with the high prices of oilseeds to permit working-class consumption to shift toward butter. The margarine makers attempted to maintain sales by cutting prices. Between 1919 and 1923 the price of margarine fell by 25 per cent.[46] The fall in raw materials prices was even more striking with Kano groundnut prices falling to below £5 per ton in December of 1920, a drop of about 83 per cent from the previous high.[47] This collapse in oilseed prices resulting from the boom and bust of 1919-20 laid bare the weaknesses of European merchant capital in Nigeria and had a devastating effect which ultimately forced its recomposition.

The structure of European merchant capital in Nigeria was based on the ready availability of credit. The time which elapsed between the purchase of groundnuts in Kano and their sale to oilseed crushers could often be as long as a year. The time between the purchase of consumer goods – such as cotton cloth – and their sale in Kano was often of a similar duration. Over this time the market price of the stocks held, either of groundnuts or of cloth could, and often did, fluctuate. Thus, there was a strong element of speculation in the trade. In order to alleviate speculation, oilseeds, such as groundnuts, could often be 'sold forward' in European markets, that is in advance of purchase in Northern Nigeria, in order to guarantee a minimum price to the seller. In a rapidly rising market, however, there was a strong temptation not to sell forward but rather to sell stocks at 'spot' or current market prices upon their arrival in

Europe. Similarly, in a falling market European buyers preferred not to buy forward but rather at spot prices in order to get stocks at the lowest possible price. In the sale of consumer goods to the merchant firms the situation was reversed, although there was in general a greater 'stickiness' to high prices and a greater tendency for merchants to contract for production in advance in order to increase the certainty of prices. This was especially the case in 1918–19 when the price of English cloth was rising. Cloth manufacturers attempted to compensate for this tendency by setting advance delivery prices which they believed would be consonant with the market price on the delivery date.[48]

In the sharp upswing of 1918–19 European merchant capital had the worst of both worlds – as buyer and as seller. Merchants' purchases constituted a small share of the market in consumer goods such as cloth and they were forced to contract well in advance for their supplies. Between 1913 and 1919 the replacement cost of cotton cloth stocks for one firm active in the Kano trade increased by nearly 300 per cent.[49] The collapse of prices in 1920 therefore found the firms with large stocks of overpriced cloth which they had purchased during the preceding period of rising prices. As sellers of raw materials, the firms found themselves in late 1920 holding stocks of produce purchased during the upswing at prices in many cases higher than those ruling in European markets at the time of their sale.[50] For a number of firms, in particular the Niger Company, the purchase of oilseeds at rapidly inflating prices during the boom had been financed by short-term commercial credit. When the bust occurred they found themselves with overpriced stocks of oilseeds and consumer goods and with the obligation to repay the principal and interest on the loans through which they had financed their purchases. The resulting credit squeeze brought the largest of the merchant houses, the Niger Company, to its knees.

In late 1920, in a secret memorandum, the situation of the Niger Company was outlined:

Now as regards the outlook for the year 1920, which has a very direct bearing on our policy regarding the 1919 profits, it is too early to make anything but a very general statement as our accounts for the past year will not be closed until next summer and much may happen between now and then. Broadly speaking, during the first 5 months of the year trade was conducted at the high prices ruling in 1919 and there was no sign of an impending break in the markets. Later, prices declined, followed by a sudden and unexpected drop in December of last year just at the time when normally the bulk of our produce begins to arrive home and from December onwards trade has been practically at a standstill. . . . the trouble is not confined to African products, it is a world trouble brought about by the poverty-stricken condition of European countries which, though eager for our own commodities, cannot afford to pay for them . . . Business with these countries was largely done on credit; today credit is greatly restricted and until it is restored we cannot expect to match the volume of trade which the company was doing in 1914.[51]

On 16 January 1920, the Niger Company, with an 'ordinary' capital of £1.25 million, was offered to Lever Brothers, the soap manufacturers, for £7.5 million in cash. Lever Brothers hesitated, but not for long. For Lever Brothers, the acquisition of the Niger Company was too great a prize to be left to possible competitors. Five days later Lever Brothers agreed to purchase the Niger Company for more than £8 million in cash. What the Niger Company's directors knew and what Lever Brothers did not know was that in addition to its trading difficulties the Niger Company was carrying a bank overdraft of about £1.5 million, a fact which was not revealed to Lord Leverhulme until after the agreement to purchase the Niger Company had been made. The directors of the Niger Company knew that it was badly overextended, their credit was at an end and even the Elder Dempster line was refusing to ship its stock on account. They were extremely lucky to be able to get out from under before the collapse.[52] For Lever Brothers, the acquisition of the Niger Company, even though heavily burdened by debt, was an important move. For Nigeria, it was the beginning of the end of the reign of competitive merchant capital and a major step in the process which would eventually give Lever Brothers and its successors a commanding presence in Nigerian commerce.

From the beginning of Lever's soap business in 1885 to the acquisition of the Niger Company in 1920, the soap manufacturing industry had been subject to the same pattern of open competition, loose co-operation and outright combination as had merchant capital in Nigeria. By the end of the First World War Lever Brothers had, however, attained a pre-eminent position, controlling not only a major share of soap production but a substantial collection of retail groceries and other assorted concerns as well. In the words of Leverhulme, the purchase of the Niger Company brought 'the largest exporter of raw materials in Nigeria into combination with the largest manufacturers of our principal products (soap) in this country.'[53]

The raw materials for the making of soap overlap considerably with those used in the making of margarine and the effect of the introduction of the fat-hardening or hydrogenation process on both was broadly the same. Thus, soap and margarine manufacturers competed in the world oilseeds market for roughly the same raw materials. Margarine making, however, demanded the use of higher quality oils and margarine commanded a much higher price than soap. As a result margarine makers could offer high prices for the best vegetable oils and had the added advantage of being able to produce soap with the residue oils from the margarine-making process. Moreover, the supply and prices of raw materials in the manufacture of both commodities were given to wide fluctuations. As both margarine and soap production were expanding, these fluctuations in turn often gave rise to severe shortages of raw materials. All of this gave Lever Brothers great cause for concern over the reliability of its sources of supply.[54] Commencing in 1901, with an abortive attempt to develop copra plantations in the South Pacific, Lever Brothers' response to this situation was to attempt to secure the control of raw materials production. This venture was faced with the problem of a shortage of labour to work the plantations. Lever's attempt to solve this problem by importing 'Hindoos from the teeming millions of India' was blocked by the Colonial Office. As a result, attention began to be focused on Africa.[55] First, Lever attempted to obtain leases in British West Africa similar to the 999-year concessions granted him in the Solomon Islands by Joseph Chamberlain. Here, however, he was thwarted by the combined forces of the Liverpool merchant houses and the followers of 'single tax' theories, which were generalized by the West African Lands Committee from the Northern Nigerian experience.[56] The Colonial Office was only prepared to issue a twenty-one year lease and to grant Lever a monopoly over oilseed crushing over relatively small areas, and not the plantation concessions he had requested. Thwarted, Lever commented:

> If the Government had offered us a twenty-one days' lease we might have been wise in buying a wheelbarrow or two, but that would be about the extent of the capital we could expend on a twenty-one days' lease. On a twenty-one years' lease we could go further, but after all, it would be comparatively a very small amount of money that we would be justified in expending holding a twenty-one years' lease. I sometimes wish that all native chiefs in the British Colonies, in Africa at any rate, were made dukes. In my opinion we should then take the sensible view that this land was theirs for development and for the advancement of civilization, and just as we will not tolerate a duke keeping his land for his own pleasure, or to lock it up, and have passed laws to make this impossible in the United Kingdom, so I can never understand why a black man should be allowed to assume a different attitude, and neither develop his own land nor allow other people to do so.[57]

Lever Brothers' proposals for plantation concessions met with a more encouraging response from the Belgian government, which had taken over the scandal-ridden Congo Free State of King Leopold. In April 1911, La Société Anonyme des Huileries du Congo Belge was born. This acquisition in the Belgian Congo was rapidly followed by another of six million acres in Congo Française, but only a small portion of this proved valuable for oilseed production.[58] In British West Africa, where Lever Brothers had been stifled in their attempt to create plantations, the firm entered the oilseed trade instead, purchasing W. B. MacIver and Company, which had traded in both Northern and Southern Nigeria, as well as two other firms which had traded in Liberia and Sierra Leone.[59]

The acquisition of direct access to oilseeds, however, meant little without the control of oilseed crushing as well. Thus, from their inception each of Lever Brothers' plantation schemes was linked to the establishment of a local oilseed crushing mill.[60] In addition, mills were erected in areas where Lever had major trading interests. Two such mills were erected in Southern Nigeria in 1910. They rapidly foundered and closed, although they experienced a brief renaissance during the First World War. The central reason for their failure was that they ran head-on into the Elder Dempster shipping monopoly.

Before the First World War the Elder Dempster/Woermann shipping ring controlled nearly 100 per cent of Nigerian shipping to and from Holland, Britain and Germany, the main consumers of Nigerian oilseeds.[61] The shipping combine maintained its power through the use of the 'deferred rebate system'. This system provided that 10 per cent of the freight rates paid by any merchant firm over a six-month period would be rebated to that firm after an additional six months if the firm used the shipping combine's vessels as its exclusive carrier. If a firm chartered a tramp steamer or used any other vessels or purchased its own, the rebate was forfeited.[62] It was the deferred rebate system, in conjunction with Lever's failure to obtain lengthy leases and monopoly control of the produce in the areas which it leased, that doomed Lever Brothers' Nigerian oilseed crushing venture to failure.

Crushing palm kernels in Nigeria could only be profitable if the resulting oil could be transported in bulk by tankers. Elder Dempster refused to supply such ships, maintaining that it did not have the requisite tankers. Elder Dempster could, no doubt, have purchased tankers, but refused to do so. The reason why they did not is fairly straightforward. Elder Dempster's monopoly position depended on its being able to deal with a large number of merchant firms, none of which was large enough to finance its own fleet of ships. The prospect of the huge Lever Brothers combine operating successfully in Nigeria posed a threat to Elder Dempster's position. Moreover, Elder Dempster was able to capitalize on the fact that the oilseed merchants were not connected financially with the oilseed crushers, largely located on the continent. The successful entry of Lever Brothers into the crushing business in Nigeria would have threatened Elder Dempster's position, while also alienating its German partner, Woermann.[63]

The outbreak of the First World War cut British soap makers off from the German oilseed crushing mills and threatened the link with those in neutral Holland, their other large supplier. This disruption seriously endangered the British war effort. Not only were the supplies of vegetable oil for the making of margarine and soap threatened but also, more crucially, the supply of glycerine, a by-product of the soapmaking process essential to the manufacture of explosives. Thus, with government support, the oilseed crushing industry was greatly expanded in Britain with Lever Brothers playing a major role.[64]

At the close of the war, Lever Brothers had an interest in every aspect of the oilseeds market from the production of raw materials to the retailing of soap. Lever Brothers also used the opportunity of the war to enter margarine production. The Niger Company fitted well into this growing vertically integrated concern. It also made Lever Brothers the largest single purchaser of Northern Nigerian groundnuts.[65] It did not, however, give Lever Brothers monopoly control of that Northern Nigerian market, for while Lever Brothers had been negotiating the purchase of the Niger Company, another important merchant combination had occurred resulting in the formation of the African and Eastern Trade Corporation. Ironically, it was Lever's movement into the West African oilseeds trade which prompted this second combination.

The firms which formed the African and Eastern had as their primary interest the coastal trade in palm produce. They were composed of a loose confederation of Liverpool firms known as the African Association and those other firms which had co-operated in pools with them. They had observed the progress of Lever Brothers with chagrin, especially its purchase of MacIvers in 1910. In response, members of the African Association and Miller Brothers, one of the other firms which had co-operated in the pools, sought an amalgamation with the Niger Company during the war. The Niger Company, however, was only willing to agree to the arrangement if it were given control over the management of the proposed combine. This the Liverpool interests refused to agree to. The proposed amalgamation was thus dropped in 1918. The remaining pooling agreements with the Niger company came to an end. The Liverpool interests did agree, however, to combine themselves, and in May 1919 the African and Eastern came into being.[66] Thus, by the end of 1920 two great trading combines stood toe to toe in the Nigerian market. Throughout the 1920s both firms continued to take over the smaller remaining independent merchants, leaving, by the end of the decade, John Holt as the only independent British firm of any consequence. The competition between these two mercantile giants, along with the entry of non-British firms, did, however, preserve an open and competitive market for groundnuts throughout the 1920s. Moreover, Lever Brothers were not the only manufacturers to enter the merchant field in search of raw materials. Its new rival was the powerful Dutch firm, Jurgens.[67]

Although the quantity of groundnuts exported from Nigeria dropped in 1922 to less than half the 1921 total of 50 979 tons and continued to drop slightly again in 1923, by the end of the 1923–4 crop year exports had increased to 60 000 tons and by 1924–5 had nearly doubled to 132 000 tons. From 1925 on the export levels remained high, the average for the crop years 1925–6 to 1929–30 being a little over 117 000 tons per annum, the total exported reaching 147 000 tons in the latter crop year. It is clear then that by the 1923–4 crop year the groundnut trade had recovered from the post-war contraction and was expanding.[68]

Groundnut prices in Europe during the period 1923–8 hovered between £20 and £25 per ton, thus recovering the level attained during the early years of the war, while prices in Kano during the same period varied from £10 to £15 per ton.[69] The Kano price, however, fluctuated greatly during any given year; prices in 1922–3 being between £7 and £14 per ton; in 1923–4, £13 to £18 10s per ton; in 1924–5, £10 to £17 per ton; and so on.[70] Both the increase in tonnage exported and the pattern of the development of commercial competition were linked to these fluctuating prices.

The groundnut trade, from its inception, had depended upon a class of middlemen who bought either from the farmer or who bought from a still lower level of intermediary. At the trade's inception the major middlemen in the trade were drawn from the indigenous merchants who had hitherto specialized in the trade in goods for the Northern Nigerian market such as kola nuts, or to a lesser extent from the remnants of the trans-Saharan trading community.[71] Until the 1920s the firms themselves remained largely in Kano itself and a few other major trading centres in the north, such as Zaria. Even the farmers from the immediately outlying areas who brought their crop into the city rarely sold directly to the firms, but rather sold to intermediaries. By the mid-1920s, however, a new group of intermediaries, usually of North African or eastern Mediterranean origin and officially labelled 'Syrians', had come to dominate the level of trade immediately below that of the European firms, and by 1926 it was reported that:

> Most of the groundnuts brought into Kano pour into the Syrian Quarters, and this community appear definitely to be becoming the middlemen to the European firms, though the latter are not pleased with the situation which has arisen.
> . . . the profits of a sudden rise in price fall neither to the native nor the European but to the Syrian trader[72]

More importantly the Syrians were now attempting to bypass the European firms altogether by trading directly to Europe. The Kano Province Annual Report for 1929–30, for example, noted that some

Syrians had 'made an abortive attempt to maintain a higher local price by exporting to Marseilles but the market, although uncontrolled, is too small to exert any appreciable difference.'[73]

The European firms were not at all happy with the situation. As early as 1923 they attempted to have the colonial state abolish the 'native' produce market in which indigenous traders bought groundnuts which they in turn later sold to the Syrians. The colonial authorities were, however, sceptical of the advantages of such a move:

> The firms ask for the produce market to be abolished and say the native producer would then go from firm to firm to ascertain the best prices and then sell goods direct to the firm. It is asserted that the firm offers a better price than the middleman. I find this hard to believe and intend next season to put it to the test. I suspect some pernicious system is at work of having different prices for different people. If the price of groundnuts is at £10 per ton the firm will pay the favoured middlemen £11 or £12. At any rate the fact remains that the average native steers clear of the European and considers he gets a fairer deal from a fellow native. It is true that the produce market and the middlemen's operation do tend to force up the price when there is competitive buying. If abolished firms could more easily combine to fix a lower price. Actually, however, with buying in progress for so many countries, Italy, France, America as well as England, the chances of a permanent combine are very small. I find the question of the market is a very difficult one to make up my mind about and want to be certain before I decide that the firms are doing all they can to get into direct touch with the producer.[74]

If the state was hesitant in coming to the firms' assistance, they were less hesitant about helping themselves. In 1928 the majority of the European firms, with the exception of the French, formed yet another groundnut buying pool.[75] In 1930 the French firms joined the pool; now only the Syrians remained outside.[76] This pool, however, like its predecessors, proved to be a failure, but for a new reason. It was faced not only with the old problems posed by middlemen but also the new threat of middlemen attempting to ship on their own to the European market.

The most successful of the Syrians was Saul Raccah who had originally come to Kano before the First World War as the agent of one of the Manchester firms active in the trans-Saharan trade. Throughout the 1920s Raccah had acted as one of the numerous middlemen in the groundnut trade. By 1928, however, he was under increasing pressure from the European firms' buying pool and thus decided to strike out on the course of independent exporting. It is likely that the Kano report cited above refers to one of his early attempts. If this first attempt was abortive, subsequent efforts were not, and throughout the 1930s Raccah made steadily increasing inroads into the European firms' groundnut tonnage.[77]

Thus throughout the 1930s the European firms were faced with two commercial opponents – their own middlemen and their former middlemen turned exporters, such as Raccah. Against both the firms seemed powerless. This state of affairs is even more striking when it is realized that in the case of their own middlemen the firms themselves financed their enemies.

Most of the middlemen, like the firms themselves, depended for their operation on the extension of credit. However, credit for the middlemen came largely from the firms. If the firms had been serious about combining against these local rivals they could have cut off credit and in fact this was unsuccessfully attempted. They could also have ended their favourable price discrimination. Yet to have done so would have necessitated a degree of co-operation even greater than that of the buying pools. If one firm or a group of firms cut off credit to the middlemen or ended favourable price discrimination while others did not, its trade would be ruined. There was no stable ground for co-operation between the firms in a competitive market, short of outright combination.[78]

By the 1929–30 crop year, the situation had, from the firms' point of view, sharply deteriorated, as a report on the groundnut trade for that year makes clear:

An increase in direct shipping to Europe by some of the more important Syrians and other independent operators has been a notable feature of the latter months of this year . . . As in recent years the Syrians have succeeded in attracting the bulk of the groundnut crop into Kano. Only some 9,000 out of 50,000 tons marketed up to the end of the year had been purchased in the township produce plots, almost the entire balance passed through Syrian hands.[79]

The same report also shows how the firms reacted to this threat to their position:

In order to reduce Syrian control, the European firms have been establishing buying stations throughout the province until at the end of 1930, 129 temporary and permanent plots had been established in Kano Emirate alone. 43 of these rights of occupancy were granted in 1930. This movement by the European firms to tap produce nearer its source has forced the Syrians to take similar action. 31 certificates of temporary occupancy have been issued to Syrians and Arabs.[80]

Thus, as a result of the competitive market and fluctuating prices in the groundnut trade, both the firms and the middlemen were forced to expand their trading territory, generalizing the trade in groundnuts not only throughout Kano Emirate and Province but eventually throughout all of Northern Nigeria where the crop could be grown.[81]

This response of the firms to the Syrian threat was not, however, without its difficulties. First, there was the cost of maintaining and staffing trading posts all over the north. Second, there was the problem of transportation. For the former there was no solution, the choice was simple – expand or die. The hope was that the increased tonnage would pay for the extra cost. As all firms attempted to expand, however, any special benefits accruing to those who were first in new areas rapidly disappeared. Moreover, the presence of the firms in a district capital rapidly created a new trading structure similar to that of Kano, only in miniature, with credit being provided to local middlemen who speculated on the changing prices. Continual attempts to prosecute offenders who had taken advances from one firm and sold to another were fruitless, as were the continuous attempts at co-operation. For the latter problem, transport, an interesting solution with far-reaching implications arose.

A report from Zaria Province for 1923 states:

> It is a remarkable fact that there is not a single motor vehicle transporting produce on the expensive Zaria–Sokoto road . . .
> The reason for this is not far to seek – motor transport cost 2/3 per ton mile. This compares with camel, donkey and oxen transport which averages out a season at 1/- per ton mile. Head transport costs 3/-.
> The amount of animal transport appears limitless, Zaria Province itself has no animal transport of any consequence, but camels and donkeys arrive in endless numbers from Sokoto, Katsina and far into French territory.[82]

By 1929 animal transport rates were reported to have dropped to 5d. per ton mile and were still displacing lorries.[83] For those who enjoy speculating on the reasons for the presence or absence of technological change it is useful to note that in 1929 four legs were still cheaper than four wheels, even if the latter were motorized.

The meeting of the Syrian threat entailed then, even allowing for the peculiarities of transport, an increase in the firms' expenditures which could only be justified by a commensurate increase in tonnage purchased and exported. There were, however, other stresses on the firms from 1925 to the end of the decade which compounded this problem. First, while it was true that the sales of manufactured goods which used oilseeds as their raw materials increased, they did not increase as rapidly as the supply of the raw materials themselves. This was especially true in margarine production. For example, margarine consumption in the United Kingdom increased from 254 000 tons in 1921 to 270 000 tons in 1927.[84] Once again the slow growth in margarine consumption was related to the low prices for butter, the consumption of which increased from 239 000 tons to 325 000 tons over the same period.[85] As a result of the slow growth of margarine consumption, inventories of unsold oilseed began to accumulate near the end of the decade. This situation had important effects on the European merchant firms in the oilseeds trade in Nigeria. Moreover, for trading concerns such as the African and Eastern Corporation this problem of oilseed oversupply was compounded by the structure of merchant capital itself, and in particular by the high degree of management rights retained by the individual firms which had formed the combine. The latter led to the proliferation of trading posts, operated ultimately by the African and Eastern but under the names of its component firms, expensively staffed, and competing with one another throughout Northern Nigeria. In addition, in the late 1920s the African and Eastern had been involved in a series of unremunerative ventures in manufacturing in Europe, which were largely attempts to diversify to meet the competition from the Lever Brothers combine. These eroded the African and Eastern's Nigerian profits and by 1928 the company was in difficult straits.[86]

This situation was exacerbated by the stock market boom in the United States which, based on speculative buying, absorbed massive amounts of credit, thus making it more difficult for foreign borrowers to find available money. By 1928 this absorption of credit had forced a chain reaction which affected British banks. In 1928 the African and Eastern informed its shareholders that no dividend would be paid for the previous year. The banks reacted by withdrawing all credit, which in turn threatened to halt the firm's trading operations. The banks suggested the appointment of an administrator whose previous history was closely linked to that of the Lever combine as a condition of resumed access to credit. This latter action set the African and Eastern on the road to combination with the Niger Company under Lever control, and on 1 May 1929 the merger was effected, the new concern being known as the United Africa Company.[87]

The formation of the United Africa Company was followed by an even more massive concentration of capital in the oilseed processing and manufacturing industry in Europe. The two largest margarine producers in Europe, the Dutch firms of Jurgens and Van den Burghs amalgamated their interests in 1927. Aside from margarine production itself, both of these firms held substantial interests in oilseed crushing, fat hardening, soapmaking, wholesaling and retailing. As with the European merchants in West Africa, the merger itself was preceded by a long history of unsuccessful marketing pool arrangements, and once again it was the competitive experience of the 1920s which forced the logic of the concentration of capital upon the two contending firms.[88]

As we have already noted, while margarine consumption continued to increase during the 1920s, that increase was modest. The primary reason for this state of affairs was the low price of butter. As a result, margarine sales were only maintained or increased by a continual price war among the manufacturers. As Charles Wilson has pointed out, by 1927 the situation was very serious:

> Two examples are sufficient to characterize the situation that resulted from the price war. In 1927 soapmakers were using margarine as a raw material for the manufacture of soap, while margarine was being given away with presents instead of presents with margarine.[89]

Eventually the firms came to see the continuation of these price wars as suicidal and thus after long negotiations the Dutch firms and their subsidiaries formed the Margarine Unie.[90]

The creation of the Margarine Unie was followed up in the next year by discussions between its principals and those of Lever Brothers. Although the main concern of the Margarine Unie was margarine production and that of Lever Brothers soap production, each made enough of the other's product to be a threat. More important, each had interests in tropical oilseeds production, milling, fat hardening, wholesale and retail shops, and most important, both competed for the same raw materials. The original intention of the 1928 discussion was to disentangle the two concerns' interests. Lever Brothers was to get out of margarine production, while the Margarine Unie was to sell off its soap-making interests. Given the complexity of the firms' operations, however, this proved to be impossible and rather than continue their competition the firms merged their interests into a new venture, Unilever. This new firm had a nominal share value of approximately £100 million and constituted the largest amalgamation in European history.[91]

One final combination of capital was attempted during 1929, but failed. This was to have been an agreement between the United Africa Company and the members of the West African Shipping Conference headed by Elder Dempster. The preamble of the abortive agreement states:

> It is the basis of this Agreement that the Merchants shall do everything in their power to support and enhance the shipowners in maintaining their paramount position in the ocean carrying trade to and from Europe and West Africa and that, on the other hand, the shipowners shall do everything in their power to support and enhance the paramount position of the merchants in their activities on the Continent of Africa and that the merchants will withdraw altogether from any direct or indirect interest as shipowners in the ocean-carrying trade to and from West Africa in consideration of the shipowners withdrawing altogether from any interest in any trading or other activity within the region marked red on the map attached hereto.[92]

The proposed agreement also called for special freight rebates for the United Africa Company as well as special normal rates. That such an agreement was even contemplated by Elder Dempster and the other members of the shipping conference is an indication of how the balance of power in the West African trade had shifted with the entry of Lever Brothers and the creation of the United Africa Company. The failure of this proposed agreement was one of the prime contributing factors in the 1930 financial collapse of the Royal Mail Shipping Group, which had acquired the Elder Dempster line on the death of Alfred Jones in 1909.[93]

The contribution of the Elder Dempster line to the collapse of the Royal Mail group can ultimately be traced to the First World War. During the war the Elder Dempster group was administered by the British government while the vessels of its principal partner in the shipping ring, the German Woermann line, were either destroyed or withdrawn as a result of hostilities. Anticipating the post-war boom, Elder Dempster, like many shippers, contracted for the building of many new ships. Yet, as a result of the massive wartime entry of the United States into shipbuilding, the conflict ended with more shipping tonnage available than at the commencement of the war. Thus, when the 1920 economic collapse hit, Elder Dempster had a large excess of new and expensive shipping tonnage as well as facing competition from the merchant houses which had built their own ships in an attempt to break the Elder Dempster monopoly. Further, the excess of world shipping prompted the entry of several new shippers into the West African trade in the early 1920s. In 1924 Elder Dempster and its fellow shippers attempted to re-establish their pre-war monopoly position through the West African Shipping Conference. They then attempted to increase shipping rates by as much as 70 per cent in the case of homeward-bound freight.[94]

In order to combat this attempt to re-establish a monopoly in the shipping trade, Lever Brothers' subsidiary, the United Africa Company, which in 1929 supplied some 40 per cent of Elder Dempster's freight, expanded its own shipping interests, which until this time had been used merely to supplement its reliance on Elder Dempster. The failed agreement of 1929 precipitated the withdrawal of the United Africa Company's business from Elder Dempster and was central to the collapse of the Royal Mail Group, of which Elder Dempster was a part. Although by the late 1930s the Elder Dempster line had recovered, as a result of the reconstruction of the Royal Mail group, the monopoly position of Elder Dempster was not restored. The entire reconstructed West African Shipping Conference was reduced to a 59 per cent share of the West African shipping trade. More important, the Unilever shipping fleet was itself admitted into the shipping conference by the 1950s.[95] Thus despite the immediate failure of 1929, the interests of shipper and merchant were eventually to coalesce under the dominance of industrial capital.

If the history of capital in Northern Nigeria from the beginning of the groundnut trade to the creation of the Unilever–United Africa Company axis in 1929 was dominated by the theme of the competition and concentration of European capital, the period of the great depression from 1929 to the beginning of the Second World War was to be dominated by the attack of the more or less united European firms on the Syrian and African middlemen. The tenacious existence of these middlemen necessitated the expensive expansion of the firms' outstations, and ensured that the United Africa Company, even with a share of the market in excess of 50 per cent, could not establish commercial hegemony. The attack on the middlemen was greatly facilitated by the extension of the rail system in the north in the 1920s and 1930s. The firms followed the progress of the line with their stations in an attempt to eliminate middlemen of all types but especially the powerful Kano-based Syrians.[96] The opening of the rail branch lines and the establishment of 'flat' or equalized through-rates for groundnuts assisted the firms by reorienting the hinterland trade away from Kano and the middlemen:

> The flat rate on the line has proved successful no doubt extending the area of outstations and cultivation. It reduces trade in Kano, however, and this has been more pronounced this season. This affects the Native and Arab traders in Kano. They will have to adjust themselves to the new conditions since it is not only on the line but in other places that trade has spread in the last ten years. This involves more distribution and the numerous middlemen of a big centre like Kano feel the pinch.[97]

The stock-market crash of 1929 and the ensuing collapse of produce prices for most primary goods in 1930, which inaugurated the economic depression in Northern Nigeria, did much to exacerbate the existing tensions between the European firms and their middlemen. More important, these tensions were to become so great in British West Africa as a whole that they were ultimately to involve the British state in such a way as to alter fundamentally the conditions of the trade in agricultural commodities and set in motion the politics which would ultimately culminate in the granting of political independence.

The price of groundnuts in the British market dropped from £20 11s 3d per ton in March of 1928 to £15 11s 3d in March of 1930 to £12 16s 3d in March of 1931. It recovered briefly in March of 1932 to £17 2s 6d but then plummetted in March of 1934 to £8 5s or less than half of what the Kano price had been in the mid-1920s.[98] This heavy decline in prices was not primarily due to a fall in the price of margarine or soap or to a lessening in the consumption of these items as one might expect, but rather to the increased production of other types of fats. In particular, whale oil, which was now benefiting from the introduction of 'factory' ships, fell rapidly in price. In addition, however, the price fall in oilseeds was generated by the producers themselves, who, when faced with falling prices, increased their output in order to stabilize their income.[99] Thus, the estimated acreage under groundnuts in India, the largest producer in the world, increased from 6 177 000 acres in 1929–30 to 8 115 000 acres in 1933–4.[100] Northern Nigeria was no exception to this trend, with exports rising from 135 000 tons in 1928–9 to 197 000 tons in 1932–3.[101] Over the same period Kano prices fell from an average of about £10 per ton in 1928–9 to an average of £2 7s in 1934, the same year in which exports increased to 244 886 tons.[102]

The increase in the groundnut crop, associated with falling prices, arose from two sources – intensified cultivation in areas in which groundnuts had become a 'traditional' staple export and the extension of groundnut cultivation for export into new areas serviced by middlemen, the European firms and the railway. The Resident for Kano Province noted in his annual report for 1933 that:

> Economically, groundnuts provide the lifestream for this Province. A falling price last year stimulated the extension of cultivation. There is a large crop, possibly larger by 25%, but the drop in price to 50/- a ton is too great to prove less than disappointing – roughly this year it takes the peasant twice as much in groundnuts to meet his tax and there has been little over for expenditures.
>
> Not only was the acreage under this crop greatly increased by the farmers already acquainted with its value as a ready money crop but in the Northern Division resident Fulani and peasants in distant buying centres planted nuts in hope of obtaining money to pay taxes . . . In consequence the acreage planted showed an increase of probably 20% over last year.
>
> It is improbable that the low prices this year will adversely affect production in the immediate future. For the bulk of the Province it is the easiest money crop and whatever the price it does represent a certain sum of hard cash.[103]

Similar sentiments were expressed by the Residents of Bornu, Sokoto, and Zaria Provinces into which the trade had now spread.[104]

In 1935 and 1936 prices rose modestly, the average buying price being £6 4s and £7 7s respectively.[105] Production, however, declined, with exports decreasing to 183 993 tons in 1935 and then climbing to 218 389 tons in 1936.[106] It is probable that this decline in production from the 1934 figure of 224 886 tons was not a response to falling prices, but rather a result of the combined effects of poor crops and a regional food shortage during these years.[107] In 1937 the average Kano price for groundnuts increased to £8 per ton and exports reached a decade high of 325 929 tons.[108] Prices, however, dropped in 1938 to an average of £4 3s and then to £3 4s in 1939.[109] The low prices for groundnuts combined with the competition from Raccah and others during the decade were translated into a profit squeeze for the firms during the 1930s. This profit squeeze was present in the import trade as well. As the incidence of taxation remained relatively steady throughout the period of decreased prices, an increasing proportion of the producers' income was directed away from the purchase of imports such as cloth into the coffers of the state.[110] Moreover, in the early 1930s the falling market for imported goods created an era of cutthroat price competition in the import trade among the remaining European firms. The main results of this competition were the continued concentration of European capital on the one hand and the extension of 'pooling' into the import trade on the other.

The first of these results of the depression may be easily disposed of. G. B. Ollivant, a British firm which had engaged in the West African produce trade, went into liquidation in 1933 and was reconstituted as a Unilever subsidiary in the same year. Ollivant had been supported both by the Liverpool soap manufacturer and Lever Brothers' competitor, Bibby, and by the Elder Dempster line which was attempting to insure itself against a United Africa Company monopoly in West Africa. By 1933 neither of Ollivant's supporters could continue to assist it and the company went the way of many we have already discussed.[111]

More important than the fate of Ollivant was the conclusion of the Staple Lines Agreement (1934) and Merchandise Agreement (1937). These agreements were made by virtually all of the major European firms in British West Africa, including the United Africa Company, G. B. Ollivant, John Holt, Compagnie Française d'Afrique Occidentale, Société Commerciale de l'Ouest Africain, Deutsche West Africanische Handelgesellschaft, De Hage Handelgesellshaft, G. L. Gaiser and Witt and Busch.[112] A memorandum in the Holt papers provides the explanation for the Merchandise Agreement:

> Consequent upon the extremely low selling prices which have been current in Nigeria for a considerable time, as the outcome of the intensive competition which has existed between the pricipal companies, discussions have taken place with the result that an agreement in respect of the main staple commodities . . . has been made amongst the following companies with the object of alleviating competition.[113]

The intent of these agreements, in particular the Merchandise Agreement, was to limit price competition through the maintenance of past market shares among the firms. They were the complement to the export pools and were an attempt to carry the commercial war against the middlemen into the import trade.

The creation of the import and export pools represented the response of capital in Northern Nigeria to the crisis of world capitalism in the

1930s. Concentration and centralization were the only means of commercial survival. Yet if these were the tools by which capital survived, they were also the tools by which the financial existence of the colonial state was threatened. The colonial state's response to this threat was to alter radically the political economy of Northern Nigeria.

NOTES

1   J. S. Hogendorn, *Nigerian Groundnut Exports: Origins and Early Development* (Zaria and Ibadan: Ahmadu University Press and Oxford University Press, 1978), p. 25. Although this chapter draws on many of the sources which Hogendorn uses, the conclusions, especially as they relate to the origins of the groundnut trade and its consequences, are radically different.
2   C. Wilson, *The History of Unilever. A Study in Economic Growth and Social Change*, 2 vols (London: Cassell, 1954).
3   J. Hogendorn, *Nigerian Groundnut Exports*, Chapter 3.
4   G. Dangerfield, *The Strange Death of Liberal England* (New York: Smith & Haas, 1935), pp. 217–18.
5   E. J. Hobsbawm, *Industry and Empire* (London: Weidenfeld & Nicolson, 1968) Chapter 9.
6   E. H. Hunt, *British Labour History 1815–1914* (London: Weidenfeld & Nicolson, 1981) p. 319.
7   Wilson, *History of Unilever*, Vol. 2, p. 24.
8   ibid., pp. 110–11.
9   ibid.
10   United Kingdom, 1922 Cmd 1600, *Report of a Committee on Trade and Taxation for British West Africa*, p. 40.
11   Intelligence Branch of the Imperial Economic Committee, *Survey of Oilseeds and Vegetable Oils*, vol. 3, 'Groundnut Products', (London: HMSO, 1935) p. 37. See also NAK SNP 9 1147/1914.
12   NAK SNP 7 4003/1905.
13   RH Mss, Afr. s. 96, RNC, vol. 12, Niger Co. to Elder Dempster, 16 March 1906.
14   ibid., s. 97, vol. 13, Jones to Scarbrough, October 1908.
15   ibid., Trigge to Scarbrough, 23 October 1908.
16   United Kingdom, 1916 Cmd 8248, *Committee on Edible and Oil Producing Nuts and Seeds*, p. 211.
17   See, for example, Jones's work on cotton in 'Minutes, African Trade Section, Liverpool Chamber of Commerce,' 26 January 1903, Liverpool Public Library.
18   P. N. Davies, *The Trade Makers. Elder Dempster in West Africa, 1862–1972* (London: Allen & Unwin, 1973), p. 125. See also RH Mss Afr. s. 86, RNC, vol. 12, Jones to Scarbrough, n.d., for Jones's undercutting of the merchants on railway materials to be sold to the government.
19   Davies, *Trade Makers*, pp. 144–68.
20   United Kingdom, 1916 Cmd 8248, *Committee on Edible and Oil Producing Nuts*

and Seeds, p. 211.

21 ibid.

22 NAK SNP 10 170p/1916.

23 United Kingdom, 1916 Cmd 8248, *Committee on Edible and Oil Producing Nuts and Seeds*, p. 211.

24 NAK KanoProf 98/1914.

25 On the working of the pools, see RH Mss, Afr. s. 86, RNC, vol. 1, 'Report of Pool's Operations', 16 July 1913; see also vol. 12 of this source Cotterell to Scarbrough, 20 December 1907; also 'Memo by Scarbrough' dated 12 December 1907 in vol. 12 of this source: also chart of pools operations in vol. 17 of the same source, undated.

26 On the inherent instability of the pools, see RH Mss, Afr. s. 96, RNC, vol. 12, Watts to Scarbrough, 18 October 1906; Scarbrough to Cotterell, 29 November 1906; Cotterell to Scarbrough, 21 December 1906.

27 United Kingdom, 1922 Cmd 1600, *Report of a Committee on Trade and Taxation for British West Africa*, p. 40.

28 RH Mss, Afr. s. 86, RNC, vol. 1, report dated 16 July 1914. See also NAK Kano Prof 98/1914, 1913.

29 NAK SNP 9 1147/1914.

30 NAK SNP 10 170p/1916.

31 United Kingdom, 1922 Cmd 1600, *Report of a Committee on Trade and Taxation for British West Africa*, p. 40. Also NAK SNP10 170p/1916 and RH Mss, Afr. s. 86, RNC, vol. 14, 'Report on the Baro-Minna Section of the Baro-Kano Railway', C. W. Hayward, 1913.

32 RH Mss, Afr. s. 86, RNC, vol. 15, entry dated 12 January 1915.

33 ibid., entry dated 18 January 1915. See also vol. 1, report dated 16 July 1914.

34 ibid., vol. 15, 'Memorandum on Profits for 1915'.

35 NAK SNP 10 170p/1916.

36 NAK SNP 10 97p/1917. The Niger Company's profits on groundnuts alone totalled some £80 000; see RH Mss, Afr. s. 86, RNC, vol. 1, report dated 18 October 1917.

37 NAK SNP 10 120p/1921.

38 *Survey of Oilseeds*, p. 37.

39 Hogendorn, *Nigerian Groundnut Exports*, p. 123.

40 D. H. Aldcroft, *From Versailles to Wall Street, 1919–1929* (London: Allen Lane, 1977) p. 65.

41 ibid., p. 62.

42 Wilson, *History of Unilever*, Vol. 2, p. 195.

43 ibid., p. 196.

44 ibid., p. 206–7.

45 ibid., p. 207.

46 ibid., Appendix 7.

47 NAK SNP 10 120p/1921.

48 This is my own understanding derived from a study of the London and Kano Company, a firm which operated in Kano during this period.

49 RH Mss, Afr. s. 86, RNC, vol. 1, entry dated 7 October 1919.

50 See note 48.

51 RH Mss, Afr. s. 86, RNC, vol. 1, 'Secret Memorandum' dated 1920.

52 Wilson, *History of Unilever*, Vol. 1, p. 252–3.
53 RH Mss. Afr. s. 86, RNC, Vol. 1, 'Report for Fall 1920'.
54 Wilson, *History of Unilever*, Vol. 2, pp. 301–10.
55 ibid., vol. 1, p. 163.
56 A. McPhee, *The Economic Revolution in British West Africa*, (1st edn 1926, reprinted London: Frank Cass, 1971), p. 151.
57 Quoted in Wilson, *History of Unilever*, Vol. 1, pp. 166–7. Lever, of course, had the wrong culprit. It was not 'black men' but colonial officials such as Girouard, Temple, and Strachey who were the enemies of industrial capitalism.
58 ibid., Vol. 1, pp. 167–83.
59 ibid., Vol. 1, p. 181.
60 ibid., Vol. 1, pp. 181–2.
61 C. Leubuscher, *The West African Shipping Trade 1909–1959* (Leyden: A. W. Sythoff, 1963) p. 99.
62 Davies, *Trade Makers*, pp. 107–10; Leubuscher, *West African Shipping Trade*, pp. 35–7.
63 Wilson, *History of Unilever*, Vol. 1, pp. 237–8; Davies, *Trade Makers*, pp. 179–81. This explanation stands in stark contrast to the usual arguments about peasant efficiency.
64 Wilson, *History of Unilever*, Vol. 1, pp. 216–19.
65 The Niger Company regularly purchased over 50 per cent of the crop.
66 F. Pedler, *The Lion and the Unicorn in Africa. A History of the United Africa Company 1787–1931* (London: Heinemann, 1974), pp. 225–39.
67 Wilson, *History of Unilever*, Vol. 2, pp. 24–50, 101–18.
68 *Survey of Oilseeds and Vegetable Oils*, p. 37.
69 NAK KanoProf 181/1925; NAK SNP 17 K105, vol. I; NAK SNP 17 K105, vol. II.
70 NAK KanoProf 181/1925; NAK SNP 17 K105, vol. I.
71 NAK SokProf 474/1925.
72 NAK SNP 17 K105, vol. II. Also NAK KanoProf 181/1925.
73 NAK KanoProf 438/1930.
74 RH Mss, Afr. s. 952, Arnett Papers, Draft of a letter from Arnett to Lugard, 17 July 1923.
75 W. K. Hancock, *Survey of British Commonwealth Affairs*, Vol. II, part 2, (London: Oxford University Press, 1942), p. 215.
76 ibid.
77 P. T. Bauer, *West African Trade. A Study of Competition, Oligopoly and Monopoly in a Changing Economy* (London: Routledge & Kegan Paul, 1963 new edn), Chapter 8; NAK KanoProf 438.
78 This was a classic case of the instability of oligopoly in a competitive market. See Bauer, *West African Trade*, Chapter 7.
79 NAK KanoProf 438.
80 ibid.
81 NAK SNP 17 9008, vol. I.
82 NAK SNP 9 100/1924.
83 NAK KanoProf 438.
84 Wilson, *History of Unilever*, Vol. 2, p. 255.

85   ibid.
86   ibid., Vol. 1, pp. 304–5. Pedler, *Lion and the Unicorn*, pp. 225–39.
87   Wilson, *History of Unilever*, Vol. 1, p. 305.
88   ibid., Vol. 2, pp. 253–70.
89   ibid., p. 252.
90   ibid., pp. 281–3.
91   ibid., pp. 303–8.
92   PRO CO 554 83/4236, Enclosure 1 to Governor Slater (Gold Coast) to Secretary of State for the Colonies, 15 March 1930.
93   Davies, *Trade Makers*, p. 170–80.
94   ibid., pp. 217–28.
95   ibid., pp. 227–8, 330–31.
96   NAK SNP 17 12127, vol. I.
97   NAK KanoProf 923, NAK KanoProf 628.
98   *Survey of Oilseeds* p. 210.
99   This phenomenon has been referred to by Kindleberger and others as a 'perverse reaction to the market'. See Charles Kindleberger, *The World in Depression, 1929–1939* (Berkeley: University of California Press, 1975), Chapter 4.
100 *Survey of Oilseeds,* p. 22.
101 ibid., p. 37.
102 NAK SNP 17 25670.
103 NAK SNP 17 21326.
104 NAK SNP 17 21303, vol. I, NAK SNP 17 21304.
105 NAK SNP 17 25673.
106 G. K. Helleiner, *Peasant Agriculture, Government, and Economic Growth in Nigeria* (Homewood, Ill: Irwin, 1966), table IV-A-8.
107 NAK SNP 17 25673.
108 NAK SNP 17 19378a.
109 ibid., also NAK SNP 17 30862; NAK SNP 17 32067.
110 NAK SNP 17 18921, vol. I.
111 F. Pedler, *Lion and the Unicorn*, p. 295.
112 RH Mss, s. 825–7, Holt Papers, File 516, 'Memo on the Formation of the Merchandise Pool', 30 November 1936.
113 RH Mss, s. 825–7, Holt Papers, File 516, 'Memorandum on Merchandise Agreement', n.d., also entry dated 10 August 1939 in the same location.

6

The Colonial State: Economic Crisis and the Origins of Development

For the colonial state, the precipitous fall in export prices and hence state revenue created a fiscal crisis in the 1930s. It has been estimated that between 1928 and 1934 the gross income of Nigeria from all sources fell from £74 million to £25 million.[1] State revenue, however, did not fall nearly so drastically. Of a total state revenue of £9 542 468 in 1927–8, indirect taxes, railway and other charges accounted for £7 917 697 while direct taxes made up the remainder with the Northern and Southern Provinces contributing £1 326 439 and £298 332 respectively. As a result of the fall in prices, these figures had declined to a total revenue of £7 601 027, comprising an indirect revenue of £5 672 000 and direct taxes for the Northern and Southern Provinces of £1 336 624 and £592 403.[2]

Thus, while the colony's income had declined by nearly 66 per cent, total state revenue had fallen by less than 25 per cent and direct taxes had actually increased substantially. The resulting situation was mercilessly, if metaphorically, described by one observer:

> The point is, however, that speaking broadly, Nigeria in *all internal respects* has not suffered from an economic depression. Her production of yams, cassava, fish, corn, and her exchange of all her produce goes on as before.
>
> Nigeria only suffers in so far as she has made or continues to make contracts in terms of money values, in other words her sufferings at the moment arise through the nerve channels of public finance and external trade alone.
>
> Prosperity does not depend on prices any more than the area of a village depends on the use of a foot or a meter to express that area.
>
> It is unjust if a particular owner of land in the village, when the

changeover from measurement in square feet to square meters is made is privileged to keep as many units as before. No wonder the village common is greatly reduced. Yet this is precisely what happens when Nigeria has to pay out double in 1932, in agricultural produce, the amount she paid for for Government services in 1926, and more than three times the amount she paid out in 1920, when the present scale of salaries was fixed . . .[3]

Government expenditure abroad has turned a favourable into an unfavourable trade balance for every year since 1929.[4]

Clearly, in the eyes of this particular observer Nigeria could no longer afford the colonial state. It did not, however, have the option of dispensing with its services. Moreover, since all but a tiny proportion of direct and indirect taxes, railway freight revenue and other sources of state income were derived from the production and sale of export crops, it was the rural agricultural producers who kept the state during this its time of trouble by producing steadily larger amounts of exports.

In the face of falling prices, the incidence of taxation in Northern Nigeria was maintained with only occasional instances of realistic remission. There were those who argued that such a situation could not persist. One wrote:

The image of a blindfolded justice has deceived many. Justice must not look to the left or to the right but it must not be ignorant . . .

Taxation is a dangerous drug for the body politic. Taxation of non-existing profits is rank poison . . .[5]

The direct taxes proposed for the Northern Provinces for 1933–34 were £1.337 millions or nearly 35% too much.[6]

The state's options for revenue sources were, however, severely limited. Aside from direct taxes there were only three other major sources of revenue – export duties, railway charges, and duties on imports. None of these could be drastically increased without lowering total revenue by killing trade. Export duties and railway charges added to the cost of exports and any substantial increase in these two areas would have made Nigerian produce uncompetitive on the world market. An increase in import duties, on the other hand, would have made imported goods such as textiles and salt uncompetitive in the local market and thus would have provided impetus for the resurgence of local production. Direct taxes were the only form of income which the state could increase to maintain its revenue. The results of such a policy were, however, open to question.

In 1934 one study indicated that agricultural producers in the Soba District of Zaria Province were paying 41 per cent of their total income in taxes while others were paying as high as 70 per cent of their cash income.

Since export crops were the single largest source of cash, it is clear that they were being produced almost entirely to meet the demands of the state.[7] However, despite this pressing burden of taxation the Nigerian government's revenue from all sources was estimated to amount in 1936–7 to only 5s 10d per inhabitant. This compared with a per capita revenue of 39s 5d for the British colony of Malaya and 28s 3d for Jamaica. Even Tanganyika had, at 6s 9d, a marginally higher revenue per head. Moreover of this 5s 10d, 1s 10d was committed to debt servicing, 4d to military expenditure and 6d to the pensions and gratuities for the colonial state's personnel. This left only 3s 5d per capita to be spent on all other facets of the colonial state's apparatus. Moreover, of the £1 876 336 which had been paid to the administrative staff in 1937–8, no less than £1 167 050 had been paid not in Nigeria, but in the United Kingdom and constituted a massive invisible export of funds by the Nigerian colonial state. It was the Nigerian peasant who bore this onerous burden.

The stark reality of this situation soon gave rise to other fears, the chief of which was famine. As the increase in export crop production to meet taxation had made definite inroads in food crop production both in terms of area and time spent, the food situation became increasingly precarious. In the District of Dawakin ta Kudu, for example, 31.45 per cent of all cultivated land was under groundnuts in 1937–8, while the Kano Annual Report for 1934 speaks of 'a real shortage of food in one of the biggest groundnut districts'.[8] The Annual Reports of 1930 and 1931 for Sokoto and Zaria Provinces openly refer to famine in these areas and cite a plague of locusts in conjunction with the overcultivation of export crops as the reasons for it.[9] In some areas even food crops had to be sold to meet the growing burden of taxes. A 1938 report on the earnings of small farmers in the vicinity of the city of Kano, the prime groundnut area, noted that 'without exception they seem to have to buy corn later on in the year the reason is that at harvest they are practically penniless. They have to sell out to pay tax'.[10] Yet it was the need to stabilize state revenue through the increased production of export crops and not the fear of famine which remained the major preoccupation of the colonial state in these years. The Resident of Bauchi Province stated this dominant view succinctly. 'As I have frequently mentioned,' he noted, 'and as the Director of Agriculture well knows, our great need is more export crops . . . We do not want more corn.'[11]

The emphasis on export crop production was the continuation of past policy and thus for good reason met with little opposition from within colonial officialdom. A preoccupation on the part of a colonial officer with food production or rural welfare was a sure route to failure, as the story of H. S. W. Edwardes, a colonial officer stationed in Sokoto Province in the late 1910s and early 1920s, suggests. Edwardes attempted to irrigate sizeable tracts of land in the Sokoto-Rima river basin in order to increase food production. Using local labour and his own engineering skills, Edwardes constructed irrigation canals to regulate flooding in order to benefit local producers. The project was, in technical terms, a success. Edwardes, however, discovered that the newly irrigated land was being appropriated by members of the Sokoto Native Administration. He was, however, powerless in the face of the sanctity of indirect rule to punish the offenders or rectify the situation. For this and other reasons Edwardes became known as what Robert Heussler describes as a 'friend of the peasant' and as such unfit for promotion. He later resigned in obscure circumstances but not before producing a stinging critique of tax assessment and collection policies as well as some of the most detailed agricultural surveys of his day.[12]

Yet if the increased production of export crops was to continue to be the primary goal of the state, it was unclear how this goal was to be achieved. The colonial state was, by past experience, singularly ill-suited for the challenge presented to it by the crisis of world capitalism – the task of cheapening the cost of export crop production, or as it came to be known, 'agricultural development'.

As has been illustrated in the earlier chapters of this work, state intervention in the economy had been largely limited to serving specific ends – the realization of taxes, the establishment of its political primacy and the somewhat dubious catering to the needs of the British textile industry. The Agricultural Department since its creation in 1916 had largely focused on produce grading to ensure high quality exports and the continual and largely futile battle to persuade Northern Nigerians to produce more cotton.[13] One of the earliest development strategies designed to mitigate the effects of the depression by cheapening production and thus exports was 'mixed farming'. The term was used to describe 'a system of animal husbandry of which the chief feature is the substitution of ploughing with bullocks for the more usual hand cultivation with a hoe'.[14] The original aim of the promotion of mixed farming was an increase in cotton production to satisfy imperial needs. Like virtually all such projects, it was a failure.[15] By the mid-1930s, however, mixed farming was being touted as a way of increasing export crop production while lowering its cost and thus securing a larger proportion of the world's market for Northern Nigerian exports. The ultimate aim of such a policy was to prop up the state's dwindling revenue. The barriers to entry to mixed farming were high. At least £10 in cash or credit was needed to purchase bullocks and a plough or the equivalent of two to three years cash earnings for the common agricultural producer.[16] Moreover, the animals had to be kept in fodder during the dry season at a cost which most producers could not bear. Even among those who were judged creditworthy, there was a high failure rate exceeding, in many years, 30 per cent.[17]

Although this strategy was first implemented in 1928, by 1935 there were only 621 'mixed farmers'. Given the funds and the time devoted to this initiative during a period which overlapped with widespread hunger, the class composition of the participants is of interest. Of the 621 mixed farmers in 1935, 119 were 'emirs and N.A. Executive Officials', 185 were village heads, while only 251 were counted as 'Peasants', leaving 65 others, who were primarily traders.[18]

The attempt to increase export crop production to stabilize revenue in the face of falling prices was not unique to the colonial state in Northern Nigeria. During the 1930s virtually all primary-goods producing states attempted it in one form or another, as did farmers, peasants and other agricultural producers around the world.[19] Yet overproduction was itself the problem and the simultaneous efforts of all to increase production only lowered prices and worsened the situation. As Drummond-Hay, the Government Agricultural Advisor, clearly saw:

> We are told that 'Mixed farming is the only hope of developing the agricultural wealth of the province'. But what does this wealth consist of? The wretched farmer has seen the introduction of cotton and groundnuts as his 'agricultural wealth', has profited by it, and has seen the value of this wealth gradually decline with increased production, until neither crop is worth the labour of cultivation. The question arises therefore whether we are introducing mixed farming in order to have ten groundnuts grow where one grew before, and increase the area under cotton . . .
>
> More production of groundnuts and cotton will only help to lower the already low price of these crops . . .
>
> What then are we attempting? It would appear that our aim is to introduce a foreign system of farming which if uncontrolled will result in large areas being cultivated, and large crops being reaped for which there are no markets. What then?[20]

If domestic 'development', in the form of mixed farming, held out little promise as a strategy for alleviating the fiscal crisis of the colonial state, neither did imperial assistance. Although in 1929 a Colonial Development Act had been passed by the British parliament it was to prove to have little effect on the colonial state's dilemma in Nigeria. The reason for its ineffectuality lay in the origins and nature of the Act itself.[21]

First, although the purpose of the Act was stated in the year of its passage by the then Secretary of State for the Colonies, Lord Passfield, to be to 'accelerate as far as possible the development of the Crown Colonies, Protectorates and Dependencies', it is generally recognized that the Act had a deeper purpose.[22] This purpose was the alleviation of industrial unemployment in Britain itself. As the Act stated: 'save in exceptional circumstances all orders for imported material should be placed in the United Kingdom; and that plant, machinery, materials etc. be of British origin and manufacture.'[23] In itself this provision might not have had a particularly negative effect had it not been combined with the Act's other more onerous provisions. One of these was the extreme paucity of the sum provided by the Act, a mere £1 000 000 per annum for the development of the colonial empire's some 66 000 000 inhabitants. Moreover, other provisions of the Act made its impact even more limited than the 'tuppence' allocated per capita suggests.[24]

Central among these limiting provisions were stipulations as to how the funds provided under the Act could be used. The use of such funds was to take either one of two forms. The first was grants or loans for the financing of a specific project. The second was grants and loans to defray the interest on a loan raised by the colonial government for the financing of a specific project for a period of ten years. In either case two important conditions applied – the funds could not be used for the financing of an existing government programme, project or service and, more important, the colonial government in question was to provide both a portion of the funding of any project and would have to find the future funds for its recurrent costs.[25]

In 1939 Sir Bernard Bourdillon, who had been Nigeria's Governor for the preceding three years recounted his experience with the Act. He stated that its interest defrayal aspect had been of little use to him in Nigeria primarily because of the large debt-servicing load which the colony already carried. Some 25 per cent of Nigeria's revenue was already devoted to servicing its debt and Bourdillon argued that adding to that burden some ten years down the road was 'too speculative a proceeding' in the absence of a guarantee that 'the resources of the country would in the meantime have increased sufficiently to offset the additional load.' In the case of direct grants or loans for specific projects he cited examples of how the Act had operated with respect to Nigeria.[2]

In one instance, on approaching the Advisory Committee set up under the Act about certain 'public health projects', he was told that 'in all projects of this nature the Colonial Government concerned should wherever possible be required to bear a reasonable proportion of the cost involved.' The result was that the Advisory Committee agreed to finance 65 per cent of the capital costs of the projects in question. However, given the sorry state of Nigeria's debt-ridden, depression finances, the Nigerian government decided to scale down the projects. Predictably, the amount allocated by the Committee was scaled down as well. In another instance, of £30 000 requested to finance a particular scheme, the Advisory Committee stated that £11 000 represented the cost 'not of new services, but of an extension of existing services' and thus was 'not a proper charge on the fund'. The remaining £19 000 was only to be forthcoming on the understanding that the Nigerian government would find the other £11 000.[27]

The problem with the Act, from the perspective of the colonial state in Nigeria, was clear. The funds provided under it could only be used for new schemes and not as a supplement to general revenue. This meant, first, that the Act had little effect in alleviating the colonial state's fiscal crisis. It also meant that in order to take advantage of the funds provided by the Act the colonial state had to commit itself both to increased current expenditure and/or increased future expenditure in the form of interest and recurrent costs. The result was that the Act was little used. Nigeria asked for and received less than a quarter of a million pounds under the Act for its estimated 22 000 000 inhabitants during the decade from the Act's inception to the outbreak of the Second World War.[28]

By the mid-1930s, in the absence of substantial external assistance and in tacit recognition of the failure of the mixed farming strategy, attention began to be focused increasingly on the marketing system itself as the source of the threat of incipient financial insolvency. In particular, the local middlemen in the export trade was singled out as the enemy for attack.[29] This view dovetailed neatly with that of the advocates of European merchant capital who were already at war with the middlemen over the division of profits. As if by magic, for the first time in its history the colonial state began to undertake a number of serious studies of agricultural production and income and discovered to its chagrin the reality of a rural population deeply in debt and periodically on the verge of famine.[30] These evils were now laid at the door of the middlemen. Co-operatives were deemed to be the answer.[31] Their main aim would be to eliminate the village moneylenders and produce-middlemen.[32]

From 1934 onward, report followed report, yet all were followed by inaction. It came to be understood clearly that were the village moneylenders and produce-middlemen to be eliminated, the sole source of rural credit would also disappear. It was also understood that only state intervention on a massive scale could replace them. As the state had neither the resources nor the inclination to embark on such an endeavour, such intervention was not undertaken.[33] However, a myriad of unenforced and indeed unenforceable regulations was passed outlawing moneylending and circumscribing the activities of middlemen as the colonial state was enlisted in the wars of capital generated by the depression.[34] No new initiatives by the state to combat the depression were undertaken. By the end of the decade external events forced the state's hand, prompted its direct intervention in the export trade and transformed the colonial state's fiscal crisis into a political crisis as well.

Despite the crushing burden of taxation, Northern Nigeria remained politically quiescent during the depression, thanks largely to the effectiveness of the Native Administration system. However, other less rigidly governed regions of the British empire did not. In particular, the

Jamaica labour rebellion of 1938 shook imperial confidence. In the large context – that of a world advancing toward war – the reform of colonial capitalism became a necessity.[35] In West Africa the need for such reform was made apparent by the Gold Coast cocoa hold-up during the 1937–8 buying season.[36] The middlemen and brokers of the Gold Coast cocoa trade faced the same purchasing pools, merchandise, and staple-good agreements as their counterparts in Nigeria. Moreover, they too were subjected to the hostile anti-middlemen campaign of the firms. However, unlike their Northern Nigerian counterparts, they did not suffer from the rigid political structure of indirect rule. With cocoa prices falling dramatically, they decided in 1937 to take action by following the lead of the cocoa farmers in playing the political card of a produce hold-up, bringing to a halt the export of cocoa. Although extended to the palm produce and cocoa trades in Southern Nigeria, the spread and evolution of this commercial 'strike', which took place far beyond the borders of Northern Nigeria, was nonetheless to play a crucial role in the restructuring of its economic and political life. Seized upon, if not instigated by, the nascent nationalists of the Gold Coast and Southern Nigeria, who found their own progress to the heights of the bureaucracy blocked by British officials, the cocoa hold-up rapidly became more than an economic gambit. For these individuals an attack upon the European firms was merely a first step in the attack upon the colonial state itself. Moreover, it provided them with a means to mobilize brokers and middlemen who might not in other circumstances have so willingly allied themselves with their personal aspirations for political power. From this point forward, the politics of independence became inextricably inter-twined with the export trade. One European merchant understood the situation in the following terms:

> Behind them all [agitators] is the editor of the West African Pilot, Mr Mnamdi Azikwe M.A. M.Sc. etc. [sic] who was turfed out of the Gold Coast. He is another 'Ghandi' [sic]. He is giving courage to people like Akinsanya . . . and has roped in the Nigerian Youth Movement. [sic]
> The pool must not be broken up – if it is, attacks will be made on every other pool and agreement until these 'red organizations' control the entire situation dictating to merchant and government alike threatening trouble at every refusal of their terms.[37]

Although the battle was seen to be essentially between the firms and the middlemen, the producer was for each a politically valuable, indeed crucial, ally. Thus in a memorandum for the head office of one European firm the following strategy was enunciated for dealing with the produce hold-up. 'Let us,' it recommended, 'put the dispute where it properly belongs and keep it there, that is between the Nigerian middlemen and the peasant producer.'[38] A reply from the firm's agent in Nigeria concurred in this strategy for 'combatting the trouble', arguing that 'the war' should be converted 'into one between middlemen, brokers and farmers'. It clearly demonstrated the political nature of the struggle as perceived by the firms.[39]

This strategy was reflected in the instructions given to the firms' agents as to the nature of the testimony they were to give to the Nowell Commission established to inquire into the Gold Coast cocoa hold-up.[40]

It has been arranged with the commission that after the first day of the first case, which will be more in the nature of a full dress parade before the public, there shall be sittings in camera. It is at these meeting that tales of the brokers' misdeeds, the political machinations behind the hold up, the inner history of the firms' experiences will be tabled.[41]

A further memorandum urged that instructions be given to all agents specifying which brokers' abuse they were to give evidence of before the commission.[42]

The European merchants' chief fear was that the commission would be sufficently frightened by the political implications of this wave of economic disturbances as to advocate some form of state intervention in the export trade either through the establishment of state marketing agencies or through the fostering of direct sales on the part of producers through co-operative selling agencies. In other words, the European firms were faced with the possibility that their anti-middleman propaganda had worked only too well and that the state, vexed with the political results of the economic war between European merchant and African middleman, would decide that the course to take in its own best interest was the radical transformation of the marketing system. Instruction to their agents reflected this fear:

Cooperative societies will not be mentioned first by us, but if the subject comes up we shall have to show a vague sympathy towards cooperation. [To do otherwise] will only strengthen the determination of the government to go ahead with cooperative marketing and will give Mr Irving the cue to recommend the introduction of government controlled marketing.[43]

The fear that the attack on the middlemen had led the European firms into the trap of state intervention is illustrated by the following exchange between Mr Irving, a key member of the commission, and Mr C. A. W. Woods, an agent for John Holt:

MR. THOMPSON: In your opinion why does the average farmer not take advantage of the facility of selling direct to the firms?
MR. WOODS: I consider that in most cases it is due to the fact that most farmers are tied to a particular middleman by reason of cash advances they have received from them.

MR. IRVING: Can you help us by suggesting any organization whereby we can insure the farmer gets true weight and value for his cocoa?
MR. WOODS: I cannot suggest any such organization unless the farmer brings his cocoa directly to the firms. As long as he is in the hands of the middlemen I do not see how he can be protected.[44]

In April 1938 the Nigerian government announced that the cocoa buying pool was to be suspended.[45] One firm's response to this move was as follows:

> We have agreed with firms on the coast, we shall co-operate with each other as fully as if the pool existed . . . In each large station agents should exchange price information and IF OUR PRICE IS HIGHER THAN UAC's OPERATING PRICE THEN WE SHOULD NOT USE IT. WE SHOULD PAY LEVEL PRICES WITH THEM.[46]

As feared by the firms, the Nowell Commission had recommended the creation of a cocoa marketing board. In addition, an attack was made upon the Merchandise Agreements as well. The firms' response was recalcitrant:

> The Staples Merchandise Agreement has been the subject of some comment in the cocoa report . . . Unless I am much mistaken this is a prelude to further inquiries in regard to the Merchandise Selling Agreement. For the salvation of that agreement also I cannot too strongly urge that its operation be transferred wholly to England. . . there is no doubt that in both the Produce and Merchandise Agreements the suspension of day to day co-operation on the coast will cost us something through the loss of local control, but the second best way of operating the agreements is infinitely better than losing the agreements altogether.
> In merchandise as well as produce, members' prices should be slightly varied as between themselves so that, in merchandise, an underseller in selling more cheaply than an overseller, there should be in both classes of agreements a semblance of coast competition.[47]

In March 1939 a committee was appointed in Nigeria to make recommendations for that colony on the basis of the Nowell Commission Report. The question which faced the committee in Nigeria was how these recommendations would be put into effect in that colony.[48] The Nigerian committee was composed of the Resident of Oyo Province, the Manager of the Bank of British West Africa in Lagos and the Director of Agriculture, Captain J. R. Mackie. One firm's agent investigated Mackie's views. He reported that 'Captain Mackie and the Government do not agree. The former shares my view [that] . . . the whole anti-pool uproar is an exercise, a reason for a test of political strength . . . Government does not share this view.'[49] However, if this assessment of Mackie's views

ave the firms some reason for cautious optimism, Mackie's assessment of
ow far the middlemen had been able to go in carrying producer support
ith them was less encouraging:

> He [Mackie] finds that whilst the agriculturalist and producer is not
> interested in the anti-pools issue, all over the country even among
> illiterates [there is] a growing hatred of the U.A.C. The veriest peasant
> appear [sic] to have an instinctive idea that the organization is getting
> a stronghold on the country, whilst the townsman is convinced that
> Government has to accede to the wishes of the U.A.C. [sic][50]

As early as the late 1930s, however, some of the firms' personnel were
essimistic about the eventual outcome of the hearings and began to
nart an alternative strategy. One wrote:

> If the government goes on with the cocoa marketing board, and our
> cooperation is invited in the formation of the scheme. [sic] We have
> two alternatives. We can be intransigent and fight a rear guard action
> with every man's hand against us and with the probability of being
> eventually coerced. Or we can show good will and give full
> cooperation, feeling that sooner or later a marketing scheme has got to
> be tried in West Africa as it has been tried in most countries of the
> world. If we are agreed that the experiment has got to come, why
> should it not come now? It will either succeed or it will fail. If it
> succeeds we shall have to adapt ourselves to this change in commercial
> evolution . . . If we give our goodwill and it fails, we shall hear nothing
> about marketing boards in West Africa for a good many years. If we
> give our goodwill and the scheme fails because of middlemen's
> opposition in Africa, then we have relieved ourselves of the charge of
> standing in the way of progress and native interest. [sic][51]

In the event, the pessimists were correct. Cocoa marketing was taken
ver by the state. The outbreak of the Second World War, however,
rofoundly altered the rationale of state intervention. War disrupted
arkets and sent cocoa prices plummeting.[52] Given the already explosive
olitical situation resulting from low prices, the British government was
rced to intervene in order to forestall the complete collapse of cocoa
rices. Rather than opposing the firms' domination of the trade, the war
rompted the British government to recruit top level staff of the
ssociation of West African Merchants (AWAM), the very individuals
ho had been responsible for the creation of the pools and merchandise
greements, to run the state marketing schemes.[53] Thus, rather than
pplanting the firms, state intervention, when it finally came, entrenched
eir position. This experience set the pattern for the mechanics of state
tervention in marketing. The European firms became licensed buying
gents of the British Ministry of Food, purchasing crops at prices fixed by
e state and selling to the Ministry of Food at guaranteed prices and thus

with a guaranteed profit.[54] In 1942, with the collapse of British resistance to the advancing Japanese throughout Asia, the rationale of state intervention changed again. Deprived of sources of Asian oilseeds Britain turned to West Africa, and in particular Nigeria, to provide this essential commodity. To fulfil this need the West African Produce Control Board was created. The WAPCB was given a complete monopoly on oilseeds purchases and brought the marketing board system into the oilseeds trade. Prices were again fixed with a 'reasonable' profit being allocated to the firms. The firms themselves once again provided the key personnel for the functioning of the scheme.[55] Under the exigencies of war, the thrust of the original impetus for state intervention in marketing was reversed, producer welfare becoming secondary to imperial needs. As one student of the period has noted, 'the arrangements of the West African Produce Control Board, so far from rectifying any of the defects of the pre-war system gave official sanction to the buying syndicates.'[56] Producer prices were kept well below world prices, the difference after the firms' profits having been deducted constituting a tax on producers to aid the war effort.[57]

Wartime controls and state marketing were also used by the firms as a weapon against upstart middlemen like Raccah in the export trade. Although marketing shares in the export trade were to be allocated on the basis of past performance, Raccah was initially denied access to export markets on spurious grounds. Although vague controls were imposed on the export side of the trade during the war these had little effect other than to discourage the entry of new competitors.[58] The AWAM merchants continued to operate the Merchandise Agreement while attempting to preserve a semblance of competition. Commenting on this strategy and refuting criticism that this semblance of competition was becoming too much like the real thing the head office of one firm wrote to its coastal agents in July of 1944:

> In the long term interest it is not altogether a bad thing that people should throw away some of their money. Nothing is more irritating to the African than to find himself faced with exactly the same terms from every firm in a station. When that happens he begins to talk about the exploitation of the pools. Let him think he is getting a little extra somewhere and he will be comparatively content. The last success of a pool does not depend upon rigid uniformity of terms and method.[59]

In the event, the European firms had little to fear from the state's entry into the marketing of export crops. The continuation of wartime state intervention into the post-war period and the creation of the statutory marketing boards did little to curtail the operation of capital directly. Rather, the state's entry into the marketing of export crops, by stabilizing prices and market shares, did what capital itself had been unable to do over almost a century of activity in the West African oilseed trade. The licensing of buying agents and the setting of fixed prices regulated profits and ended cutthroat competition.

Running parallel with the state's intervention in marketing there was a resurgence of interest in development, culminating in the Colonial Development and Welfare Acts of 1940 and 1945. In order to understand fully the reasons for this new developmental thrust it is once again necessary to situate the Nigerian reality in a larger context – that of British imperialism as a whole. The colonial state in Nigeria was not alone in its troubles. Rather, the political ramifications of the depression were empire-wide.

During the 1930s serious political upheavals occurred in Malaya, Northern Rhodesia and Jamaica, to name only some of the most important. In each case the fall in primary commodity exports was a central causative factor. In the late 1930s as war approached, two fears haunted the London-based administrators of Britain's colonial empire – colonial rebellion from within and subversion from without. The fear of internal rebellion was given voice by the writings of a senior Colonial Officer advisor in 1939, the year following the Jamaica labour rebellion. He wrote:

> At intervals during the past year there have been discussions on the possibility of our adopting a more vigorous Colonial policy . . . As I understand it, there have been two motives behind this proposal, the one a desire to avert possible trouble in certain Colonies, where disturbances are feared if something is not done to improve the lot of the people, the other a desire to impress this country and the world at large with our consciousness of our duties as a great Colonial Power.[60]

The desire to 'impress this country and the world' had been given a sharpened meaning in 1938 by Malcolm MacDonald, the Secretary of State for the Colonies when he stated that 'in future, criticism of Great Britain would be directed more and more against her management of the Colonial Empire . . . It was an essential part of her defence policy that her reputation as a colonial power be unassailable.'[61] In 1942, Bourdillon, still Governor of Nigeria, returned to the theme when he referred to:

> another class of the inhabitants of Nigeria, a large class, whose ability to make their needs known and to insist on their recognition is rapidly growing, whose position, none too good before the war, is deteriorating as a result of war conditions. I refer to the daily wage earner and to low-salaried employees.[62]

He went on to make the source of his concern about this group abundantly clear:

Twice since I came to Lagos six years ago has a threatened strike in the Government Colliery resulted in an improvement in conditions of employment, twice has the same thing happened in the Railway. On each occasion I have no hesitation in saying that the demands which were granted were not only reasonable but modest, and would have been granted before they had been made had Nigeria been a richer country.[63]

Referring to the trade union movement, Bourdillon went on ominously:

The growth of the movement, though rapid, has been surprisingly healthy, a fact which is due in no inconsiderable extent to the war, and to a genuine desire not to embarrass the Government in any way which might hinder the war effort. The conclusion seems to me inevitable that we shall in the future be compelled to pay adequate wages and salaries to Africans as well as to Europeans, whether we can afford to or not; it would surely be wise to assume the obligation voluntarily rather than at the point of the bayonet.[64]

The course and strategy of post-war British imperial colonial development and welfare strategy lies beyond the confines of the present work. However, as should now be clear, the impetus for state intervention in marketing and in development were in origin both the products of the capitalist crisis of the interwar years and not an altruistic response to the poverty of colonial peoples. Nor were they the creation of post-war labour 'socialists'. Development and state control began as an attempt to save imperial capitalism, not to supplant it. State control of capitalism did, however, mark the beginning of a new era in the political economy of Nigeria as a whole.

For the state itself, the creation of the marketing boards engendered a massive new source of revenue. Producer prices were kept well below steadily rising post-war prices, the difference being appropriated by the state. Over the period 1947–54 approximately £25 million was appropriated from this source. When combined with purchase taxes and export duties this appropriation amounted – in the case of groundnuts – to a withdrawal of nearly £62 million or about 25 per cent of potential producer incomes.[65] During the war itself prices were kept so low that forced labour had to be instituted to meet imperial demand.[66] What was this hoard used for? In theory and by law 70 per cent of the funds was to be banked for future payment to producers during periods of low prices, 22.5 per cent was to be allocated to 'development' and 7.5 per cent was to be devoted to research.[67] A glimpse behind these regulations, however, reveals the true use of much of the 70 per cent of these funds ostensibly held for price stabilization. Emerging from the Second World War, Britain was nearly bankrupt. In particular, it needed banked funds to stabilize the value of sterling. By 1954 some £66 million of potential Nigerian cocoa, groundnut, palm kernel and oil producers' incomes had been invested in British securities. Thus, funds supposedly earmarked for the stabilization of peasant incomes were in reality used for the stabilization of the British economy.[68] As to the 22.5 per cent of the funds earmarked for 'development', this was primarily used along with grants and loans acquired under the Colonial Development and Welfare Acts of 1940 and 1945 as state capital invested in schemes designed to increase primary product output. Such increases were in turn sought as a means of earning more dollars, again with sterling stabilization in mind.

The report of the World Bank mission to Nigeria of 1954 marked a major turning point in the utilization of marketing board funds. The Bank declared that far too much was being held by the marketing boards for the purpose of price stabilization. Dominated by American interests, who were frustrated by British reluctance to open the empire to American trade, the Bank report played on the increasingly nationalistic and anti-British sentiments of the rising Nigerian bourgeoisie.[69] In response to the Bank report and to growing criticism in Nigeria, price stabilization funds began to be channelled into 'development' under the auspices of those Nigerians who would soon inherit state power. Through this action the floodgates of politics were opened. In the north and in the south the regional marketing board surpluses were raided for 'development' expenditures which became synonymous with the use of these funds as a major tool in the construction of the political parties of independence.[70] The reaction of the European firms to the changing and increasingly nationalistic post-war scene was prescient. As early as 1943 an employee of John Holt wrote:

> it seems to me that there is no fundamental difference of business interests between business people in West Africa of no matter what race . . . I do not know if the African has changed very much since I knew him so well at close quarters, but unless he has it will be found that, although he may at times be touchy, he really responds to European leadership as long as he is fully convinced that it is disinterested, honest and enlightened, and that it is serving his interest as well as our own. It seemed to me therefore that the proper field in which all of this can be fertilized would be a chamber of commerce with the widest possible reach . . . if Europeans want to continue to exert an influence on economic policy they will have to do so with the aid of Africans . . .[71]

By the mid-1950s, sensing the move toward independence, more drastic measures were taken. The firms slowly began to extricate themselves from direct involvement in the produce trade and import retailing – their two most politically vulnerable fronts. By the early 1960s the United Africa Company had virtually withdrawn from the produce trade, selling its rural stores to former employees and encouraging former middlemen to set up as independent licensed buyers. There were economic as well as political gains in this move, as one United Africa Company director described:

> In the mid 1950s the local board in Nigeria was beginning to think about the time when it would be extremely difficult for the local company to sell a lot . . . in the consumer goods field . . . profitably. It was also argued by the local board that a time was coming when we would have to move out of the produce buying trade because this was a trade that could be equally well done by Nigerians . . . In 1959, 1960, 1961 it was decided that UAC should gradually move out of the produce buying and out of semi-wholesaling and retailing. We should be thinking of employing the capital that we invested in something else, mainly industry . . . within two years we were out of the produce buying trade . . .[72]

However, the European firms' withdrawal from the produce buying trade did not mean a withdrawal from the Nigerian economy. Rather the firms hitched their capital to the development dreams and party politics of Nigeria's politicians of independence, providing capital equipment and entering into a partnership with the state on import substitution and other ventures, the funds for which were provided, of course, by the agricultural export producers through the marketing boards. 'Development' had become the new means of surplus appropriation.

The concentration and centralization of capital which both generated and resulted from the inter-war crisis of capitalism, provoked both the wrath of the incipient bourgeoisie in West Africa and direct state intervention in the Nigerian economy. These, in conjunction with the post-war crisis of British capitalism, not only set the stage for independence, but as a result of American pressure applied through the World Bank, provided the financial wherewithal for that incipient bourgeoisie to assume political independence and state power. The sixty-odd years of colonial rule in Northern Nigeria would now come to an end. These years had wrought massive changes in Northern Nigerian society. It is the nature of some of these changes that will be the subject of the final chapter.

NOTES

1   RH Mss, Afr. t. 16, S. M. Jacob, 'Report on Taxation and Economics of Nigeria', 1934, p.34. Hereafter cited as 'Jacob's Report'.
2   Jacob's Report, figures calculated from tables 1.1 and 1.2.
3   ibid., pp. 86-7.
4   ibid., p. 91.
5   ibid., pp. 12-13.
6   ibid., p. 35.
7   ibid., pp. 35-8. See also NAK KanoProf 438.
8   NAK KanoProf 30361. See also NAK SNP 17 29664.
9   NAK SNP 17 11159 vol. II.
10 NAK SNP 17 11159, vol. II and NAK SNP 17 14818, vol. I.
11 NAK SNP 17 11703, vol. I.
12 RH Mss, Afr. s. 769, Edwardes Papers, pp. 123-7, 155-6.
13 See R. W. Shenton and L. Lennihan, 'Capital and class: peasant differentiation in Northern Nigeria', *Journal of Peasant Studies*, vol. 9, no. 1 (1981), pp. 47-70.
14 NAK SNP 17 11703, vol. III.
15 NAK KadMinAgric 757.
16 NAK KadMinAgric 1100, vol. II.
17 ibid.
18 ibid.
19 Charles Kindleberger, *The World in Depression, 1929-39* (Berkeley: University of California Press) Chapter 4.
20 NAK SNP 17 11703, vol. III.
21 See PRO CO 583/243/30415, Governor Bourdillon to Secretary of State for the Colonies, 5 April 1939. See also CO 852/214/13 for other evidence of Bourdillon's views on Nigeria's development and the Colonial Development Act.
22 ibid.
23 Ian Drummond, *British Economic Policy and the Empire, 1919-1939* (London: Allen & Unwin, 1972), p. 51.
24 For the specific problems involved in making use of the funds in Nigeria see PRO CO 583/243/30415, Governor Bourdillon to Secretary of State for the Colonies, 5 April 1939.
25 ibid.
26 ibid.
27 ibid.
28 ibid.
29 See, for example, NAK SNP 17 21304.
30 NAK KanoProf 628.
31 NAK KadMinAgric 621.
32 NAK SNP 17 20070, vol. I and NAK KadMinAgric 2600
33 T. Forrest, 'Agricultural policies in Nigeria 1910-1978', unpublished paper, Zaria, 1977.
34 NAK SNP 17 37094 and KadMinAgric 20207.
35 RH Mss, s. 825-7, Holt Papers, File 516, entry dated 18 July 1939.

36 See B. Beckman, *Organising the Farmers: Cocoa Politics and National Development in Ghana* (Uppsala: Scandinavian Institute of African Studies, 1976) and R. Howard, *Colonialism and Underdevelopment in Ghana* (London: Croom Helm, 1978).

37 RH Mss, s. 825–7 Holt Papers, File 92 (v), entry dated 25 January 1938.

38 ibid., 'Memo by Rawlings', dated 11 January 1938.

39 ibid., entry dated 25 January 1938.

40 For a discussion of the point see Howard, *Colonialism and Underdevelopment*.

41 RH Mss, s. 825–7, Holt Papers, File 516, entry dated 2 April 1938.

42 ibid., 'Memorandum from Winter to all agents', 22 August 1938.

43 ibid. See also the entry dated 31 May 1939 in the same source.

44 ibid., extract of Cocoa Commission hearings, dated 4 May 1938.

45 ibid., entry dated 28 April 1938.

46 ibid., 'Memorandum from Winter to all agents', 22 August 1938.

47 ibid., 'Memorandum by Rawlings to District Agents', 15 November 1939.

48 Nigerian Sessional Paper 20 of 1939.

49 RH Mss, s. 825–7, Holt Papers, entry dated 4 March 1938. See also Cotgrave to Home Office, 17 March 1939.

50 ibid., entry dated 4 March 1938.

51 ibid., 'Memorandum on cocoa commission report', 1 November 1938.

52 RH Mss, s. 825–7, Holt Papers, Rawlings to District Agents, 15 November 1939. 11–39.

53 P. T. Bauer, *West African Trade. A Study of Competition, Oligopoly and Monopoly in a Changing Economy* (London: Routledge & Kegan Paul, 1963, new edn), Chapter 19.

54 ibid., pp. 246–59.

55 ibid., p. 250.

56 ibid., p. 266.

57 G. K. Helleiner, *Peasant Agriculture, Agriculture, Government, and Economic Growth in Nigeria* (Homewood, III: Irwin, 1966), p. 154.

58 Bauer, *West African Trade*, p. 255.

59 RH Mss, s. 825–7, Holt Papers, File 516, entry dated 3 July 1944.

60 PRO CO 852/250/10, Memorandum by G. L. M. Clauson, 7 July 1939.

61 PRO CO 852/190/10, Minutes of a Department Meeting, 9 December 1938.

62 PRO CO 583/262/30519, Govenor Bourdillon to Secretary of State for the Colonies, 24 January 1942.

63 ibid.

64 ibid.

65 Helleiner, *Peasant Agriculture*, p. 163.

66 NAK KadMinAgric 31731N.

67 Helleiner, *Peasant Agriculture*, p. 168.

68 ibid., p. 169.

69 International Bank for Reconstruction and Development, *The Economic Development of Nigeria* (Washington, DC, 1955). See also Helleiner, *Peasant Agriculture*, pp. 169–70.

70 This use of marketing board funds is cautiously alluded to in Helleiner,

Peasant Agriculture, pp. 170–72.

71 RH Mss, Holt Papers, s. 825–7, File 516, Rawlings to Goddard, 24 August 1943.

72 RH Mss, Afr. s. 1428, Davies Papers, p. 21.

7

'Changelessness' and 'Development'

As far as Northern Nigeria is concerned, Karl Marx's depiction of colonialism as a hothouse for the development of capitalism is especially apt. During the sixty-odd years of colonial rule the social formation of Northern Nigeria was dramatically transformed. Although this transformation was of a massive and decisive nature, much of Northern Nigerian society continues to this day to leave the casual and even the scholarly observer with the impression of changelessness. Emirs still rule, peasants still till the soil with hoes. Yet behind this superficial continuity a world has changed.

Perhaps the greatest obstacle to comprehending this change has been the historical sources themselves – in particular the archives of the colonial state. In working through these records it becomes abundantly clear that, aside from its callousness and venality, one of the most striking aspects of the colonial state was its consummate ignorance of the society which it ruled. Despite the overwhelmingly rural character of Northern Nigerian society, little systematic study of the sociology and economics of agricultural production was ever undertaken, and when such work was done, little heed was paid to the results unless they fitted into some immediately pressing state need. From the households of the emirs to the lowliest rural *gida*, Northern Nigerian society remained and in many ways continues to remain a closed book to outside observers, both foreign and Nigerian – hence the dominant impression of changelessness.

As we shall see in this chapter, contrary to this impression, major alterations of the fundamentals of social and economic life were afoot. How was changelessness important to the mythology of colonialism in Northern Nigeria? First it is essential to note that the impression of changelessness was a central element in the ideology of the colonial state. Continuity, especially in the realm of politics, was a highly valued political commodity, for the acceptance of the appearance of political continuity presented the ruled with the impression of the political legitimacy of their rulers, and hence guaranteed stability and peace. The success of this policy can be adduced from the almost complete absence of rural revolt in Northern Nigeria from the conquest on.

Yet although it was one of the poles of colonial rule, the emphasis on changelessness was matched by an emphasis on 'development' – its diametric opposite in the ideological framework of colonialism. In fact it is reasonable, without stretching the point too far, to speak of changelessness and development as the polar elements of the dialectic contained in that great centrepiece of British colonialism in Africa, Lugard's *Dual Mandate*, the bible of expansion and preservation, modernization and tradition.[1]

Second, it is crucial to remember that both beneath and intertwined with the ideology of colonialism lay a material reality from which that ideology was in part abstracted and over which it was superimposed. This material reality had two predominating aspects. The first among these was the reality of the pre-capitalist nature of the social formation of Northern Nigeria at the moment of the colonial conquest. The second was the reality of capitalist development, the reproduction of capital, accomplished through the ever-increasing commoditization of not only the produce of human labour itself, but of the relationships between man and man, penetrating the household itself and permeating the social relations of ruler and ruled from the village to the state.

It is upon entering this world of material reality that we may cast aside the illusion of changelessness and come to grips with the ever-more intense struggle of a social formation and the human beings which composed it to survive the transformation from pre-capitalist to capitalist society. It was and continues to be a socially violent world of ceaseless turmoil.

For those who sat at the top of this world, the political mandarins and commercial barons of colonialism, the essential problem at the outset of colonial rule was the transformation of the quality, magnitude and destination of the surplus product of the agricultural producer without bringing about the destruction of the indigenous political system which guaranteed political acquiescence. The central reason for the expansion of capitalism through colonialism was profit, and profit itself was in turn dependent upon the expanded commoditization of production and ultimately production relations. Yet if political stability was to be maintained, the political relations between the pre-capitalist ruling class of sultans, emirs, district and village heads and the subordinate agricultural producers had somehow to be made impervious to the acid of commoditization.

Translated into colonial policy, this meant that while the old sources of surplus appropriation of the indigenous ruling class were to be increasingly circumscribed by the gradual abolition of slavery, the regularization of taxation, the prohibition of forced labour and the ensuing decline of the old ruling class estates, the political position of this class was to be continually bolstered by the ceremony of indirect rule. Durbars imported from India, and the mandatory public obeisance of even British colonial officers before the top level of the local ruling class were all-important to the success of this policy – as was corruption.

The corruption of the indigenous ruling class was an essential aspect of the transformation to capitalism under colonial rule. Its main source is readily comprehended. It was colonial policy to reduce the number of individuals who were directly dependent upon the state for their livelihood in order to free society's surplus product for the capitalist market. Thus, by reducing both the sources and the amount of the surplus which could be appropriated by local rulers it was hoped that these rulers would – in Lugard's words – 'gradually recognize that the retention of a number of useless or ornamental officials, together with a number of head slaves and court satellites, forms a heavy drain on their incomes, [and] they will doubtless be more disposed to reduce their number.'[2] However, as the old sources of surplus appropriation dried up or were outlawed, indigenous rulers were placed in an increasingly untenable position. What appeared to be 'useless officials' and 'court satellites' to the colonial mind were in reality the objects of largesse necessary to guarantee political security in a world of palace cliques and succession disputes. This was all the more true in a situation in which many claims to office rested almost solely upon the favour of the colonial authorities. Caught in this dilemma, only the continued surreptitious tapping of the pre-colonial sources of unpaid goods and labour or the cultivation of new ones in harmony with the development of capitalism could provide a solution. In the eyes of the colonial state both implied political corruption.

Reports of such corruption and depositions for it are a constant theme in the records of the colonial state. In Wurno District in 1911 we hear of 'farmers . . . who in addition to paying the general tax . . . are also paying annual sums of money to . . . hakimi [district heads] . . . in return for the permission to farm plots of land under the control of those hakimi.'[3] In the same year in Gonyoro District we are told that while 'the hakimi were almost word perfect in their theory of the methods of assessment,' they 'were almost undoubtedly collecting sums very largely in excess.'[4] In 1914, the Emir of Zaria was reported not to be paying the local labour which was conscripted for 'Government projects', but personally appropriating the funds so designated.[5] The forced decortication of groundnuts from his official farms was the charge against the *mai gari* of Karofi in 1923.[6] In 1922, 20 per cent of the wages due to the labourers on the Zaria–Sokoto road disappeared into official hands.[7]

The collection of taxes was an area rife with corrupt practices, many of which were officially encouraged. As Mary Bull has noted:

> Revenue figures were commonly taken as the yardstick by which to measure success in administration both because they indicated financial progress toward self-sufficiency and because of the general belief that only by paying taxes did the African acknowledge himself to be under the control of the government.[8]

Given the stress on the prompt collection of taxes, even at the level of senior British officers, the niceties of anything like remotely equitable assessment often went by the board. Edwardes, the 'peasant's friend' mentioned earlier, wrote in 1917:

> The variety of methods employed to arrive at the taxable capacity of the village is remarkable . . .
> In only two cases have the officers compared their estimate of total yield with the total consumption of the inhabitants, in no case has an officer suggested that the corn produced in the district was insufficient for the feeding of the people though in nine cases production works out at less than consumption.[9]

There are serious doubts as to whether even these officers themselves, with the occasional exception, such as Edwardes, took their own estimates of the taxable capacity of their districts seriously. Writing confidentially, one officer showed amusement at the official commendation he had received for his assessment of Fika District. 'His Honour's comments on my Fika report were,' he remarked, 'very funny . . . which – remembering my eyewash and tongue in cheek method will tickle you as much as it does me.'[10]

Such attitudes could not help but percolate down to indigenous officials, especially when it was continually made clear to them that their salaries and positions were dependent on getting the tax in promptly, and with a minimum of trouble. The comments of one British official in Kano in 1915 are instructive:

> It will be seen . . . that in 1915 the Hakimi or District Heads have had less money than in 1914, the fact that the total revenue has not fallen appreciably in spite of trade depression, famine . . . is due I think to the loyal and vigorous action of the Central Native Administration when it was brought home to them that unless active measures were taken there would be a serious drop in revenue.[11]

Under the pressure of dwindling resources, it was merely a short step from these attitudes to the outright peculation of funds. As one official noted:

It is extremely difficult to inculcate the idea that Government is interested in the method as opposed to the result of collection, and the native mind considers the Government has no right to complain if a chief renders to Caesar as much as Caesar can find out is due even though he incidentally makes a good deal for himself.[12]

Compounding the ambiguity in the attitude of the colonial state toward corruption was the realization that in order to maintain political stability much that was even identified as corruption had to be tolerated. Charles Temple, writing in 1918, expressed the view that for reasons of state:

an important chief must not be made to work among a gang of felons from the common herd, even though his crimes be far blacker than theirs . . . it is hard to get some officials to realize that it is right to punish by imprisonment a policeman who, when travelling every evening demands, and is given by the villagers, free of charge, a fowl for his supper; while it may be crass folly so to punish a native chief travelling with perhaps a number of followers, who does the same thing, on an infinitely greater scale.[13]

The reasons for such tolerance were stated clearly in 1923 by the then Governor Clifford. Writing to a trusted fellow official, Clifford remarked that he feared that his colleague was right to suggest that 'we have not heard the last of Mahdist activities in the Northern Provinces, but our truest safeguard lies in the identity of the Emir's and Native Administration's interests with our own.'[14]

British fears of rebellion were, however, no guarantee against deposition from office, which was frequent and must have seemed for many, when it came after years of officially ignored or sanctioned corruption, as a whim on the part of the colonial rulers. Thus, many turned to the expanding commoditization of the agricultural surplus, to the market itself, as a new means of surplus appropriation. The expansion and redirection of commodity production in agriculture provided vastly increased opportunities for surplus appropriation on the part of the office-holding class. In order to understand why this should have been so it is necessary to turn to a brief examination of the development of indigenous merchant capital in Northern Nigeria.

As has been explicitly argued in Chapter 1, any search for a 'natural economy' in the pre-colonial Sokoto Caliphate would be fruitless. Rather, a high degree of commodity production and surplus appropriation by indigenous merchant capital was ultimately blocked by the political and economic power of the pre-colonial ruling class. The policies of the colonial state, both explicit and implicit, had uneven effects on the development of indigenous merchant capital. In some cases, such as the accumulation of landed property, the explicit policies of the colonial state created new barriers to surplus accumulation. In others, such as the implicit policy of increasing the commoditization of agricultural production, new opportunities were opened up to this class. Thus, while the transition of merchant to agricultural capital was blocked, the continued expansion of merchant capital itself was encouraged, especially in the realm of the marketing of goods for export.

The expansion of indigenous capital in the export trade meant, however, that it was increasingly subsumed by European merchant capital. The case of the Dan Tata family, today one of the richest families in Northern Nigeria, is an example. In the nineteenth century the Dan Tatas were primarily long-distance merchants, dealing in kola nuts, a local stimulant, produced in what is now Ghana.[15] The social organization of this long-distance trade was based on three kinds of networks, the family, the *asali* and the brotherhood. The use of family links to cement trading networks over long distances is a common enough device and needs no elaboration here. The *asali* is only slightly more unusual. The *asali* which might be likened to a 'clan', is essentially a recognized group of families who all claim a common origin and has the effect of increasing the size of the 'kin' group whose members could be counted upon to conduct business in a reliable manner. The third kind of merchant network, the religious brotherhood, complemented, enlarged and extended the merchant network beyond the family and the *asali*. The Islamic brotherhood provided trading links across ethnic boundaries and, perhaps more crucially, provided the merchant class with access to the Muslim clerisy, who were often called upon to mediate commercial disputes. In addition, the brotherhood provided important links to the agricultural producer, again mediated by the Muslim clerics. These latter links were central in the enforcement of debts and the regularization of marketing in general.[16]

For the Dan Tatas and other important merchant families, such as the Abu Lafiyas, these links were crucial. The latter, for example, were involved from early in the twentieth century in the trans-Saharan trade, which was organized along brotherhood lines.[17] The reduction of the trans-Saharan trade and the growth of the relative importance of the trade in such commodities as groundnuts signalled a new era of expansion for the Dan Tatas and Abu Lafiyas. It also ushered in the period of their subsumption by European merchant capital. Both, in the first two decades of the twentieth century, became agents of the firm of Raphaello Hassan and Company, one of the European protégés involved in the trans-Saharan trade.[18] By 1920, however, Hassan's firm had been absorbed into what would eventually become the United Africa Company, itself destined to become a part of the Unilever commercial empire.[19] The United Africa Company provided the Dan Tatas and others with an immensely increased market and line of credit, while families like the Dan Tatas provided the United Africa Company with access to the brotherhood, *asali*, and family networks which were crucial to its own operation. Similar patterns prevailed among other buyers and intermediaries.

Due to the centrality of credit to the successful operation of the trading system, access to the indigenous merchant capitalist networks was especially crucial to the European firms operating in Northern Nigeria. Large sums, and as the colonial period progressed, increasingly larger sums of both cash and goods had to be advanced to village middlemen well before the produce buying season began in order to secure the purchase of the crop. More important, because of the lack of indigenous private property in land, these sums often had to be advanced and re-advanced from the European firms, through families like the Dan Tatas, to the village middlemen, and eventually to the producer himself, with little or no security. It was here that the maintenance of the pre-colonial trading networks proved essential.[20]

As the colonial period progressed, these advances also increased, not simply because of the growth of export crop production, but also because the increased commoditization of the social relations of production in the household and the village led to greater and greater rural indebtedness. Taxation was often the initial force in the creation of indebtedness. Thus, we find in 1944 that:

> The practice of collecting tax in Zaria and Katsina Provinces in October, before the crops have been harvested definitely drives the farmer to accept advances from middlemen and firms' clerks. District Heads must produce the tax for their Districts or they get into trouble. The obvious corollary is that they go to the middlemen and clerks for the money, selling their crops in advance at probably *half the true value*. Thus apart from encouraging the pernicious practice of making advances for produce most of the money for crops is going into the pockets of middlemen and not the farmer.[21]

Taxation and the associated need for cash on the part of the rural producer was also the means through which the office-holding class appropriated a portion of merchants' profits. In some cases district and village heads themselves purchased crops in advance, holding the tax receipts of the debtors as security for delivery.[22] Alternatively tax money was used for commodity speculation. As early as 1914 a complaint was made that 'The headmen, in many cases this year have had their share [of the tax] in hand for some time and have started trading with it.'[23] Although practices such as these were frowned upon, they persisted throughout the colonial era. As should now be clear, material reality was starkly in opposition to the impression of changelessness. Both the office-holding class and indigenous merchant capital had been transformed, the pattern for that transformation being set by the interaction of pre-capitalist relations of production, the pace of commoditization and capital accumulation, and the particular policies of the colonial state. The transformation of the office-holding and merchant classes cannot, however, be understood in isolation from that of the rural producers themselves, for it was the latter who produced the surplus on which the colonial state and economy were based. It is ironic that at the level of the rural producer the impression of changelessness is strongest for it was in the everyday life of the village and the rural household that the transformation resulting from the development of capitalism was most profound.

The lives of the agricultural producers of Northern Nigeria had never been easy. The land itself is hard and unyielding, giving up a harvest only through the application of much backbreaking work with much attention and care. Rainfall is concentrated in a period of four to five months of the year and it is during this period that the vast bulk of agricultural labour must be undertaken. Insects and disease attack the planter as well as the plant and most of the population which survives birth and childhood suffers from chronic gastroenteritis, malaria and general debilitation.

Yet despite all of these hardships, the rural population of Northern Nigeria has for countless centuries provided enough food, not only for itself, but for the urban areas as well. The achievement is immense. A survey of the fields surrounding Kano or Zaria from one of the high rock outcrops in this otherwise flat land provides the observer with a panorama of miles upon miles of neatly hand-ploughed fields. One cannot help but be awed by this sight.

Given the enormity of this achievement of human survival under such bleak conditions it is ironic that we know so little of how it has been achieved. Pre-colonial records of the organization of agricultural production and rural life are, with one or two exceptions, non-existent. The records of the colonial state are little better. It was in the interests of the producer to reveal as little as possible. It was also in the interests of the local agents of the colonial bureaucracy to disclose as little as possible about rural life and production in order to maintain their own sphere of appropriation and power. Moreover, as has been demonstrated, the colonial state was far more interested in the results of tax collection than the methods employed and hence even less interested in the material reality which produced tax revenue. Yet, allowing for this paucity of sources it is still possible to reconstruct a tentative, if schematic outline of rural life and to suggest some of the major changes which it underwent during the colonial period.

As has been noted, rural life and agricultural production were hazardous. Yet rural society had developed a number of buffers between

127

its own existence and the hazardous environment. The first of these was the household itself. Northern Nigerian agricultural households at the dawn of the colonial period were for the most part extended rather than nuclear. They were made up of varying combinations of a senior male along with his married and unmarried sons and brothers, their sons and brothers and possible slaves and clients, along with the wives and children of these men. In a rare survey of five villages in one district made in 1909 the average population per household was calculated at 10.3 to 15.3, and households with 40 to 50 inhabitants were noted.[24] Agriculture within these extended farming units was divided between communally worked grain farms and smaller individual plots. The communal plots were worked under the direction of the household head, who also oversaw the distribution of its harvest. In addition, it was out of the communal harvest that taxes, tithes and social obligations such a marriage expenses, naming ceremonies and expenses relating to religiou festivals were met.

The importance of the structure of the rural household was twofold. First, it was large and multi-generational, which alleviated the burden of the young on the household and made it easier for the household to weather the burden of the illness of death of one of its productive members. Second, the labour of the household was clearly focused on its primary aim, the production of sufficient food for its own reproduction. In addition to the structure of the family itself, the particular kind of agriculture practised, with its ecologically adapted multi- and inter-cropped patterns and its careful maintenance of a wide variety of different seed strains of the crucial grain crops, provided some measure of security. Moreover, the variety of different craft pursuits in a household also offered some hedge against uncertainty.[25]

Important as was the household itself, however, this unit did not exist in isolation. Rather, households were knitted together in a web of market and non-market relationships with other households in the hamlet or village. The local village markets, which often brought together a number of villages or hamlets, were places to dispose of domestic craft production, livestock and agricultural surpluses which circulated locally. The market was also a window on the outside world, as regional and long-distance traders bought and sold regional manufacturing specialities as well as salt and grain. Thus, the market could help to alleviate regional distress. In addition to the market, but by no means of lesser importance, were the revolving credit schemes, communal work groups, and bonds of kinship between households, which could all help to alleviate a crisis in an individual household.[26]

At an even higher level than the village itself, the indigenous state apparatus in the pre-colonial and early colonial period had of necessity to consider the well-being of its rural subjects. A certain degree of largesse was necessary in building and maintaining the political following necessary to gain or maintain political office. As important was the nature of the pre-colonial and early colonial taxation system. Tax farming, the means of collection, ensured that a certain amount of the agricultural surplus appropriated as taxes would stick in the hands of local, regional, and state functionaries and thus remain in the countryside. This, together with injunctions to practise Islamic charity and the local cultural revulsion towards the rich but miserly man at least made possible some measure of local famine relief. Yet to say this is not of course to deny that there were rapacious and greedy officials, nor to imply that there was no war or slave-raiding nor to deny that rural life encompassed the oppression of women. However, the existence of these forms of oppression did not negate the existence of the redistributive mechanisms referred to above. Indeed, existing together, oppression and redistribution, whether at the level of the household, the village or the state reflected the contradictions inherent in the pre-capitalist social formation.[27]

The most important aspect of the household, village, and regional economy was neither its oppressive nor its redistributive character but rather its high degree of self-subsistence. In general, wealth which was produced and consumed within these economic units may have changed hands but it had a great propensity to remain within reach of its point of production. Yet despite this fact, it was ultimately the low level of the development of the means and relations of agricultural and craft production which was to blame for social crises. Crises were, by and large, a result of underproduction, not exploitation. As always, men and women did the best they could to survive and prosper within the society and economy of which they were a part.[28]

What does this phrase 'the best they could' mean in real life terms? The data are scanty and thus the introduction of what is admittedly an anachronistic illustration from 1939 may be permissible. For one village in Daura Emirate, we are provided for that year with a small glimpse of a 'wealthy', an 'average' and a 'poor' household. The wealthy household, described as having a 'very high standard of living' was headed by a low-level member of the state bureaucracy. In it, 3.3 lb of grain per head per diem were available with 'condiments and meat'. In the 'ordinary' household 1.3 lb of grain per head per diem were available with no mention of meat although there may have been a little. The third case is that of a 'poor peasant'. In this household only 0.83 lb of grain per head per diem was available for consumption and the comment was made that this was only available for five months of the year and that so desperate was this family for grain that it often ate the fruits of the harvest before the grain had been properly dried. The grain ration accepted by the colonial state for the meeting of minimal nutritional standards was 2.2 lb per head per diem. One did not have to be 'poor' to go hungry.[29]

These figures represent the scene in the midst of a worldwide depression. The situation may well have been a good bit better in the earlier and later days of colonial rule. Still, they do provide us with an impression of the orders of magnitude with which we are concerned. The difference between rural wealth and poverty may seem to us quite small – a pound of grain a day – but it represented the vast gulf between health and illness, a full stomach and chronic hunger, to those who were the subjects of these dry statistics.

What did the introduction of colonial rule and the parallel development of capitalism in Northern Nigeria mean for the precarious position of the rural agricultural producer? This is a large question. Let us begin to answer it with the conquest itself.

There is no doubt that the conquest of Northern Nigeria, and the ensuing, if brief, period of political chaos which it engendered, had a deleterious effect on production of and trade in agricultural produce. More important, however, it left the rural population more vulnerable than it might otherwise have been to the crop failure of 1904. The colonial state, more concerned with the cementing of its political authority than with social issues, and with little means either in personnel or transport at its disposal, did little or nothing to alleviate the situation. The attitude of the Colonial Office was harsh. Commenting on a request for famine assistance from Lugard, a Colonial Office official pointed to the advantages to colonial rule of hunger. 'If there is a famine,' he noted, 'it ought to solve temporarily the difficulties which exist in obtaining labour for transport.'[30]

The next major rural crisis, the crop failure and ensuing famine of 1907–8, found the colonial government now concerned with making Northern Nigeria a going financial proposition, and still unprepared to assist the rural producer, even though it was the rural producer on whom the hopes for colonial financial self-sufficiency rested. The effects of the 1907–8 famine were well-known to the colonial bureaucracy. One report from Kano states:

> During 1907–08 a famine occurred in Kano. The inevitable result here as elsewhere is always that a considerable number of slaves have been transferred, the possessors being unable to support them and the slaves hungry and anxious to be transferred.

Another states:

> I do not wish to labour this question particularly as there is no remedy for what has happened. It is useless to appeal to the better feeling of District Heads and even village heads who will not report want lest they themselves should suffer; as a matter of fact the gates of the towns in these particular districts are shut against the wretched people who

have supplied what little foodstuffs is inside their walls.[32]

As we have seen, the period 1909–14 witnessed a number of major changes in the Northern Nigerian economy; the construction of the railway to Kano, the groundnut boom, the demand of the colonial state for the conversion to British coinage, and the beginnings of increasingly streamlined and higher rates of tax assessment and collection. What did this mean for the rural producer and the rural economy? Some of the effects of these transformations, such as the change in the quality and the quantity of the tax demanded, we have touched upon, others remain to be explained.

As early as 1907 the market disruptions associated with the withdrawal of cowries and their replacement with British silver were recognized. In particular, the smallest British coin was still of too high a value to accommodate the petty transactions of the market. Drinking water might cost 'a single cowrie for a small bowl, pieces of sweetmeat, 2 cowries; small pieces of boiled cassava, 5 cowries; small bundles of firewood, 5 cowries'.[33] Yet the rate of exchange was 300 cowries to a 3d piece. Moreover, the British currency that did come into local circulation literally had to be purchased from the British economy by a surplus of agricultural exports over imports. Even once such currency was in circulation, the demands of the colonial state operated in such a way as to denude the countryside of its stock of the means of exchange. Commenting on the massive *export* of British currency from Sokoto Province in 1915, the Resident noted that 'our specie problems are due to the fact that we are taking a handsome revenue out of the province in excess of our expenditures'.[34]

Yet, in the short and the long run, it was the increasing level and redirection of commodity production in the rural areas, through which currency was purchased and taxes paid, which was the most devastating result of the 1909–14 period. In Northern Nigeria, as elsewhere, urban areas and their immediate environs were not self-sufficient in food production. In 1908 this truth was recognized in what was to become the centre of the groundnut trade when it was reported that Kano, 'never self-supporting in foodstuffs, is yearly becoming less so.'[35] Even before 1914, the attraction of Kano as a focus of colonial administration and as a commercial centre was increasing its population. The ripple effects of the burgeoning demand for food were felt far afield. A Divisional Report for 1912 reported that 'during the past month the price of a bundle of dawa [guinea corn] has varied between 1/- and 1/6 in the Kazaure market. The reason is the large export trade to Kano'.[36]

The effects of this growing urbanization were compounded by other changes. The 1912 Kano Annual Report noted that:

The increased demand for corn in the mining districts coupled with what amounted to a practical prohibition from French territory caused a considerable rise in prices all over the province. For some months during the rains the price of corn was about 1d per lb. in the Kano market, and even at that price only a small quantity, in proportion to the needs of the inhabitants, was available.[37]

Yet, despite what was acknowledged to be a grave situation, the push for colonial fiscal self-sufficiency continued. Taxes were increased and the commoditization and redirection of the agricultural surplus in the form of groundnuts continued. The result was famine. The lack of adequate rain over the years proceeding 1913 combined with the exactions of the colonial state, the new demands of the mines and groundnut exporters and the disruption of regional trade to produce a famine on such a scale as to make the 1904 and 1908 food shortages pale into insignificance.

We do not have comprehensive figures for the mortality rate during the 1913–14 famine. In Kano Division alone the number of deaths was variously estimated at 30 000 to 40 000.[38] There is, however, subjective but eloquent testimony on the effects of the famine from one observer:

> This year the effect of the shortage showed itself in all of its ghastliness. The gaunt ghost of famine stalked abroad through Kano and every other part. The stricken people tore down the ant hills in the bush to get at the small grains and chaff within these storerooms. They wandered every where collecting the grass burrs of the Kuangia to split the pod and get the tiny seed. They made use of every poor resource their ingenuity could think of, and ravenous in their hunger, seized on anything they could steal or plunder. Mothers could not feed their babies at their breasts and cows' milk lacked, for the pasture had dried up and cattle were just skin and bone. The great city of Kano drew the starving thousands from the country in the faint hope of scouring in the streets and markets to pick up what they might, or beg the charity of the townsfolk . . . One came across them in the town markets emaciated to skeletons, begging feebly for sustenance, or collapsed where they sat, and one poor wretch died, in the Residency garden where he had crept at night with his last strength.[39]

The famine was followed by disease:

> There was an epidemic form of dysentery called 'mai bashi' by the natives, during the late summer and autumn it is believed that a large number of natives died of this complaint, but as it was most prevalent at a time when the famine was at its worst it is possible that many of the deaths attributed to this complaint were really the result of destitution and starvation.[40]

Famine relief was minimal and 'tardy' and did little, despite the new

Kano railway, to check mortality.

Yet in the aftermath of the famine, groundnut exports continued to increase. Why? We are provided with a clue by a comment made in the 1915 Sokoto Annual Report which noted that 'some farmers are still badly off having got into debt last year so that much of this year's good crop went to repay their creditors.'[41] Groundnuts were not only the easiest way to pay taxes but also debts incurred during the famine. Moreover, the increase in groundnuts exports from 1914 to 1920 was paralleled by an increase in the price of food. Commenting on this trend, one colonial official noted in 1914 that the 'general cost of living has increased considerably here during the last two years, caused not only by the partial failure of the crops but by export, and as far as I can see this export trade will grow larger each year.'[42]

The dramatic increase in groundnut prices over the period 1915–20 might on their own suggest that the period was one of rural prosperity. A more detailed look at food prices, however, provides a different story. Food prices were rising dramatically and nearly every observer linked this increase to the growing production of crops for export and the increase in the prices of what were now becoming necessary import items. The 1921 Nupe Province Annual Report noted that the 'day is long gone when the Northern Native produced all his own requirements in the shape of food, clothing, utensils, implements, etc. He is daily becoming a large consumer of imported wares – chiefly cloth'.[43]

The breakdown of the regional and local self-sufficiency of the rural producers of Northern Nigeria was at hand and its effects were felt throughout the entire economy. The Kano Annual Report for 1918 notes:

Foodstuffs both for Europeans and natives have been plentiful in Kano; the prices of local foodstuffs rose steadily throughout the year and at the time of writing have not yet fallen and this condition of affairs is no doubt largely due to the prices paid for groundnuts and the fact that the means of transport and the energies of the populace are absorbed in the harvesting and marketing of the groundnut crop. It is extremely doubtful though if they will ever go back to the pre-war local prices. The imports which the native buys are 2 and 3 hundred per cent dearer than they were and he must pay for them with his products.[44]

Another reason for the high price of food disclosed by the author of the Zaria Annual Report for 1919 was the neglect of cereal production:

That the price of corn . . . is somewhat high cannot be denied . . . Every encouragement is being given to farmers to increase the acreage under cultivation, but the prices obtainable for cotton and groundnuts naturally make them plant more of these crops somewhat to the neglect of cereals.[45]

The increase in food prices was compounded by the currency policy of the colonial state. In response to the wartime shortage of British coin, currency notes were introduced, but these pieces of paper found little favour with the populace. Commissions of '2/- in the pound' were frequently charged for changing them. Paper currency at one point fell to the value of '6d for the shilling'.[46] The author of the Zaria Annual Report for 1920 speaks of the ensuing market disruption:

> The price of food commodities became very high and was severely felt by the wage earning classes. Paper currency was one of the causes of this high rise. Copper coins were difficult to obtain and the market people were unable to give change.[47]

In 1918 and 1919 the increase in agricultural exports and the rise in food prices once more evoked the spectre of famine. In 1918, the Resident of Zaria reported a growing dearth of food. 'The shortage,' he wrote, 'is said to be due to two causes: the increased cultivation of cotton and groundnuts and the ever increasing non-farming communities.'[48] The fears of famine were given emphasis by the food production shortfall in Sokoto Province in 1921:

> The western and northern districts of the Sultanate suffered most severely getting but 10% to 30% of their normal crop. Fortunately, the dawa in Zamfara and the south-east did well and rice gave a bumper crop in Argungu and Birnin Kebbi so that the province as a whole will be able to feed itself.
> *The possibility of a disastrous famine is by no means remote in this province* and each year the sowing and harvesting months are times of great anxiety.[49]

The shortfall in food was compounded by the extraction of wealth from the province in the form of taxes:

> At least £50,000 per annum, (£64,000 in 1921) leaves the Province, in payment of taxes and can only be replaced by means of exports. Wealth is much more evenly distributed here than in England but the margin over the subsistence line is very small.[50]

As a result of the famine scare of the war years, a plan to collect a portion of taxes in kind to be held against the danger of famine was put forth by District Officer Browne of Katsina.[51] The plan was, however, quashed in extremely harsh and almost unbelievable terms by Lieutenant Governor

Goldsmith who argued that there had been 'no cause for serious alarm [about famine] in the last 20 years . . . a famine policy is unwarranted.'[52]

The proponents of the plan did not have long to wait for events to vindicate their views. Famine struck rural Northern Nigeria once again in 1927. Once more, comprehensive statistics are unavailable. However, the brief note of one colonial official will perhaps provide an adequate substitute for hard figures. 'It is undoubtedly true,' he wrote, 'that considerable quantities of cotton seed distributed last season were used as food in some of the northern districts where supplies were particularly short owing to the failure of the rains in 1926.'[53]

There were only a few years of respite between the famine of 1927 and the onset of the great depression of the 1930s. During the depression food prices fell in tandem with those of export crops. Yet this did little to alter the steadily worsening position of the rural producer. For as we have seen, groundnut production was dramatically increased in the face of falling prices to meet taxation. One report for a major groundnut producing area provides us with an insight into what was happening. In Dan Zomo District in northern Kano Province the total acreage under cultivation 'declined considerably' between 1917 and 1932 concurrently with the general adoption of groundnut cultivation for the export market. Average farm size fell from eight acres in 1917 to approximately five acres in 1932, of which 'a little over 4 acres' was devoted to food production. For the farmers of Dan Zomo District the adoption of groundnut cultivation halved the acreage under food.[54]

As a result of the changeover from grain to export crop production, fears of famine were revived. In 1930 a grain storage plan was again raised and again the proposal was followed by studied inaction.[55] As with the earlier attempt, the reality of famine followed closely on the heels of the fear. The author of the assessment report for Arewa Gabbas, Sokoto Province for 1930–31 wrote:

> The locust invasion of 1930–31 and the subsequent shortage of food resulted in a reduction of the area in farmland. The normal acreage was not sown in 1931 for three reasons. 1) The farmers' stamina was weakened by a year on short commons. 2) Shortage of seed as the grain had been eaten. 3) Temporary migration of farmers.[56]

Yet the rate of taxation in this district was *increased* from 4s 7½d in 1929–30 to 5s in 1930–31![57] For the rural producer the choice was stark – either increased crops of groundnuts had to be produced to fulfil the demands of the state or an alternative form of earning cash had to be found. The diaries of W. R. Crocker, a member of the colonial service in Northern Nigeria, demonstrate why the major alternative, wage labour, was uninviting. Labour, although nominally free, was continually

referred to as 'political', or forced labour, and myriad devices were used
to bilk the labourers of their wages. As Crocker noted:

The District Head 'forces' the labour, every household has a
quota . . .
At the end of a job . . . the normal Hausa labourers go away
without a penny.
Families and 7 year old girls at the earthworks. Virtually no
labourer has any real idea of what was due to him at the end of the
month.
Each labourer is theoretically paid 8d per day, but only if he finishes
the days task set for him. I suppose there has never been seen here the
day or the labourer who did his task in one day. Normally the day's
task takes from 4–7 days and there are cases, by no means rare, of 9
days being taken. Why is it that too when possibly a month or more
salary is owing to them . . . ?
Originally, (according to a contractor) he built a camp adequate for
1000–1200 men. Now could only hold 300. Why? . . . with the coming
of the rains men have pulled down two huts to make waterproof the
hut they were inhabiting.
Distribution of profits at an earthwork. Contractors, 1/9 for 3 yds
earth moved; Subcontractor 1/6 ditto; Labourer 1/- ditto.[59]

Little comment need be made on the reasons for the overwhelming
preference for tax payment through increased groundnut production
over wage labour during the depression years.

The outbreak of the Second World War, which, it is often claimed,
brought the world crisis of capitalism of the 1930s to an end, did little to
assist the rural producer in Northern Nigeria. On the contrary, Northern
Nigerians in their millions were called upon to produce 'a groundnut a
day to keep Hitler at bay'. The Groundnut Campaign, a mixture of
propaganda and coercion, along with food requisitioning and the
recruitment of forced labour for the tin mines of the Jos Plateau, once
again created famine conditions. Once again relief was limited. Once
again there was no famine policy in place.[59]

By the 1950s, with the birth of the development dreams based on
marketing board surpluses extracted from the groundnut producers of
Northern Nigeria, food shortage had become an accepted part of the
rural scene. A 1957 survey of thirty-eight villages, in four provinces,
showed that between 53 per cent and 80 per cent of all households had
run out of grain by May, the middle of the *planting* season. Moreover, it
showed that 47 per cent of all loans were made for food at a mean rate of
90 per cent to 100 per cent interest. Debt was chronic, the average period
that a loan was outstanding being twelve to twenty-four months, with
either grain or wage labour being the security for the loan in 79 per cent

of all cases. The rural producers of Northern Nigeria had emerged from a century and a half of colonialism as an impoverished and chronically indebted peasantry.[60]

This is not the full story, however, for the very forms of rural existence had been transformed. The mechanism of this transformation was the increase and redirection of the agricultural surplus which altered the regional, village and household political economy. At the regional level, the pressure to commoditize the agricultural surplus created a massive withdrawal of Northern Nigeria's social surplus and replaced it, in part, with inedible British currency and imported manufactured goods. The latter, over the long run, decreased the relative importance of regional craft production and thus the scope of the potential market of rural craft producers. Together with the land tenure and labour laws which were biased toward the continued expansion of merchant capital and against the development of the means and social relations of agricultural production, this extraction of the social surplus increased the vulnerability of the regional economy to drought, disease, and famine. Conversely, the development of merchant capital, through increased commoditization and extraction of the social surplus eroded regional grain stores and non-commodity relationships, as well as the political and moral obligations of the rulers to the ruled, and in doing so made the regional economy more vulnerable to the classic capitalist crises of over-production.

At the level of the village, self-sufficiency was again eroded while individual households became increasingly polarized between the few rich and the many poor, the many debtors and the few creditors. A comparison of data collected in 1937 and 1957 is relevant. While in 1937 a study of the rural economy stressed that the sale of agricultural labour was a rare and stigmatized sign of abject poverty, the 1957 report stated that 13.7 per cent of all loans made were for the purpose of employing wage labour. In order to understand the growth of wage labour and the corresponding decline in communal village work groups, and other forms of redistribution, it is necessary to focus our discussion on the household.[61]

As will be recalled, it was ideally the obligation of the head of the extended farming household to provide its members with seed, tools, tax, marriage and childbirth expenses, shelter, food, a personal plot of land and free time to work it. In return it was the obligation of subordinate members of the household to work the common grain farm, together with, and under the direction of, the household head. By the 1950s and 1960s clear evidence began to emerge that these social relations of household production and reproduction had broken down. In many households subordinate males began to be expected to pay their own taxes from the proceeds of personal plots, subsidiary crafts, or wage labour. In other households, the control of common fields was decentralized, each member having a share and personally providing food and tax requirements while still under the nominal control of the household head. In many other cases the extended household had simply disappeared, giving rise to a larger number of nuclear households.[62]

What were the reasons for this social dissolution? Given the reciprocal and redistributive nature of the extended household, a household head' inability to meet his social obligations to household members would be met with a similar reduction in their social obligations to him and hence the household itself. This would constitute a basic restructuring of the relations of production within the household. It is not hard to imagine the position of a household head in control of the redistribution of a grain reserve that ran out before or during the planting season or who was unable to pay the household's taxes or to provide for the social expenses of marriage or naming ceremonies.

With the erosion of relative regional and village self-sufficiency due to the increasing commoditization and redirection of the social surplus more and more households found themselves vulnerable to a crisis of simple reproduction in which the food needs of the household, taxes, and social obligation could not be met. Moreover, as commoditization increased, the nature of the goods necessary to meet these social obligations was altered as well. Taxes had to be paid in British silver, and the young man who went in search of a wife with carved calabashes and shea nut oil stood little chance against suitors who offered umbrellas and other imported wares. The obvious long-term result of these changes, and the household head's inability to meet them, was the dissolution of the household.

This process of household dissolution could often be initiated by the effects of drought, famine or disease alone or in combination with the effects of market disruptions such as the post-First World War boom and bust, the depression of the 1930s or the Second World War. The immediate result of such a crisis was to ensnare the rural household in the clutches of the village moneylender and/or produce-buying agent, who would offer loans or advances against groundnuts still unripe and unharvested at 50 per cent to 100 per cent interest. Once ensnared, it was all but impossible to escape chronic indebtedness, given the high rates of interest and the minimal returns to rural wage labour. Indeed, the latter only compounded the problem, for rural labour was only in demand at planting, weeding, and harvest periods, when to labour on an employer' farm meant to neglect one's own and thus lessen its harvest.[63]

One study of five elderly men has traced the progressive weakening of extended households over two or three generations. The author concludes

> The failure . . . to provide the social obligations of members has precipitated the further decline of large family groups and the decentralization of economic control in those that remain . . . without

the benefits to be derived from a substantial form of income to provide the social obligations [of the household], there is little attraction for either the father or the sons to remain together.[64]

This alteration in the form of the household has had grave repercussions for Northern Nigerian society. Now, nuclear families, far more liable to crises of simple reproduction because of their demographic structure, face the prospect of drought, disease, starvation and capitalist crises in isolation. As such, they became increasingly easy prey to the moneylender and the exploitive rural employer. Thus, the commoditization of agricultural production of Northern Nigeria has reproduced rural society in a fundamentally different form and has given birth to the agricultural crisis Nigeria now faces.

To conclude, the development of capitalism, fostered by the hothouse of colonial rule, transformed Northern Nigerian society from top to bottom. The brilliance and success of British colonial policy was to transform Northern Nigerian society while preserving a facade of changelessness. The price of the success of this policy is only now becoming apparent. Independence and oil have together shattered the illusion of stability and the development dream of the 1960s has, for many, become a nightmare. Hunger stalks the cities and the countryside, the bounty from oil providing only a fragile shield in the form of food imports. In the final analysis, the price of the success of colonialism may well come to be understood in terms of the dissolution of Northern Nigerian society itself.

NOTES

1 F. D. Lugard, *The Dual Mandate in British Tropical Africa* (Edinburgh & London: Blackwood, 1922).
2 Lugard, *Political Memoranda* (1906), no. 6, para. 39
3 NAK SNP 7 1140/1911.
4 NAK SNP 7 2991/1911.
5 NAK SNP 8 55/1914 and NAK SNP 10 175p/1915.
6 NAK SNP10 254p/1916.
7 NAK SokProf 26/1922.
8 Mary Bull, 'Indirect rule in Northern Nigeria, 1906–1911' in K. Robinson and F. Madden (eds), *Essays in Imperial Government* (Oxford: Blackwell, 1963), p. 79.
9 RH Mss, Afr. s. 769, Edwardes Papers, p. 123.
0 R. Heussler, *The British in Northern Nigeria* (London: Oxford University Press, 1968), p. 41.
1 NAK SNP10 170p/1916.
2 ibid.
3 C. Temple, *Native Races and Their Rulers* (Cape Town: Argus, 1918), p. 83.

14 RH Mss Afr. s. 1149, Clifford Papers, Clifford to Gowers, 30 December 1923

15 P. Lovejoy, 'The Kamberin Beriberi: the formation of a specialized group of Hausa kola traders in the nineteenth century', *Journal of African History*, vol 14, no. 4 (1973), pp. 633–52.

16 I. A. Tahir, 'Scholars, sufis, saints and capitalists in Kano 1904–1974: the pattern of bourgeois evolution in an Islamic society' (PhD thesis, Cambridge University, 1977), p. 454.

17 RH Mss Afr. s. 86, RNC, vol. 15, Memo to Agent General, dated December 1915.

18 ibid.

19 RH Mss Afr. s. 86, RNC, vol. 1, entry dated 18 October 1917.

20 RH Mss Afr. s. 1428, J. B. Davies Papers, p. 13.

21 NAK KadMinAgric 2110, vol. II.

22 NAK KadMinAgric 22815, vol. II.

23 NAK SNP 10 476p/1914.

24 NAK SNP 7 5555/1909.

25 R. W. Shenton and L. Lennihan, 'Capital and class: peasant differentiation in Northern Nigeria', *Journal of Peasant Studies*, vol. 9, no. 1 (1981), pp 47–70.

26 ibid.

27 This is my own synthesis of the arguments contained in James C. Scott, *The Moral Economy of the Peasant: Rebellion and Subsistence in Southeast Asia* (New Haven: Yale University Press, 1976) and S. Popkin, *The Rational Peasant: the Political Economy of Rural Society in Vietnam* (Berkeley: University of California Press, 1979)

28 Bob Shenton and Mike Watts, 'Capitalism and hunger in Northern Nigeria', *Review of African Political Economy*, nos. 15/16 (May–December 1979), pp. 53–62.

29 NAK SNP 17 20007.

30 PRO CO 446/40, Minute by C. Strachey, 3 September 1904 on Lugard to Secretary of State for the Colonies, 31 August 1904 (telegram).

31 RH Mss, Afr. s. 230, Brice-Smith Papers.

32 NAK SNP 7 5490/1908.

33 NAK SNP 7 1765/1907.

34 NAK SNP 10 102p/1915.

35 NAK SNP 7 5490/1908.

36 RH Mss, Afr. s. 230, Brice-Smith Papers, entry dated 21 February 1912.

37 NAK SNP 10 134p/1913.

38 NAK SNP 9 447/1914.

39 A. Hastings, *Nigerian Days* (London: John Lane, 1925), p. 111.

40 NAK KatProf 1978.

41 NAK SNP 10 102p/1915.

42 NAK SNP 10 476p/1914.

43 NAK SNP 10 125p/1921.

44 NAK SNP 10 93p/1919.

45 NAK SNP 10 273p/1919.

46 NAK SNP 10 148p/1917.

47 NAK SNP 10 105p/1921.

48 NAK SNP 10 95p/1919.
49 NAK SokProf 26/1922.
50 ibid.
51 NAK KatProf 109.
52 ibid.
53 NAK SNP 17 10199, vol. I.
54 M. V. Backhouse, *Reassessment Report on the Dan Zomo District of Gumel Emirate* (Lagos, Government Printer, 1932).
55 NAK KadMinAgric 9900 and NAK KadMinAgric 14429.
56 NAK SNP 17 21336.
57 ibid.
58 RH Mss, Afr. s. 1073(1), Crocker Papers, diary entries dated 12 March 1932 to 8 July 1932.
59 Shenton and Watts, 'Capitalism and hunger', pp. 59–60.
60 NAK MSWC s5, vol. I, table 14.
61 ibid., Tables 3 and 4. NAK ZarProf 1468a.
62 Shenton and Lennihan, 'Capital and class', pp. 64–5.
63 ibid.
64 A. D. Goddard, 'Are Hausa-Fulani family structures breaking up?', *Institute for Agricultural Research Newsletter*, no. 11, 3 June 1969, Ahmadu Bello University, Zaria, Nigeria.

Bibliography

Primary Sources

Archives

Government Archives, Northern Nigeria

Series consulted in the National Archives, Kaduna (NAK) include
records of the Northern Nigerian Secretariat (SNP); of the provincia
administrations (KatProf, SokProf, ZarProf, MuriProf, KanoPro
BornuProf etc.); of the technical departments (NAK KadMinAgri
MSWC, etc.) and of the local authorities (KanoLA, ZariaLA, etc.). I
the list below, file descriptions refer to issues covered, not to the actu
titles of files.

1899–1900
NAK SNP 15 Acc. 7a, Major Festing's report
1901
NAK SNP 1/1, vol. 1, no. 130, Currency questions
NAK SNP 7 789/1901 Barter
NAK SNP 1/1, vol. 4, Maria Theresa dollars
1901
NAK SNP 1/1, vol 1 no. 264, Currency in Northern Nigeria
NAK SNP 1/1, vol. 1 Correspondence regarding Way and Co.
1903
NAK SNP 1/1, vol. 3, Notes on cotton growing
NAK KatProf 1769, Reports by H. R. Palmer
1904
NAK SNP 7 510/1904, Tripoli–Kano trade
NAK SNP 15 Acc. 73, Way–Lugard Correspondence
1905
NAK SNP 7 761/1905, Store at Kachia
NAK SNP 7 3823/1905, London and Kano House inside Kano
NAK SNP 6 4286/1905, Plantations

NAK SNP 7 29/1905, Samples of native cloth
NAK SNP 7 671/1905, Mohmadu Nasuru's arrival at Zungeru
NAK SNP 7 757/1905, Freights and cables, Kano–Tripoli
NAK SNP 7 1218/1905, Freight rates to Jebba
NAK SNP 7 1307/1905, London and Kano Co.
NAK SNP 7 1521/1905, Niger Co. ginnery proposal
NAK SNP 7 2033/1905, Circulation of copper coinage
NAK SNP 7 2136/1905, Reduction of fortnightly currency imports
NAK SNP 7 4000/1905, Sciama and Co.
NAK SNP 7 4003/1905, List of produce purchased by Niger Co.
NAK SNP 7 4545/1905, Abolition of caravan and canoe tax
NAK SNP 15 Acc. 395, Caravan trade
NAK KatProf 1797, Monthly reports, Katsina Division

906

NAK SNP 7 8/1906, Warning by Lugard concerning commercial
activity on the part of government officials
NAK SNP 7 41/1906, Banking in Nigeria
NAK SNP 3194/1906, Collection of tolls in Northern Nigeria
NAK SNP 3687/1906, Application for wasteland by the London and
Kano Company
NAK SNP 7 116/1906, Counterfeit coin
NAK SNP 7 918/1906, Complaints about Niger Co. prices at provincial
stations
NAK SNP 7 1552/1906, Pledges made regarding cotton growing in
Northern Nigeria

907

NAK SNP 6 64/1907, Kiara, political agent
NAK SNP 6 81/1907, Intelligence report
NAK SNP 6 102/1907, Land tenure and revenue in Northern Nigeria
NAK SNP 6 136/1907, Kano provincial assessment
NAK SNP 6 c162/1907, Memorandum on land tenure
NAK SNP 7 881/1907, Customs revenue
NAK SNP 7 991/1907, Trade from the north coast
NAK SNP 7 1086/1907, Trader Muklam Ben Zeglam
NAK SNP 7 1514/1907, Niger Co. acting as agents for Bank of Nigeria
NAK SNP 7 1557/1907, Sir Alfred Jones's proposal to give medals for
cotton growing
NAK SNP 7 1765/1907, Tour of Commercial Intelligence Officer,
Birtwistle
NAK SNP 7 1818/1907, Caravan traffic between Ghat and Zinder
NAK SNP 7 1859/1907, Proposed transport policy
NAK SNP 7 1867/1907, Kano Annual Report for 1907
NAK SNP 7 2390/1907, Fawa District assessment report

NAK SNP 7 2410/1907, Possibilities of cotton growing in Northern Nigeria

NAK SNP 7 2442/1907, Salt rates

NAK SNP 7 2732/1907, Enquiries regarding cotton growing

NAK SNP 7 2813/1907, Native and Resident assessment

NAK SNP 7 2978/1907, Cadastral survey of Northern Nigeria

NAK SNP 15 Acc. 369, Land tenure in Hausa states

NAK SNP 15 Acc. 372, Salaries for district sarkis

NAK SNP 15 Acc. 374, Memorandum on land tenure

NAK SNP 15 Acc. 376, Native Administration proposals

NAK SNP 15 Acc. 380, Native Administration proposals

NAK SNP 16 c4002, Memorandum on land tenure

NAK KatProf 1802, Katsina Province Reports

NAK KatProf 1813, Katsina Province Annual Report for 1907

NAK KatProf 1263, Quarterly Report, Katsina Province

1908

NAK SNP 1908a, Estate of Abdurahman ben Jak Ahmed Sharko (Ahmed el Baff) (AS 15)

NAK SNP 6 102/1908, Elder Dempster freight rates

NAK SNP 7 525/1908, Imports and exports for 1907

NAK SNP 7 3120/1908, Ostrich farming by the London and Kano Company

NAK SNP 7 5490/1908, Kano migration report

NAK SNP 7 6103/1908, West African leather

NAK SNP 7 6350/1908, Tribute Assessment, Argungu Division, Sokoto Province

NAK SNP 7 6559/1908, Niger Company river transport

NAK SNP 7 6565/1908, Land tenure and assessment

NAK KatProf 1289, Taxation in Katsina

NAK KatProf 1828, Katsina Quarterly Reports

1909

NAK SNP 7 2084/1909, Bebeji District Assessment

NAK SNP 7 1050/1909, Cowries as legal tender

NAK SNP 7 1787/1909, Tripoli caravans

NAK SNP 7 4252/1909, Taxation in Zaria province

NAK SNP 15 Acc. 166, Memorandum on customs stations

NAK SNP 7 5555/1909, Gora District Assessment

NAK SNP 15 Acc. 384 a18, Correspondence regarding indirect rule in Kano

NAK SNP 16 cc0109, Documents of historical interest

NAK KatProf 1836, Katsina Quarterly Reports

NAK KatProf 1898, Yandaka District Assessment

1910

NAK SNP 7 1515/1910, Notes on Kano

IAK SNP 7 6242/1910, London and Kano Company litigation
IAK SNP 7 6255/1910, Quarterly Report, Muri Province
IAK SNP 15 Acc. 167, Kano Annual Report for 1910
IAK SNP 17 50897, Native land proclamation
IAK KatProf 1842, Katsina Province Quarterly Report
IAK MuriProf 6255/1910, Quarterly Report, Muri Province
911
IAK SNP 6 39/1911, Possible railway to Zinder
IAK SNP 7 1140/1911, Wurno District Assessment
IAK SNP 7 2384/1911, Yerima and Galadima District Assessments
IAK SNP 7 2991/1911, Gonyoro District Assessment
IAK SNP 7 3973/1911, Trade in Sokoto Province
IAK SokProf 12/1911, Wababi District Assessment
IAK SokProf 69/1911, Salame District Assessment
IAK SokProf 265/1911, Chafe District Assessment
IAK SokProf 385/1911, Badawa District Assessment
IAK SokProf 387/1911, Bazai District Assessment
IAK SokProf 542/1911, Gumi District Assessment
IAK SokProf 553/1911, Bukwium District Assessment
912
IAK SNP 7 7521/1912, Nafada District, Gombe Emirate, Central
  Province Assessment
IAK SNP 7 3326/1912, Inheritance
IAK SNP 7 5225/1912, S. and V. Naham–Maria Theresa dollars
IAK SNP 7 6689/1912, Industrial taxation
IAK SNP 9 6249/1912, Azare District Assessment
IAK SNP 10 134p/1913, Kano Annual Report for 1912
IAK SNP 10 152p/1913, Sokoto Annual Report for 1912
IAK SNP 10 182p/1913, Borno Annual Report for 1912
IAK SokProf 344/1912, Sanyinnan District Assessment
913
IAK SNP 7 6713/1913, Estate of Ali of Gao
IAK SNP 9 1147/1914, Report for Northern Provinces, 1913
IAK SNP 10 92p/1914, Bornu Province Annual Report for 1913
IAK SNP 10 104p/1914, Report on Argungu for 1913
IAK SNP 10 105p/1914, Talata Mafara District Assessment,
IAK SNP 10 134p/1913, Kano Annual Report for 1913
IAK SNP 10 137p, Chiroma's District Assessment
IAK SNP 10 260p/1913, Creation of sub-district heads
IAK SNP 10 261p/1913, Hired labour
IAK SNP 10 262p/1913, Emir's relations with non-natives
IAK SNP 10 332p/1913, Barter
IAK SNP 363p/1913, Baiawa District Assessment
IAK SNP 364p/1913, Argungu District Assessment

NAK SNP 10 366p/1913, Argungu and Lalabi Districts Assessment
NAK SNP 10 410p/1914, Zaria Annual Report for 1914
NAK SNP 10 414p/1914, Sulibawa and Ingawa Districts Assessment
NAK SNP 10 567p/1913, Denge District Assessment
NAK SNP 10 631p/1913, Jemaari District Assessment
NAK SNP 10 689p/1913, Kebbi District Assessment
NAK SNP 10 705p/1913, Kaura Namoda District Assessment
NAK SNP 10 708p/1913, Kaoji District Assessment
NAK SNP 10 743p/1913, Dambam District Assessment
NAK SNP 10 769p/1913, Dogondaji District Assessment
NAK SNP 10 770p/1913, Jega District Assessment
NAK SNP 16 c4002, Land tenure in Northern Nigeria
NAK KanoProf 98/1914, Kano Annual Report for 1913

1914
NAK SNP 8 55/1914, Native labour
NAK SNP 9 447/1914, Kano Province Reports
NAK SNP 9 1147/1914, Report for Northern Provinces
NAK SNP 10 102p/1915, Sokoto Annual Report for 1914
NAK SNP 10 175p/1915, Zaria Province Annual Report for 1914
NAK SNP 10 231p/1914, Kano food prices
NAK SNP 10 250p/1914, Nassarawa Province Reports
NAK SNP 10 431p/1914, Ningi Division Assessment
NAK SNP 10 476p/1914, Sokoto Province Reports
NAK SNP 10 609p/1910, Raba District Assessment
NAK SNP 10 681p/1914, Zaria Town Assessment
NAK KatProf 1978, Katsina Annual Report for 1914

1915
NAK SNP 8 139/1915, Non-natives in native areas
NAK SNP 8 167/1915, Skins bought in Kano
NAK SNP 10 54p/1915, Kwiambana District Assessment
NAK SNP 10 55p/1915, Bondugu District Assessment
NAK SNP 10 93p/1915, Kaura District Assessment
NAK SNP 10 138p/1916, Zaria Annual Report for 1915
NAK SNP 10 152p/1916, Bornu Annual Report for 1915
NAK SNP 10 170p/1916, Kano Annual Report for 1915
NAK SNP 10 274p/1915, Sale of land
NAK SNP 10 465p/1915, Gummi District Assessment
NAK SNP 10 474p/1915, Kano Reports
NAK SNP 10 535p/1915, Karayew District Assessment
NAK SNP 10 536p/1915, Jega District Assessment
NAK SNP 10 553p/1915, Gwangwan and Karaye District Assessment
NAK SNP 10 795p/1915, Village heads' share of excess tax
NAK SNP 10 85p/1915, Murgu

1916

NAK SNP 8 133/1916, Max Klein of Marseilles
NAK SNP 8 183/1916, Aliens trading in pagan districts
NAK SNP 10 252p/1916, Bingi District Assessment
NAK SNP 10 254p/1916, Deposition of certain sub-district headmen
NAK SNP 10 419p/1910, Kware District Assessment
NAK SNP 10 511p/1916, Gando District Assessment
NAK SNP 10 518p/1910, Kano Reports
NAK SNP 10 607p/1916, Instructions to district heads from Emir
NAK SNP 10 637p/1916, Sabon Birni District Assessment
NAK SNP 10 768p/1916, Taxation of private property of emirs
NAK SNP 10 97p/1917, Zaria Annual Report for 1916
NAK SNP 10 145p/1917, Bornu Annual Report for 1916
NAK SNP 10 148p/1917, Sokoto Annual Report for 1916
NAK SNP 14 2742/1916, Undesirability of touts and middlemen
1917
NAK SNP 8 189/17, Intelligence Report
NAK SNP 10 203p/1917, Comparison of taxes paid in Sokoto, Katsina, Zaria and Bida
NAK SNP 10 365p/1917, Sarkin Yaki Assessment Report
NAK SNP 10 162p/1918, Zaria Annual Report for 1917
NAK SNP 10 179p/1918, Kano Annual Report for 1917
NAK SNP 10 200p/1918, Sokoto Annual Report for 1917
NAK SNP 10 531p/1918, Nupe Annual Report for 1917
1918
NAK SNP 9 2846/1919, Report for Northern Provinces
NAK SNP 10 45p/1918, Zaria Town Assessment
NAK SNP 10 297p/1918, Ibi Division Assessment
NAK SNP 10 481p/1918, Tudun Wada Village Assessment
NAK SNP 10 44p/1918, Barde District Assessment
NAK SNP 10 487p/1918, Jere District Assessment
NAK SNP 10 491p/1918, Kano Reports
NAK SNP 10 945p/1918, Sokoto Province Reports
NAK SNP 10 511p/1918, Illo District Assessment
NAK SNP 10 93p/1919, Kano Annual Report for 1918
NAK SNP10 94p/1919, Nupe Province Assessment for 1918
NAK SNP 10 95p/1919, Zaria Province Report for 1918
NAK KatProf 44/1918, Katsina Division reports
NAK KatProf 1922, Katsina Reports
NAK SokProf 70/1919, Sokoto Annual Report for 1918
NAK ZarProf 482/1918, Zaria Reports
1919
NAK SNP 7 236/1919 Soba District Assessment
NAK SNP 8 6/1919, Cash shortage

NAK SNP 8 11/1919, Abensur, agent of Hassan
NAK SNP 8 106/1919, H. R. Palmer's journey to Jeddah
NAK SNP 8 130/1919, Colonial bank
NAK SNP 9 2846/1919, Northern Provinces Report
NAK SNP 10 40p/1919, Arabic letters to the Emir of Kano
NAK SNP 10 273p/1919, Zaria Reports
NAK SNP 10 289p/1919, Sokoto Reports
NAK SNP 10 318p/1919, Kano Reports
NAK SNP 10 370p/1919, Principles of taxation
NAK SNP 10 399p/1919, Clerks of the London and Kano Co.
NAK SNP 10 448p/1919, Children of Kano Arabs
NAK KatProf 1923, Katsina Reports
NAK SokProf 105/1920, Sokoto Annual Report for 1919
1920
NAK SNP 9 1609/1920, Attitudes towards cotton growing
NAK SNP 9 3329/1920, Cotton
NAK SNP 10 34p/1920, Islamic law and insolvent estates
NAK SNP 10 93p/1920, Paper currency and tax
NAK SNP 10 119p/1920, Hadj Kolo, trader
NAK SNP 10 211p/1920, Dan Marusa District Assessment
NAK SNP 10 105p/1921, Zaria Province Annual Report for 1920
NAK SNP 10 120p/1921, Kano Province Annual Report for 1920
NAK SNP 10 121p/1920, Kontagora Annual Report for 1920
NAK SNP 10 126p/1921, Sokoto Annual Report for 1920
NAK ZarProf c4003, Gayya and forced labour
1921
NAK SNP 16 c17, Status of Tripolitanian Arabs in Kano
NAK KatProf 109, Katsina Division Report
NAK KatProf 1972, Trade inquiries
NAK SokProf s379, Dundaye District Assessment
NAK SokProf 26/1922, Sokoto Annual Report for 1921
NAK SNP 10 125p/1921, Nupe Province Annual Report for 1921
1922
NAK SNP 7 387/1923, Zaria Annual Report for 1922
NAK SNP 9 1040, Estate of Ali Elhamre
NAK SNP 9 73/1923, Zaria Annual Report for 1922
NAK KatProf 1607, Katsina Division Assessment
NAK KadMinAgric 600, Cotton regulations
1923
NAK SNP 9 98/1924, Sokoto Annual Report for 1923
NAK SNP 9 100/1924, Zaria Annual Report for 1923
NAK ZarProf 368/1923, Ikara District Assessment
NAK KadMinAgric 600, Cotton regulations
NAK SNP 17 10199 vol. I, Reports on cotton growing

1924

NAK SNP 9 525/1924, Ungogo District Assessment

NAK SNP 9 603/1924, Sumaila District Assessment

NAK SNP 9 687/1924, Anchau District Assessment

NAK SNP 9 705/1924, Report on groundnut trade in Kano Province

NAK SNP 9 632/1925, Zaria Annual Report for 1924

NAK SNP 9 640/1925, Bornu Province Annual Report for 1924

NAK KanoProf 181/1925, Kano Annual Report for 1924

1925

NAK SNP 7 1458/1925, Kiawa District Assessment

NAK SNP 7 1460/1925, Dutse District Assessment

NAK SNP 17 K102, vol. I, Bornu Province Annual Report for 1925

NAK SNP 17 K105, vol. I, Kano Annual Report for 1925

NAK SNP 17 Klll, Zaria Province Annual Report for 1925

NAK KanoProf 1708a, Taki Assessment

NAK KanoProf 410/1925, Tudun Wada District Assessment

NAK SokProf 474/1925, Sokoto Annual Report for 1925

1926

NAK SNP 17 K105, vol. II, Kano Annual Report for 1926

NAK SNP 17 Klll, vol. III, Zaria Annual Report for 1926

NAK SNP 17 K2151 Principal famines of Hausaland

NAK SNP 17, vol. I,II Sokoto Annual report for 1926–27

NAK SokProf 229/1926, Sokoto Annual Report for 1926

NAK KadMinAgric 606, Cotton middlemen

NAK KadMinAgric 2600, Haig Report

1927

NAK SNP 17 K1653, Zaria Annual Report for 1927

NAK SNP 17 K5093, Kano Province Reassessment

NAK SNP 17 3270, vol. I, Sokoto trade returns

NAK SNP 17 6808, vol. I, Bornu Annual Report for 1927

NAK SNP 17 20070, Cooperatives

NAK KanoLA 28/1927, Food prices

1928

NAK SNP 17 9008, Bornu Province Annual Report for 1928

NAK SNP 17 9159, Zaria Province Annual Report for 1928

NAK KanoLA 74/1928, Employment and wages

1929

NAK SNP 17K8823, Yandaka District Assessment

NAK SNP 17 1894, vol. 1, Zaria Annual Report for 1929

NAK SNP 17 12004, Kano Annual Report for 1929

NAK SNP 17 12270, Bornu Annual Report for 1929

NAK KanoProf 9118, Bichi District Assessment

NAK KanoLA 8/1929, Food prices

NAK KatsinaNA w765, Dan Yusufu District Assessment

NK SNP 17 12127 vol. I, Sokoto Annual Report
1930
NAK SNP 17 14603, vol. I, Bornu Annual Report for 1930
NAK SNP 17 14818, vol. I, Sokoto Annual Report for 1930
NAK SNP 17 14830, Zaria Annual Report for 1930
NAK SNP 17 21336, Arewa Gabbas District Assessment
NAK SNP 17 25673a Kano food prices
NAK KatProf 1976, United Africa Company
NAK KadMinAgric 9900, Guinea corn storage
NAK KadMinAgric 12676, Cotton inspection
NAK KadMinAgric 14429, Famine relief
NAK KadMinAgric 20207, Advances for purchase of produce
NAK KanoProf 438, Kano Annual Report for 1930
1931
NAK SNP 17 16670, vol. I, Sokoto Annual Report for 1931
NAK SNP 17 16678, vol. I, Zaria Annual Report for 1931
NAK KanoProf 628, Kano Annual report for 1931
NAK KanoProf 1708, vol. I, Land system and taxation in Kano
NAK KadMinAgric 16817, vol. I, Bornu Annual Report for 1931
NAK KadMinAgric 19735, Advances
1932
NAK SNP 17 18921, vol. I, Sokoto Annual Report for 1932
NAK SNP 17 18939, vol. I, Zaria Annual Report for 1932
NAK SNP 17 19187, Bornu Annual Report for 1932
NAK SNP 17 29652a, Kano food prices
NAK KanoProf 923, Kano Annual Report for 1932
1933
NAK SNP 17 21303, vol. I, Sokoto Annual Report for 1933
NAK SNP 17 21304, Zaria Annual Report for 1933
NAK SNP 17 21325, vol. I, Bornu Annual Report for 1933
NAK SNP 17 21326, vol. I, Kano Annual Report for 1933
NAK BauchiProf 449, Crop yield statistics
NAK KanoProf 926, Minjibir District Assessment
NAK KanoProf 2007, Groundnuts and taxation
NAK ZarProf 1712, Ikara District Assessment
NAK KadMinAgric 757, Cotton and mixed farming
1934
NAK SNP 17 11703 Mixed farming
NAK SNP 17 19378a Groundnut prices 1934-8
NAK SNP 17 20070, vol. I, Cooperation and advances
NAK SNP 17 23562, Zaria Annual Report for 1934
NAK SNP 17 23585, Sokoto Annual Report for 1934
NAK KanoProf 1324, Kano Annual Report for 1934
NAK ZarProf 1269, vol. II, Incidence of taxation

NAK ZarProf 1706, Zaria Annual Report for 1934
NAK KadMinAgric 621, Strickland Report
NAK MinLocalGov 22179 Durbi District Assessment
1935
NAK SNP 17 11703, vol. II, Agricultural extension
NAK SNP 17 21336, Arewa Gabbas Assessment
NAK SNP 17 25673, Kano Annual Report for 1935
NAK SNP 17 25757, Sokoto Annual Report for 1935
NAK KadMinAgric 1118, Credit and mixed farming
NAK KadMinAgric 2110, Cotton Advisory Committee
NAK KadMinAgric 2403, Agricultural development
NAK SNP 17 25670, Zaria Annual Report for 1935
1936
NAK SNP 17 27810, Kano Annual Report for 1936
NAK KadMinAgric 2600, Haig Report
1937
NAK ZarProf 1486a, Giles Report
NAK SNP 17 11703, vol. III, Agricultural extension
NAK SNP 17 29615, Zaria Annual Report for 1937
NAK SNP 17 29652, Kano Annual Report for 1927
NAK SNP 17 29664, Sokoto Annual Report for 1937
NAK KadMinAgric 2838, vol. II, Crop Yield Statistics
1938-1957
NAK SNP 17 30862, Zaria Annual Report for 1938
NAK SNP 17 11159 vol. II, Farm and family budgets
NAK SNP 17 30847a, Kano Annual Report for 1938
NAK KadMinAgric 31657a, Kano Annual report for 1938
NAK KadMinAgric 31731, Wartime produce buying
NAK KanoProf 4094, Inheritance
NAK KatProf 128, Moneylending
NAK KadMinAgric 606, Cotton regulations
NAK SNP 17 32067, Zaria Annual Report for 1939
NAK SNP 17 20007, Farm and family budgets
NAK SNP 17 1864, Advances
NAK KadMinAgric 31731N, Groundnut campaign
NAK KadMinAgric 3157s3, Food storage
NAK KadMinAgric 4205, Economic aspects of groundnut growing
NAK SNP 17 34242, Kano Annual Report for 1940
NAK SNP 17 33147, Kano Annual Report for 1941
NAK KadMinAgric 4200, Groundnut and cotton production
NAK KanoProf 398 vol. III, Food storage
NAK KanoLA 51/1927, Groundnut control scheme
NAK KadMinAgric 2110 vol. 2, Advances
NAK SNP 17 31183, Zaria Annual Report for 1943

NAK SNP 17 30007, Grain prices 1943–6
NAK KanoProf 30361, Dawakin Ta Kudo Assessment Report
NAK SNP 17 37094, Mortgaging of standing crops
NAK KadMinAgric 22815, vol. II, Cotton Advisory Committee
NAK SNP 17 31079, Relative cost of groundnut and guinea corn production
NAK SNP 37005, Kano Annual Report for 1943
NAK KanoProf 211, Advances
NAK KadMinAgric 1100 vol. I, Mixed farming
NAK SNP 17 41986, Kano Annual Report for 1946
NAK SNP 43599, Kano Annual Report for 1948
NAK KanoProf 6179, vol. II, Middlemen
NAK KadMinAgric 283, Development schemes
ArgunguNA 1018, Rural indebtedness
NAK KatProf 398s2, Rural indebtedness
NAK KadMinAgric 10028, Tempany report
NAK KadMinAgric 760, Conference of Directors of Agriculture
NAK KadMinAgric 1121, Mixed farming
NAK KadMinAgric 1100, vol. II, Mixed farming
NAK KadMinAgric 2839, vol. I, Northern Region Development Loans Board
NAK MSWCs 5, vol. I, Vigo Report

Public Record Office, Kew (PRO)
Documents in the following series were consulted:
BT 31 Board of Trade company records
CO 446 Northern Nigeria, Original Correspondence.
CO 465 Blue Books of Statistics, Northern Nigeria
CO 554 West Africa, Original Correspondence
CO 583 Nigeria, Original Correspondence
CO 586 Government Gazettes, Northern Nigeria
CO 660 Annual Reports and Trade Statistics, Nigeria
CO 763 Nigeria, Registers of Correspondence
CO 852 Economic

Rhodes House Library, Oxford (RH Mss)
Documents in the following series were consulted:
Abadie, G., Mss, Afr. S. 1337, letters, 1897–1904
Arnett, E.J., Mss, Afr. s. 952, papers on Northern Nigerian exports, etc. 1902–40
Backhouse, M.V., Mss, Afr. s. 601, Birniwa assessment, 1930
Baker, J.E.A., Mss, Afr. s. 312, Kano revenue survey, 1943–8
Brice-Smith, H.M., Ms, Afr. s. 230, Kano Province reports, 1909, 1912–13, 1915

Burdon, A, Mss, Afr. s. 1037, ff. 19–22, letters on the slave trade, 1902

'Bushwhacker', Mss, Afr. r. 177, Nigerian reminiscences, 1928–46 (anon. at author's request)

Carr, F.B., Mss, Afr. s. 546, Nigerian reminiscences, 1919–49

Carrow, J.H., Mss, Afr. s. 1443 and s. 1489, Nigerian reminiscences, 1919–43; correspondence with R. Heussler on indirect rule, 1965–7

Cary, J., Mss, Cary Adds 4 f.54, letters to his father and wife, 1900–23 Central Secretariat Office, Mss, Afr. s. 1585, kola trade, 1906–33

Clifford, H.C., Mss, Afr. s. 1149, correspondence with Sir William Gowers, 1920–24

Cragg, V.E., Mss, Afr. s. 1588, memoirs of a wife of a political officer in Northern Nigeria, 1924–33

Crocker, W.R., Mss, Afr. s. 1073, touring diaries, 1931–4

Davies, J.B., Mss, Afr. s. 1428, service with the United Africa Company, 1930s

Edwardes, H.S.W., Mss, Afr. r. 106 and s. 769, diaries, 1905-15, 1921–4; papers, 1906–24

Gowers, W.F., Mss, Afr. s. 662, notes on trade in Sokoto Province, 1911

Grier, S.M., Mss, Afr. s. 1379, service in Nigeria, 1906–25

Guy, J.C., Mss, Afr. r. 95, r. 96, touring diaries, 1937–8, 1939–43

Harford, J.D., Mss, Afr. s. 897, report on Konduga District, Bornu Province, 1926

Holt, J., Mss, Afr. s. 1526 t. 21, Holt Papers, 1909–21

Holt Papers, Mss, Afr. s. 825–7, correspondence, 1922–7

Jacob, S.M., Mss, Afr. t. 16, report on taxation and economics of Nigeria, 1934

Kirby, H.M., Mss, Afr. r. 44, reminiscences of the wife of a Director of Agriculture, 1912–14, 1916–18

Lugard, F.D., Mss, Brit. Emp. s. 30–99, Lugard Papers

Mackie, J.R., Mss. Afr. s. 822, s. 823, personal correspondence, 1927–8, 1939–45

Maxwell, J.L., Mss, Afr. s. 1112, diaries of a Sudan United Mission missionary, 1908–34

Nicholson, R.P., Mss, Afr. r. 81, Northern Nigerian notes, 1900–05

Patton, J., Mss, Afr. s. 571, life in Nigeria as a railway pioneer, 1914–27

Rawson, P.H., Mss, Afr. s. 1421, letters on medical matters, 1925–8

Rosedale, W.O.P., Mss, Afr. s. 582, correspondence etc., Northern Nigeria, 1927–33

Royal Niger Company Papers, Mss, Afr. s. 85–101, 1898–1930

Smith, J.H., Mss, Afr. s. 1232, touring reports, 1951–4

Stevens, T.J., Mss, Afr. s. 834, papers, 1903–42

Temple, O., Mss, Afr. 1531, notes for a Northern Nigerian handbook, *c.* 1912–16

Turner, R., Mss, Afr. s. 424, ff. 325–9, proposal for ten-year development plan for Niger Province, 1946

Walker, C.R., Mss, Afr. s. 433–45, diary of an assistant district officer, Northern Nigeria, 1915–20

Ward. J.F., Mss, Afr. s. 1036, diary of an agricultural officer, 1928–30

Watt, L.S. Mss, Afr. s. 1412, diary of an agricultural officer in Northern Nigeria, 1939–59

Wilson G., Mss, Afr. s. 2549, touring diaries, 1936–9

Woodhouse, C.A., Mss, Afr. s. 236–66, diaries, 1908–33

Liverpool Public Library

Minutes of the African trade Section of the Liverpool Chamber of Commerce

Guildhall Library, London

Minutes of the African Trade Section of the London Chamber of Commerce

Royal Commonwealth Society, London

Papers relating to colonial administration in Northern Nigeria

Manchester Public Library

Minutes of the Manchester Chamber of Commerce

Northern History Research Scheme, Ahmadu Bello University Zaria, Nigeria

London and Kano company papers

Lugard, F., *Political Memoranda* (1906)

Printed Primary Sources

Command Papers

1904 Cmd 1433, *Correspondence Relating to Kano*

1906 Cmd 2875, *Mineral and Economic Products Reports. Northern Nigeria*

1910 Cmd 5101, *Northern Nigerian Lands Committee*, 'Minutes of Evidence'

1910 Cmd 5102, *Northern Nigerian Lands Committee*, 'Summary of Conclusions and Recommendations'

1910 Cmd 5103. *Northern Nigerian Lands Committee*, 'Proceedings'

1916 Cmd 8247, *Committee on Edible and Oil Producing Nuts and Seeds*, 'Report'

1916 Cmd 8248, *Committee on Edible and Oil Producing Nuts and Seeds*, 'Evidence'

1922 Cmd 1600, *Report of a Committee on Trade and Taxation for British West Africa*

Secondary Sources

Books

Abun-Nasr, J.M., *A History of the Maghrib* (Cambridge: Cambridge University Press, 2nd edn. 1975)

Adeleye, R. A., *Power and Diplomacy in Northern Nigeria 1804–1906* (London: Longman, 1971)

Aldcroft, D.H., *From Versailles to Wall Street, 1919–29* (London: Allen Lane, 1977)

Amin, S., *Accumulation on a World Scale*, 2 vols (New York: Monthly Review Press, 1974)

Anderson, P., *Lineages of the Absolutist State* (London: New Left Books, 1974)

Baden-Powell, B.H., *The Land Systems of British India*, 3 vols (Oxford: Oxford University Press, 1892)

Bargery, G., *A Hausa-English Dictionary and English–Hausa Vocabulary* (London: Oxford University Press, 1934)

Barth, H., *Travels and Discoveries in North and Central Africa*, 5 vols (1st edn 1857, reprinted London: Frank Cass, 1965)

Bauer, P.T., *West African Trade. A Study of Competition, Oligopoly and Monopoly in a Changing Economy* (London: Routledge & Kegan Paul, new edn, 1963)

Beckman, B., *Organizing the Farmers: Cocoa Politics and National Development in Ghana* (Uppsala: Scandinavian Institute of African Studies, 1976)

Boahen, A.A., *Britain, the Sahara and the Western Sudan* (Oxford: Clarendon Press, 1966)

Bovill, E.W. (ed.), *Missions to the Niger*, Vol. 1 (Cambridge: Cambridge University Press, 1965)

Boxer, C.R., *Four Centuries of Portuguese Expansion 1415–1825; A Succinct Survey* (Johannesburg: Witwatersrand University Press, 1961)

Braudel, F., *The Mediterranean and the Mediterranean World in the Age of Philip II*, 2 vols. (London, Collins, 1972–3)

Chayanov, A., The Theory of Peasant Economy (Homewood, Illinois: Irwin, 1966)

Clapperton, Hugh, *Journal of a Second Expedition into the Interior of Africa, from the Bight of Benin to Soccatoo* (1st edn 1829, reprinted London, Frank Cass, 1966)

Cookey, S.J.S. *Britain and the Congo Question, 1885–1913* (London: Longmans, 1968)

Corrigan, Philip, Ramsay, Harvie and Sayer, Derek, *Socialist Construction and Marxist Theory: Bolshevism and its Critique* (London: Macmillan, 1973)

Crowder, Michael, *West Africa under Colonial Rule* (London: Hutchinson, 1968)

Curtin, P., *The Image of Africa; British Ideas and Action, 1780–1850* (Madison: University of Wisconsin Press, 1964)

G. Dangerfield, *The Strange Death of Liberal England* (New York: Smith & Haas, 1935)

Davies, P.N., *The Trade Makers. Elder Dempster in West Africa, 1862–1972*

(London: Allen & Unwin, 1973)

Davies, P.N., *Sir Alfred Jones: Shipping Entrepreneur Par Excellence* (London: Europa, 1978)

Dike, K. Onwuka, *Trade and Politics in the Niger Delta 1830–1885* (Oxford Clarendon Press, 1956)

Drummond, Ian, *British Economic Policy and the Empire, 1919–1939* (London: Allen & Unwin, 1972)

Echard, Nicole, *L'expérience du passé, histoire de la société paysanne hausa de L'Ader* (Niamey: Institut de Recherche en Sciences Humaines, Etudes nigériennes no. 36, 1975)

Flint, J. E.. *Sir George Goldie and the Making of Nigeria* (London: Oxford University Press, 1960)

Frankel, S.H., *Capital Investment in Africa* (London: Oxford University Press, 1938)

Geertz, C., *Agricultural Involution: Processes of Ecological Change in Indonesia* (Berkeley: University of California Press, 1971)

George, Henry, *Progress and Poverty* (London: Routledge & Kegan Paul, 1981), p.154.

Goody, J., *Technology, Tradition and the State in Africa* (London: Oxford University Press, 1971)

Greenberg, J., *The Influence of Islam on a Sudanese Religion* (Monographs of the American Ethnological Society, no. 10, New York: Augustin, 1946)

Hancock, W.K.. *Survey of British Commonwealth Affairs*, Vol. II, Part 2 (London: Oxford University Press, 1942)

Hastings, A.. *Nigerian Days* (London: John Lane, 1925)

Helleiner, G. K.. *Peasant Agriculture, Government, and Economic Growth in Nigeria* (Homewood, Ill: Irwin, 1966)

Heussler, R.. *The British in Northern Nigeria* (London: Oxford University Press, 1968)

Hill, Polly, *Studies in Rural Capitalism in West Africa* (Cambridge: Cambridge University Press, 1970)

Hill, Polly, *Rural Hausa. A Village and a Setting* (Cambridge: Cambridge University Press, 1972)

Hill, Polly, *Population, Prosperity and Poverty: Rural Kano 1900 and 1970* (Cambridge, Cambridge University Press, 1978)

Hiskett, Mervyn, *The Sword of Truth. The Life and Times of the Shehu Usuman Dan Fodio* (New York: Oxford University Press, 1973)

Hobsbawm, E.J., *Industry and Empire* (London: Weidenfeld & Nicholson, 1968)

Hogendorn, J.S.. *Nigerian Groundnut Exports: Origins and Early Development* (Zaria and Ibadan: Ahmadu Bello University Press and Oxford University Press)

Hopkins, A.G., *An Economic History of West Africa* (London: Longman 1973)

Howard, R., *Colonialism and Underdevelopment in Ghana* (London: Croom Helm, 1978)

Hunt, E.H., *British Labour History 1815–1914* (London: Weidenfeld & Nicolson, 1981)

Intelligence Branch of the Imperial Economic Committee, *Survey of Oilseeds and Vegetable Oils* (London: HMSO, 1935)

International Bank for Reconstruction and Development, *The Economic Development of Nigeria* (Washington, DC: IBRD, 1955)

John, A.H., *A Liverpool Merchant House: Being the History of Albert Booth and Company, 1863–1958* (London: Allen & Unwin, 1959)

Kay, Geoffrey, *Development and Underdevelopment: A Marxist Analysis* (London: Macmillan, 1975)

Kindleberger, Charles, *The World in Depression 1929–1939* (Berkeley: University of California Press, 1975)

Kirk-Greene, A.H.M., *Lugard and the Amalgamation of Nigeria: A Documentary Record* (London: Frank Cass, 1968)

Kjekshus, Helge, *Ecology Control and Economic Development in East African History, the Case of Tanganyika 1850–1950* (Berkeley: University of California Press, 1977)

Koubebel, L.E., *The Songhay Empire: Essay in the Analysis of its Socio-Political Structure* (Moscow, n.d.)

Krader, L., *The Asiatic Mode of Production: Sources, Development and Critique in the Writings of Karl Marx* (Assen: Van Gorcum, 1975)

Last, M., *The Sokoto Caliphate* (London: Longmans, 1967)

Leubuscher, C., *The West African Shipping Trade 1909–1959* (Leyden: A.W. Sythoff, 1963)

Low, V.N., *Three Nigerian Emirates: A Study in Oral History* (Evanston: Northwestern University Press, 1972)

Lugard, F.D., *The Dual Mandate in British Tropical Africa* (Edinburgh and London: Blackwood, 1922)

McPhee, A., *The Economics Revolution in British West Africa* (1st edn 1926, reprinted London: Frank Cass, 1971)

Martel, A., *Les confins saharo-tripolitaines de la Tunisie, 1881–1911* (Paris: Presse Universitaire de France, 1965)

Meillassoux, Claude (ed.), *L'Esclavage en Afrique précoloniale* (Paris: Maspéro, 1975)

Morel, E.D., *Nigeria: Its Peoples and its Problems* (1st edn 1911, reprinted London: Frank Cass, 1968)

Muffett, D.J.M., *Empire Builder Extraordinary: Sir George Goldie* (Ramsey, IOM: Shearwater Press, 1978)

Myint, H., *The Economics of Developing Countries* (London: Hutchinson, 1967)

Nicolas, G., *Dynamique sociale et apprehension du monde au sein d'une société Hausa* (Paris)

Onimode, Bade, *Imperialism and Underdevelopment in Nigeria: Dialectics of Mass Poverty* (London: Zed Press, 1983)

Orr, C.W.J., *The Making of Northern Nigeria* (1st edn 1911, reprinted London, Frank Cass, 1965)

Palmer, H. Richmond *Sudanese Memoirs* (1st edn 1929, reprinted London Frank Cass, 1967)

Panikkar, K.M., *Asia and Western Dominance. A Survey of the Vasco da Gama Era of Asian History, 1498–1945* (London: Allen & Unwin, rev. edn 1959)

Pedler, F., *The Lion and the Unicorn in Africa. A History of the United Africa Company 1787–1931* (London: Heinemann. 1974)

Perham, M. *Lugard: The Years of Authority 1898–1945* (London: Collins 1960)

Perham, M., *Native Administration in Nigeria* (London: Oxford University Press, 1937)

Popkin, S., *The Rational Peasant: The Political Economy of Rural Society in Vietnam* (Berkeley: University of California Press, 1979)

Poulantzas, Nicos, *State, Power, Socialism* (London: New Left Books, 1978)

Raynaut, C., *Quelques données de l'horticulture dans la vallée de Maradi* (Etudes Nigériennes, no. 26, Paris: CNRS, 1969)

Reuke, L., *Die Maguzawa in Nordnigeria* (Freiburg: Bertelsmann, 1969)

Rodney, Walter, *How Europe Underdeveloped Africa* (London: Bogle L'Ouverture, 1972)

Salifou, A., *Le Damagaram ou sultanat de Zinder au XIX₍ siècle* (Etude Nigériennes, no. 27, Niamey, CNRSH, 1971)

Schatz, P., *Nigerian Capitalism* (Berkeley: University of California Press 1977)

Schon, J., *Magana Hausa* (London, 1885)

Scott, James C., *The Moral Economy of the Peasant: Rebellion and Subsistence in Southeast Asia* (New Haven: Yale University, Press, 1976)

Shanin, T., *The Awkward Class. Political Sociology of Peasantry in a Developing Society: Russia 1910–1925* (London: Oxford University Press, 1972)

Smaldone, J., *Warfare in the Sokoto Caliphate: Historical and Sociological Perspectives* (Cambridge, Cambridge University Press, 1977)

Smith, Mary, *Baba of Karo: A Hausa Woman of the Moslem Hausa* (London Faber, 1954)

Smith, M.G., *The Economy of Hausa Communities of Zaria* (Colonial Research Series, no. 16, London: HMSO, 1955)

Smith, M.G., *Government in Zazzau* (London, Oxford University Press 1960)

Smith, M.G. *Affairs of Daura* (Berkeley: University of California Press 1978

Stenning, D.J. *Savannah Nomads: A Study of the Wodaabe Pastoral Fulani of Western Bornu Province* (London: Oxford University Press, 1959)

Temple, C., *Native Races and Their Rulers* (Cape Town: Argus, 1918)

Van Apeldoorn, J., *Drought in Nigeria*, 2 vols (Zaria: Centre for Social and Economic Research, 1978)

Williams, Eric, *Capitalism and Slavery* (London: Andre Deutsch, 1964)

Williams, Gavin (ed.), *Nigeria: Economy and Society* (London: Rex Collings, 1976)

Wilson, C., *The History of Unilever. A Study in Economic Growth and Social Change*, 2 Vols (London: Cassell, 1954)

Wolf, E., *Peasant Wars of the Twentieth Century* (New York: 1971)

Chapters in Collective Volumes

Bull, Mary, 'Indirect rule in Northern Nigeria, 1906–1911', in K. Robinson and F. Madden (eds). *Essays in Imperial Government* (Oxford: Blackwell, 1963), pp.47–87

Buntjer, B.J., 'Rural society: the changing nature of gandu', in M. Mortimore (ed.) *Zaria and its Region* (Zaria: Department of Geography, Ahmadu Bello University, 1971), pp.157–69

Denzer, La Ray, 'Sierra Leone-Bai Bureu in M. Crowder (ed.), *West African Resistance* (London: Hutchinson, 1971), pp.233–67

Forde, D., 'The north: the Hausa', in M. Perham (ed.), *The Native Economies of Nigeria*, Vol. 1 (London: Faber, 1946), pp. 119–70

Godelier, M., 'The concept of the Asiatic mode of production', in D. Seddon (ed.), *Relations of Production* (London: Frank Cass, 1978)

Smith, Abdullahi, 'The early states of the Central Sudan', in J.F.A. Ajayi and M. Crowder (eds). *History of West Africa*, Vol. 1 (London: Longman, 1971), pp. 158–201

J. Suret-Canale, 'Les sociétés traditionelles en Afrique tropicale et le concept du mode de production asiatique', in J. Suret-Canale (ed.). *Sur le 'mode de production' asiatique* (Paris: Editions Sociales, 1974)

Williams, G., 'Rural development', in E. Akeredolu-Ale (ed.), *Social Development in Nigeria: A Study of Research and Policy* (Ibadan: 1977)

Articles

Baier, Stephen, 'Trans-Saharan trade and the Sahel: Damergu, 1870–1930', *Journal of African History*, vol. 18, no. 1 (1977), pp. 37–60

Barkow, Jerome H., 'Muslims and Maguzawa in North Central State, Nigeria: an ethnographic comparison', *Canadian Journal of African Studies*, vol. 7, no. 1 (1973), pp. 59–66

Bernstein, Henry, 'Underdevelopment and the law of value: a critique of Kay', *Review of African Political Economy*, no. 6 (1976),pp. 51–64

Bernstein, Henry, 'Notes on capital and peasantry', *Review of African Political Economy*, no. 10 (1977), pp. 60–73

Coquery-Vidrovitch, C., 'Recherches sur les modes de production africaines', *La Pensée*, no. 144 (1969), pp. 61–78

Corby, H., 'Changes brought about by the introduction of mixed farming, Bomo village, Zaria', *Farm and Forest* vol. 2 (1941)

Crummey. D., 'Abyssinian feudalism', *Past & Present*, no. 89 (November 1980), pp. 115–38

Faulkner, O.T. and Mackie, J., 'The introduction of mixed farming in Northern Nigeria', *Empire Journal of Experimental Agriculture*, vol. 4 (1936)

Goddard, A.D., 'Are Hausa-Fulani family structures breaking up?', *Institute for Agricultural Research Newsletter* (Ahmadu Bello University, Zaria, Nigeria). no. 11. 3 June 1969

Goddard, A.D., 'Changing family structure among the rural Hausa', *Africa*, vol. 43, no. 3 (1973), pp. 207–18

Greenberg, J., 'Islam and clan organization among the Hausa' *Southwestern Journal of Anthropology*, vol. 3, no. 3 (1947), pp. 193–211

Grove, A.T., 'A note on the remarkably low rainfall of the Sudan zone in 1914'. *Savanna*. vol. 2. no. 2 (1973). pp 133–8

Hill, Polly, 'The myth of the amorphous peasantry: a Northern Nigerian case study', *Nigerian Journal of Economic and Social Studies*, vol. 10 (1968), pp. 239–60

Hill, Polly, 'Hidden trade in Hausaland', *Man*, vol. 4, no. 3 (1969), pp. 118–35

Hill, Polly, 'Big houses in Kano emirate', *Africa*, vol. 44, no.2 (1974), pp. 118–35

Hill, Polly, 'From slavery to freedom: the case of farm slavery in Nigerian Hausaland', *Comparative Studies in Society and History*, vol. 18, no. 3 (1976), pp. 395–426

Hopkins, A.G., 'The creation of a colonial monetary system: the origins of the West African Currency Board', *African Historical Studies*, vol. 3 (1970), pp. 101–32

Johnson, M., 'Cotton imperialism in West Africa', *African Affairs*, vol. 73, no. 291 (1974), pp. 178–87

Johnson, M., 'Calico caravans in the Tripoli–Kano trade after 1880', *Journal of African History*, vol. 17, no. 1 (1976), pp.95–117

Klein, M., 'Slavery, the slave trade and legitimate commerce in late nineteenth-century Africa', *Etudes d'Histoire Africaine*, vol. 2 (1971), pp 5–28

Lovejoy, P., 'The Kamberin Beriberi: the formation of a specialized group of Hausa kola traders in the nineteenth century', *Journal of African History*, vol. 14, no. 4 (1973) pp. 633–52

Mery, M., 'Renseignements commerciaux', *Bulletin du Comité de l'Afrique française* (1893)

Nicolas, G. 'Une forme atténue du "potlach" en pays hausa (République du Niger): le "dubu", *Economies et sociétés* vol. 2 (1967), pp. 151–214

Northrup, David, "The compatibility of the slave and palm oil trades in the Bight of Biafra', *Journal of African History*, vol. 18, no. 3 (1976), pp. 353–64

Nworah, K.D., 'The West African operations of the British Cotton Growing Association, 1904–1914', *African Historical Studies*, vol. 4, no. 2 (1971), pp. 315–30

Raynaut, Claude, 'Transformation du système de production et inégalité economique: le cas d'une village haoussa (Niger)'. *Canadian Journal of African Studies*, vol. 10 no. 2 (1976), pp. 279–306

Raynaut, Claude, (Circulation monétaire et évolution des structures socio-économiques chez les haoussas du Niger', *Africa*, vo. 47, no. 2 (1977), pp. 160–71

Roseberry, W., 'Rent differentiation and the development of capitalism among peasants', *American Anthropologist*, vol. 78, no. 1 (1976), pp. 45–58

Shenton, R.W., 'A note on the origins of European commerce in Northern Nigeria', *Kano Studies*, vol. 1 no. 2 (n.s.) (1974/77), pp. 63–7

Shenton, R.W. and Lennihan, L., 'Capital and class: peasant differentiation in Northern Nigeria', *Journal of Peasant Studies*, vol. 9, no. 1 (1981), pp. 47–70

Shenton, Bob [R.W.] and Watts, Mike, 'Capitalism and hunger in Northern Nigeria', *Review of African Political Economy* nos 15/16 (May-December 1979), pp. 53–62

Smith, Abdullahi, 'Some considerations relating to the formation of states in Hausaland', *Journal of the Historical Society of Nigeria*, vol. 5, no. 3 (1970), pp. 329–46

Smith, H.F.C., 'A neglected theme of West African history: the Islamic revolutions of the 19th century', *Journal of the Historical Society of Nigeria*, vol. 2, no. 2 (1961), pp. 169–85

Smith, M.G., 'Slavery and emancipation in two societies', *Social and Economic Studies*, vol. 3, nos 3 & 4 (1954), pp. 239–90

Tambo, D.C., 'The Sokoto caliphate slave trade in the nineteenth century', *International Journal of African Historical Studies*, vol. 9, no. 2 (1976), pp. 187–217

Waldman, M.R., 'The Fulani jihad: a reassessment', *Journal of African History*, vol. 6, no. 3 (1965), pp. 333–55

Wallace, Christine C., 'The concept of gandu: how useful is it in understanding labour relations in rural Hausa society?', *Savànna*, vol. 7, no. 2 (December 1978), pp. 137–50

Unpublished Theses

Aliya, A., 'The establishment and development of emirate government in Bauchi, 1805–1903' (PhD thesis, Ahmadu Bello University, Zaria, 1974)

Alkali, M.B., 'A Hausa community in crisis. Kebbi in the nineteenth century' (MA thesis, Ahmadu Bello University, Zaria, 1969)

Baier, S.B., 'African merchants in the colonial Period: a History of Commerce in Damagaram (Central Niger), 1880–1960' (PhD thesis, University of Wisconsin, 1974)

Barkow J.H., 'Hausa and Maguzawa: processes of group differentiation in a rural area in North Central State, Nigeria' (PhD thesis, University of Chicago, 1971)

Charlick, R.B., 'Power and participation in the modernization of rural Hausa communities' (PhD thesis, University of California, Los Angeles, 1974)

Collins, J.D., 'Government and groundnut marketing in rural Hausa Niger: the 1930s to the 1970s in Magaria' (PhD thesis, Johns Hopkins University, 1974)

Dunbar, R.A., 'Damagaram (Zinder, Niger) 1812–1906: history of a central Sudanic kingdom' PhD thesis, University of California, Los Angeles, 1970)

Faulkingham, R.H., 'Political support in a Hausa village (PhD thesis, Michigan State University, 1970)

Ferguson, D.E., 'Nineteenth-century Hausaland, being a description by Imam Imoru of the land, economy and society of his people' (PhD thesis, University of California, Los Angeles, 1973)

Fika, A., 'The political and economic reorientation of Kano emirate, Northern Nigeria, 1882–1940 (PhD thesis, University of London, 1973)

Hogendorn, J., 'The origins of the groundnut trade in Northern Nigeria' (PhD thesis, London School of Economics, 1966)

Hull, R.W., 'The development of administration in Katsina emirate, Northern Nigeria, 1887–1944' (PhD thesis, Columbia University, 1968)

Matlon, P.J., 'The size, distribution, structure and determinants of personal income among farmers in the north of Nigeria' (PhD thesis, Cornell University, 1977)

Na Dama, Gaba, Rise and collapse of a Hausa state: social and political history of Zamfara' (PhD thesis, Ahmadu Bello University, Zaria, 1976)

Okedeji, F. A., 'An economic history of Hausa-Fulani emirates of Northern Nigeria 1900–1939' (PhD thesis, Indiana University, 1972)

Saulawa, A., 'British colonial administrative policies and migration in the Birnin Katsina 1903–1954' (BA thesis, Ahmadu Bello University, Zaria, 1976)

Shea, P., 'The development of an export oriented dyed cloth industry in Kano Emirate in the nineteenth century' (PhD thesis, University of Wisconsin, 1975)

Smith, M.G., 'Social and economic change among Hausa communities,

Northern Nigeria' (PhD thesis, University of London, 1950)

Tahir, I.A., 'Scholars, sufis, saints and capitalists in Kano 1904–1974: the pattern of bourgeois evolution in an Islamic society' (PhD thesis, Cambridge University, 1977)

Usman, Y.B., 'The transformation of Katsina, *c.* 1796–1903: the overthrow of the sarauta system and the establishment and evolution of the Emirate' (PhD thesis, Ahmadu Bello University, Zaria, 1974)

Unpublished Manuscripts, Conference Papers etc.

Abubakar, S., 'A survey of the eastern emirates, Sokoto Caliphate, during the nineteenth century, paper presented to the Sokoto Seminar, June 1975

Benoit, Y., 'The start of the growing season in Northern Nigeria', Ahmadu Bello University, Zaria, 1977

Clough, P., 'Farmers and traders in rural Hausaland', Oxford University, 1977

Ehrensaft, P., and Brown, B., 'The West African mode of production in colonial Nigeria, 1884–1945', Montreal, 1973

Forrest, T., Agricultural policies in Nigeria 1910–1978', unpublished paper, Zaria, Nigeria, 1977

Harris, B., 'Going against the grain', Zaria, 1978

Kadzai, A., 'Operation Feed the Nation as an aspect of Nigeria's economic and social strategy for industrialisation'. Ahmadu Bello University, Zaria, 1974

King, R., 'Farmer's cooperatives in Northern Nigeria: a case study used to illustrate the relationship between economic and institutional change', University of Reading, 1976

Longhurst, R., 'Calorie expenditure and cropping patterns', Institute of Development Studies, Sussex, 1977

Lovejoy, Paul, 'Plantation economy of the Sokoto Caliphate', paper presented to the American Historical Association, 1976

Mason, M., 'Industry and empire: a note on the Manchester Cotton Supply Association and West Africa 1857–1872', unpublished manuscript

Mason, M., 'Trade and state in nineteenth century Nupe', paper presented to the Seminar on the Economic History of the Central Savanna of West Africa, Zaria, Nigeria, 1977

Na Dama, G., 'Urbanization in the Sokoto Caliphate', Sokoto, 1975

Na Dama, G., 'Legends, rituals and ceremonies connected with agricultural activity and craft production in Zamfara during the nineteenth century', Zaria, 1976

Nkom, S., 'Class formation and rural development: a critique of rural development programmes in Nigeria', Zaria, 1976

Mahdi, A. 'The genesis of Kano's economic prosperity during the nineteenth century', Zaria, 1978

Palmer-Jones, R., 'Peasant differentiation in Northern Nigeria', Zaria, 1978

Palmer-Jones, R., 'The Gicci system of intercropping', Kano, 1978

Pflaummer, T., 'Railway policy in Nigeria: the first phase', paper presented to the Nigerian Historical Society Conference, University of Benin, 1978

Stewart, C., 'Toward an Islamic factor in West African history', Zaria, 1975

Stewart, C., 'Shehu Usman dan Fodio's social revolution reassessed', Urbana, Illinois, 1977

Swainson, O., 'Irrigation in Sokoto', manuscript, 1938

Tahir, I., 'Learning and prosperity in Kano', Zaria, 1976

Tukur, M., 'The role of emirs and district heads in the imposition, assessment and collection of kudin kassa and jangali in the emirates, 1903–14, Zaria, 1977

Usman, Y.B., 'Some conceptual problems in the study of the economy of political communities of the central Sudan', Zaria, 1973

Usman, Y.B., 'The transformation of political communities; some notes on the perception of a significant aspect of the Sokoto jihad', Sokoto, 1975

Usman, Y.B., 'Some notes on three basic weaknesses in the study of African cultural history', paper presented to the Seminar on the History of Culture in West Africa in the Second Millennium AD, Zaria, Nigeria, 1977

Usman, Y.B., 'The assessment of primary sources: Heinrich Barth in Katsina', Zaria, 1977

Waterman, P., 'The jihad as an episode in African history', Zaria, 1970

Watts, M., 'The sociology and political economy of food shortage in Northern Nigeria', Sussex, 1978

Watts, M. and Shenton, R., 'Capitalism and hunger in Northern Nigeria', Zaria, 1978

Index

2210　　　　2088